*It is better to limp along
the path of God's Word
than to dash with all speed
outside it.*

John Calvin, the *Institutes*

To Serena
This is our book, not only mine.
As poet, evangelist, and twin theologian,
you inspired it, helped to write it.
In this as in every way, you are my helpmate,
indispensable both in theology and in life.

Limping Along . . .

CONFESSIONS OF A PILGRIM THEOLOGIAN

Béla Vassady

GRAND RAPIDS, MICHIGAN
WILLIAM B. EERDMANS PUBLISHING COMPANY

Unless otherwise noted, all biblical citations are from the Revised Standard Version of the Bible, copyrighted 1946, 1952, © 1971, 1973.

Library of Congress Cataloging-in-Publication Data

Vassady, Béla.
Limping along.

1. Vassady, Béla. 2. Theologians—Hungary—Biography.
3. Theologians—United States—Biography. I. Title.
BX4827.V37A35 1985   230'.044'0924 [B]   85-20905
ISBN 0-8028-0095-5 (pbk.)

TABLE OF CONTENTS

CONTENTS

PREFACE

This theological autobiography was written in the winter of my life, as I continued to limp along the path of God's Word. It was prepared with fear and trembling as God transformed my remembrances into confessions. I wrote it because "necessity was laid upon me" to testify to God's triumphing grace in all the dimensions of my earthly life.

In my preparation of this book, three devoted persons were of special help to me. First of all, there was and is Serena, my beloved of more than half a century. Because she labored with me step by step on the manuscript, her refreshing thoughts and poetic style became thoroughly intertwined with the systematic, somewhat scholarly thoughts and elaborate style of the professional theologian. Without her, this book certainly could not be what it is.

In Alnita H. Dyall (from Los Altos, California), God provided us a friend and a sister in Christ. With her flawless English she weeded out grammatical errors and restructured sentences construed according to the pattern of our native Magyar language. She also gave us many invaluable suggestions. Not only that, but she insisted on typing the entire manuscript herself. In her devoted and unsparing labor of love, she certainly walked not only that second mile but also a third and a fourth. Thank you, dear Nita. We praise God for you.

Last but not least, our deep gratitude goes to Bill Hillegonds, a minister of the Word of God (*verbi divini minister*) in the truest sense of this biblical phrase. Despite the physical distance that now separates him from Serena and me, he remains our pastor. His vitamin-rich messages, which we now hear on tape recordings, continue to feed our souls. I asked him to write the Foreword during what was (unbeknownst to Serena and me) a most difficult period of his life. Yet his answer was an unhesitating "yes." In thanking him, we cannot help but think of Proverbs 17:17, Proverbs 18:24, and John 15:13. He is the kind of friend these verses describe.

I would like to close with the same three words with which John Calvin ended his monumental work, the *Institutes*. For vision, time, and energy; for helpmate, fellow workers, and publisher—that is, for everything, God alone be praised:
SOLI DEO GLORIA.

Béla Vassady

*Readers may write to the Vassadys at 2759 Leonard NW, D-7, Grand Rapids, MI 49504

FOREWORD

This is a book that allows the reader to touch with increasing intimacy two people who choose not to die while still alive. It is a book about two people who don't believe that the worst thing about life is to grow older every day. It is a gift of two people who believe there is nothing that takes on the sight and sound of death so much as regularity. In these pages we meet two people who see beyond the boundless shore a God who one day will remove the limp and transform the pilgrim and his beloved into persons whose traveling will continue in a place where pain and sorrow and war and walls between people will be no more. This will be the ultimate in ecumenicity.

There is movement in these pages. There is the stumbling of a man who views his journey through the years as a pilgrim's delight. But he does not journey alone. Early on, the story turns into the story of two people: Béla and Serena, whose life together becomes the bloom of growing happiness. In their marriage they discover that the more they give each other, the more alive they become. They discover in times of relative plenty and considerable want what it means to be always of each other and for each other. Their marriage, of which these pages give us a lingering look, tells us of times marked by much laughter and great joy, by heavy disappointment, by the shattering of certain hopes and the realization of more of them, by the awareness that God's miracles are but God's raising the level of what seems impossible in the heart and to the human eye, and by the realization that the heart of the Christian faith is the willingness to act upon glorious assumptions. What a beautiful and fitting epitaph they record for someone else to say one day on their behalf: "Now we see God 'in a mirror dimly,' but then and there we shall see him 'face to face.' . . . We shall reach him and limp no more." To that can be added what François Mauriac said before his death—lines that also speak eloquently of our two pilgrims:

> I believe, as I did as a child, that life has meaning, a direction, a value; that no suffering is lost, that every tear counts, each drop of blood; that the secret of the world is to be found in Saint John's "God is love."

This book is about real people and places that can be visited. It mirrors familial love shaped and made strong by abounding grace. It is a book about ideas whose parameters change like the colors of the sky at sunset—sometimes gently, sometimes turbulently. In it are lines about war and peace, psychology and theology, about two people living and loving when they are together and when they are separated by half a planet. Their walk with God is not a walk when the dew is still on the roses, not a walk in the cool of the evening, but it is a walk with God nonetheless. This is a book about people in search of the meaning of a refrain that won't release its hold on their souls: "God of grace and God of glory." As the fibers of that search become the fabric of long life together, there is great celebration, a celebration of life and love that gives to every person everywhere what God chooses to give those whom he calls according to his purpose.

Theology is the stumbling pilgrim's main theme, a theology that speaks of a God "complete in himself while for us he is continually being born," a theology that sometimes has the theologian trying to cover eight windows with seven screens. This is the reason why the words that Béla uses frequently to describe his long journey with God—*openness, courage, patience, love*— seem so very right. These are words that can be used to describe the theologian who believes that God always has new light to shed upon his grand declaration of love for the world, a declaration made concrete and eternal in Jesus Christ. There are, however, two other words that describe the man and woman who give us this book, one of which is the key word in the book's title and in much of what follows. Béla Vassady describes himself as a *pilgrim,* "a person who journeys, especially a long distance, as an act of devotion." There is purpose in this dictionary definition. It suggests that one becomes intent on finding meaning and purpose in all that happens along the way. It suggests that even along the unexpected, mostly unwanted detours, there are things to glean from the passing days and changing scene. The word *pilgrim* is to be set down in contrast to the word *nomad,* or the person who is apt to drift endlessly, guided only by the attractiveness of a particular spot. He seldom thinks much about tomorrow and what marvelous things might lie on the farther side of its dawning. It is a pilgrim (or pilgrims) about whom we read in this book, a pilgrim whose whole life is to be seen in terms of not resting very long or very comfortably where "little systems have their day." What we have in these pages is a portrait of a man who does become "totally involved and thus wholly active, while all the while utterly passive" in the receiving of God's expansive and ever-expanding word on love, Jesus Christ.

Let this last word on the lives of two people—whose greatness has developed in part because they use gracefully their large and small gifts—be a personal one. I am grateful that these pilgrims limped my way. They came out of the winter of their days into the autumn of mine and touched my life with charm and grace. They have affirmed my ministry. Their strong belief that the church is first and foremost a mission has helped to reinforce in me the conviction that the church is essentially new light with Christ and in Christ. And that what matters most, in both our striving and our rest, is that Christ should be seen taking form in the midst of God's people. Serena and Béla's courage in the face of both plenty and want has challenged me to revisit with a new and richer understanding the conviction that the future belongs to those who offer it the greatest hope.

So, begin the reading of these pages with a grand *Te Deum* in your heart. Begin your journey with these limping pilgrims in the spirit in which, at book's end, they rest their pens: Alleluia. Amen.

WILLIAM HILLEGONDS
Pastor, First Presbyterian Church
Ann Arbor, Michigan

Limping Along . . .

1

IN SEARCH OF A TITLE

At a large family dinner-party, conversation turned to "Who does what?" When I stated that I was writing my theological autobiography, the news was received with a murmur of approval, the kind of general reaction that boosts the ego and warms the heart. Amid this soothing chorus, Susie, a niece of mine, chirped, "Uncle Béla, I guess I know what an autobiography is. You simply write about the events of your life, out of memory. But what is a *theological* autobiography? I mean, what is the difference between a theological autobiography and a regular, normal one?"

Her question was prompted partly by genuine curiosity and partly, I suspect, by youthful suspicion, even scorn, for what is usually regarded as lofty, ivory-tower mumbo-jumbo: theology.

Susie's remark again brought to the surface the need for something so seldom provided by professional theologians: a simple, straightforward explanation of the word *theology*. It is most unfortunate that its original meaning has deteriorated into a vague, scientific concept. Many bona fide Christians meekly believe that theology is something out of their league, irrelevant to their daily lives, and thus better left to professionals. This misperception creates a gulf of misunderstanding between the so-called professionals and the nonprofessionals, a misunderstanding that slowly festers beneath the surface and poisons the whole body of believers.

I explained to Susie (while the older generation around the table also listened with eager ears) that the word *theology* comes to us from the Greek language. It is a compound word derived from *theos* (meaning "God") and *logos* (meaning "word" or "language" or "science"). *Theology* thus has a twofold meaning. Primarily it means God's speaking to us, and secondarily it means our speaking about God. Interpreting, explaining, broadcasting the Word of God in our words—that's what theology is all about. In this sense, then, basically every true Christian is a theologian by avocation. Unfortunately, whatever filters through the sieve of fallen human minds is apt to go amiss. Therefore, our speaking about God (our theologizing), like everything else we do, requires constant self-examination, honest recognition, and humble confession.

An autobiography of the kind Susie called "normal" and "regular" usually moves on the level of sheer reminiscence. Introspective though it may be, it seldom chooses as its *raison d'être* the act of confession. On the other hand, a theologian's very identity is characterized by the statement "I confess, therefore I am." At the same time that a theologian confesses, he is of course also reminiscing. In Greek philosophy the basic word for reminiscence is *anamnesis*. In our Christian liturgy this expression refers to the eucharistic prayer that recalls the sacrifice of Christ, ending with the words "Do this in remembrance of me."

That is why the autobiography of a theologian is more than a string of recollections, however meaningful these may be. It is more because the events disclosed in it always point beyond themselves to God's grace and power in the life and word of one who dares to call himself a theologian. His stories are bound to turn into an all-pervasive and all-embracing *anamnesis*, a constant remembrance of him who died for us all and who reminds us each day, "Apart from me, you can do nothing." In him and in him alone our memories irresistibly turn into confessions.

"Confessions" must be in the plural, because the word *confession* has two meanings. It refers both to our acknowledging our sins before God and to our declaring our faith. And since the process of our spiritual existence is a continual interplay of both of these actions, confessions are necessarily present in all our life situations. This is especially true if the confessor happens to be a pilgrim theologian.

I first called myself a "pilgrim theologian" in an inaugural address I delivered in 1930 at the Reformed Theological Seminary in Sárospatak, Hungary. I raised these questions: Could anyone be a true theologian without being a pilgrim at the same time? Could he lead others if he himself was not led by the Spirit? Could he be followed if he himself was not a follower of Christ? And could he move others if he himself was not on the move?

I repeatedly advised my students to follow my way of thinking only insofar as they felt that my interpretation of the Word of God was true to the source. I told them to regard it as their duty to contradict or correct me whenever I tried to substitute a tightly closed system of doctrines for God's living Word. We all need the humility of a pilgrim who is constantly on the road, continually plodding forward but fully aware that he has not yet arrived.

In 1961, thirty years after I delivered this address, the same note echoed in the preface I wrote for my book *Light Against Darkness*:

> For more than thirty years, both in Europe and in America, I have been working on my "system" of theology. I am grateful to the Lord that his Word has always been a lamp to my feet and a light to my path and did not allow me to shut myself up in an artificially constructed, closed system of thought. The light-overcoming-darkness motif will remain to the end of my life the guarding principle of my theological thinking. In due time it will also help me to pass over from here to eternity. Until that day I shall not cease to remember with a humble mind and a joyful heart Tennyson's quatrain:
>
> > Our little systems have their day;
> > They have their day and cease to be:

They are but broken lights of Thee,
And Thou, O Lord, are more than they.

Just now I am on the last stretch of my earthly pilgrimage: I am definitely and consciously on the homeward journey. With "contrite heart" and "uplifted head" I try to take in stride what is commonly called the aging process. But my wife, Serena, and I prefer to speak of it as "the period of making haste slowly." In my heart I still feel young enough to say, with John Dewey, "Anticipation is more important than recollection." At the same time, I am old enough and I hope wise enough to agree with a dictum of Søren Kierkegaard: "Life can only be understood backwards; but it must be lived forwards." And this I know: God is the One who enables the theologian in me to remain ever a pilgrim, and the pilgrim to remain ever a theologian.

But woe to the self-revealing theologian should his advance turn him into a self-reliant traveler. Trying to dash ahead in his own direction and under his own power would merely result in his running in circles. The only way he can make real progress is by *limping* along the path of God's Word. He limps because it is not possible to glide along that path smoothly and easily; it entails relapses and renewals. Captivity and liberation, abasement and exaltation, repentance and forgiveness, being pruned and experiencing spurts of growth—these go hand in hand in the pilgrimage of an authentic theologian. For the Lord disciplines him whom he loves, but whomever he wounds, he also heals.

Do you remember, dear reader, Jacob's wrestling with that mysterious stranger? How that someone touched his thigh and put it out of joint? Yet Jacob clung to him and would not let him go until he received the blessing. And the stranger told him, "Your name shall no more be called Jacob, but Israel, for you have striven with God and with men, and have prevailed." Jacob called the place Peniel (which means "the face of God"), saying, "For I have seen God face to face." And "the sun rose upon him as he passed Penuel, *limping* . . ." (Gen. 32:22–32).

In my own life I too have wrestled with God and with men. In these spiritual struggles I too have been hurt, wounded in the very depth of my being. I too have passed my own Penuels, limping. Yet, paradoxically, it has been through such limping that I have found my wholeness again and again.

I remember (could I ever forget) the summer of 1944 in our native country, Hungary. My family and I were spending the summer on the vineyard-clad slopes of our mountain in a picturesque villa. We had just finished building it, planning to use it whenever we needed rest and recreation for mind and body in the years to come. But man proposes, and God disposes. . . .

It happened one sweltering August afternoon. At first we heard only a distant, ominous rumbling; then we heard the muffled sound of falling bombs and exploding shells. The Russian troops had crossed the Carpathian Mountains and were approaching us through Transylvania. Dazed, incredulous, we finally let the truth sink in. We would not be the ones to harvest the grapes in the fall. We would have to leave everything behind us and become homeless refugees in our own country.

In that state of acute insecurity, in two desperate weeks, I jotted down the first draft of my theological autobiography. That first draft has since undergone many changes, but its motto has never changed. I borrowed it from John Calvin's *Institutes*: "It is better to *limp along* the path of God's Word than to dash with all speed outside it" (I, 6, 3; italics mine). It is just as appropriate now as it was in 1944—perhaps even more so. This motto is echoed in my title: *Limping Along . . . Confessions of a Pilgrim Theologian*. It suggests my overriding purpose: to invite readers to limp along with me on God's pathways, so that we may journey together in this gravely divided world.

2

TAPPING THE TAPROOT
(1902–1912)

Three Lateral Roots

The taproot is the central lifeline of a plant that draws nourishment through its many lateral roots. In our human existence the self is that central portion: a mind that has a body, a psychosomatic root-unity doing two things at once. It burrows its way downward, seeking the infinity of depth, the Source of all being. At the same time, it thrusts upward, seeking the infinity of height, the End of all being.

The lateral roots of our existence are many, but the three most prominent are nation, religion, and family. And in his inscrutable way God extends his divine covenant-relationship to us all primarily through these human relationships.

To tap my own taproot in both its downward and its upward reach is one reason for writing this autobiography. Get behind me, self-centeredness and pride! Let this message radiate through every page: "Our competence is from God" (2 Cor. 3:5).

My Nation. Present-day Hungary, which is about the size of the state of Indiana, has as its bordering neighbors Austria, Czechoslovakia, the Soviet Union, Romania, and Yugoslavia. Though primarily an agricultural country, it became rapidly industrialized after World War II. It has about ten million inhabitants. Another three million Hungarians live under the rule of the neighboring nations, and about two million more are scattered around the world. Half of these live in America.

Hungarians call themselves Magyars and their country "the land of the Magyars" (*Magyarország*). Their language is neither Germanic nor Slavic: together with Finnish, it belongs to the Ural-Altaic language group. It is one of the most phonetically rich languages of the world—clear, rhythmical, and sonorous—but it is hard to master. In Roman Catholic hierarchical circles one sometimes hears the humorous remark, "The Magyar language is so difficult to learn that not even the pope would venture to utter a sentence in it."

The Magyars originated in the Russian steppes, then gradually migrated westward. Finally, in A.D. 896, they settled down in the Danube basin. In A.D. 1000 Pope Sylvester II

9

recognized Hungary as a Christian nation and crowned Stephen I, a descendant of the Árpád dynasty, as the first Christian king of the country. Then and there began the history of Hungary, a martyrdom of geography.

Each century brought new aggressors to attack the nation. They came from the east and the west, from the north and the south to threaten and invade the land. First came the Germans, then tribes of Turkish origin, then the Greek Empire, then the Mongolian hordes, and then again the Ottoman Turks. The Turks occupied the southern and central sections of Hungary for 150 years during the sixteenth and seventeenth centuries. At the same time, the northwestern region was under Hapsburg rule, and only the eastern part of the country, Transylvania, could safeguard the historic continuity of Hungary as an independent state. In the seventeenth century, after the Turks were expelled, all of Hungary fell under the dominion of the Hapsburgs. In the middle of the nineteenth century the Magyars, led by Louis Kossuth, were finally able to revolt successfully against the rule of Austria and defeat its army. But this success didn't last: the Austrian emperor Franz Joseph asked the Russian Czar Nicholas I for military assistance, and the combined Austrian and Russian armies finally succeeded in crushing the Hungarian struggle for independence. Nevertheless, the Magyars' yearning for freedom survived, and their passive resistance continued. Finally, in 1867, they forced the Austrian emperor into a compromise. Hungary thus regained its independence, and a dual monarchy was established, the so-called Austro-Hungarian Empire.

Several decades later came World War I. Because of its restricted geographical and political situation, Hungary was dragged into the war on the side of Austria and Germany. As a result, it ended up being the greatest loser among the principal losers. The baneful Treaty of Trianon, which disregarded national identity and the right of self-determination, sliced off three-fourths of Hungary's historic territory, dividing it among its (partly newly created) neighbors: Czechoslovakia, Romania, and Yugoslavia. With the restructuring of Transylvania alone, more than two million Magyars were lumped into Romania.

The bitterness evoked by the injustices of the Treaty of Trianon kept ticking away like a time bomb in the Magyar soul for more than twenty years, fated to explode sooner or later. But the country managed to survive, now as "a kingdom without a king," under the ill-fated governorship of Admiral Horthy. In fact, it made a remarkable recovery both economically and culturally. Yet the "trunk"—what was left of Hungary—kept bleeding, and it never relinquished its hope to be reunited with its severed limbs.

In the meantime, Germany regained its strength. Under the obsessive and hypnotic leadership of Hitler, it grew into a seemingly invincible force. Before and during the first half of World War II, Hitler's military might swallowed up one country after another. For strategic reasons he needed Hungary as a satellite. But to gain its help he used the carrot of attractive promises and the stick of blackmail instead of guns and bombs. He offered the Hungarian government the territories it had lost at the end of World War I in return for letting him use Hungary as his strategic military base. This offer split the Hungarian government and the whole nation right down the middle. Some, thoroughly repulsed by Hitler's despicable policies, were adamantly opposed to accepting his offer. Others, dazzled by his spectacular first conquests and his rosy promises, were eager to agree with him. Viewed in perspective, of course, the whole issue was quite theoretical. Hitler's army would have marched into and through Hungary no matter what decision had been reached—as indeed it did.

Distressed and defenseless, the premier of Hungary, Count Paul Teleki, expressed his protest by committing suicide, and under German pressure the country ended up with a pro-Nazi government. Those who resisted this outcome were ousted, imprisoned, or executed. A massive deportation of Hungarian Jews was engineered. Protesting church leaders were promptly silenced; masses of people were intimidated. Ultimately, with German efficiency, the whole country was turned into a battleground, a no-man's-land between the German-Nazi and the Russian-Communist armies. Surely the people of Hungary wanted neither of them—in fact, they hated both armies. Yet ironically, in the eyes of a misinformed world, the Hungarians were perceived as sympathizing with one or the other—or both.

The battles on Hungarian territory started in the summer of 1944 and ended by April 4, 1945. The actual siege of Budapest lasted for more than four months, and it left the city in a shambles.

After World War II Hungary was declared a Communistic People's Republic. Ever since then it has been "protected" by the Soviet Union. Thus Hungary has had to endure another period of geographical-political martyrdom, this time as a regimented satellite of one of the great world powers.

I am aware that this patchy presentation of mine is bound to be incomplete and may raise puzzling unanswered questions. The vitally important social, cultural, ethnic, and economic factors cannot even be touched upon in so condensed a review. But I hope that I have been able to demonstrate at least one thing: the unquenchable thirst of the Magyars for their national political independence. No vicissitudes of history can ever extinguish this yearning. It is a basic characteristic of the Magyars, one that has consistently influenced my personal life too.

One of Hungary's great thinkers once exclaimed, "It is a miracle of God that our country is still alive!" Of course, not all Magyars are religious in the narrower sense of the word. But oddly enough, even some of the so-called atheists and nonbelievers nurture a stubborn, atavistic faith in *some kind* of divine providence that somehow always protects their nation from any logically predictable extinction. Mention of faith necessarily leads to the discussion of a second lateral root in my earthly existence. And as my entire autobiography demonstrates, from my early youth onward this next has been the most important molding factor in my personal life.

My Church. Those nomad Magyar horsemen, roaming down to the Danube valley at the end of the eighth century, had their own religion and worshiped one god as peculiarly theirs. To seek his favor the Magyar sacrificed his most precious possession: a favorite horse. It had to be a horse par excellence, flawless and snow-white. In the ninth century Stephen I converted his people to Christianity. Although he used coercive measures that met with considerable resistance, Hungary slowly but surely became a Christian nation. Some of its kings participated in—even led—the Crusades, and the country produced a number of saints.

By the fifteenth and sixteenth centuries Hungary served as the easternmost bulwark of the Christian West. But by the time the waves of the Reformation reached the land, the greater part of it was already under Turkish rule. Aristocrat and peasant alike suffered at the hands of the Moslem invaders. Consequently, the Hungarian people looked for an inner strength, the kind offered in the Gospel. Itinerant preachers roamed the country, and by the end of the sixteenth century about ninety percent of the Magyars had accepted the Reformed (Calvinistic) faith. In 1590 Gáspár Károlyi published the entire Bible in Hungarian, and by that time Reformed colleges and seminaries had been founded in Pápa, Sárospatak, and Debrecen.

Hungary was the first country in Europe to formally proclaim complete religious liberty (in 1568, at Torda). Yet when the Turkish occupation had ended and Hungary suffered under the oppressive rule of the Hapsburg dynasty, the nation had to face a ruthless, bloody Counter-Reformation. During the centuries that followed, the fight for liberation from Hapsburg rule and the fight for religious freedom were one and the same struggle. The princes of Transylvania were at the forefront of this heroic resistance, but their fight was in vain. Whether by alluring promises or by enforced measures, a large number of the people were reconverted to Roman Catholicism.

Repression of the Protestant churches continued even in the nineteenth century, but so did Protestant resistance. Although the "compromise" of 1867 finally acknowledged equal rights for all churches, in reality the Roman Catholic Church never yielded its superiority. With its political influence and its spiritual wheeling and dealing—especially in regard to the religious upbringing of the offspring of mixed marriages—it continued its proselytizing efforts even into the first half of the twentieth century.

Meanwhile, in the Protestant churches the signs of spiritual renewal began to appear. And by the time World War II broke out, and especially during its aftermath, Hungarians were ripe for a deep spiritual awakening, ready to witness and to serve.

This theological autobiography mirrors both the tragic and the beneficent effects of these twentieth-century events in my own life and religious development, first in Hungary and later in America. But now let me trace the third lateral root of my taproot.

My Family. I was born on December 30, 1902, the second child of a family belonging to the so-called highly cultured middle class of Hungary. My father earned three diplomas. My mother was an accomplished painter and a good pianist, but she was most outstanding in creating or unearthing original patterns of intricate embroidery. Her skill in designing and stitching petit-point pictures and weaving Gobelin-style tapestries was especially admired. My parents had been married in 1900, when the world looked rosy, especially in Hungary. Talleyrand's famous saying—"He who has not lived before 1789 has not known the sweetness of life"—was rightly applied by Hermann Sasse, a German theologian, to the two decades preceding the outbreak of World War I: "Not to have lived before 1914 is not to know how happy life can be."

An exuberant optimism prevailed in those years throughout the whole of Europe. During the dire years of World War I, I heard many glowing stories from my parents about how joyful, how proud the Hungarian nation had been to celebrate the one-thousandth anniversary of Magyar statehood, the so-called "millennium," in 1900, the very year in which they were married.

My parents' union was made more challenging because my father was a Protestant and my mother was a Roman Catholic. My father had originally wanted to be an ordained minister in the Reformed Church. But when he decided to marry my mother, his serving a Protestant congregation became unthinkable. He had to settle for a secular profession, so he became a superintendent of education. My parents also had to decide what sort of religious training to give their children. Six years before they were married, a new state law had established guidelines for determining the religious affiliation of the offspring of mixed marriages. Prior to their marriage a couple could decide in which religion their children were to be raised. According to their agreement, children could follow the faith of either the father or the mother. But if no formal official agreement had been made, the boys followed the father's religion and the girls followed the mother's religion. My parents worked out a compromise. My father chose another profession so that he could marry a Roman Catholic girl, and my mother agreed that all their children would be raised in the Reformed faith.

Altogether there were six children in the family: four boys and two girls. Jestingly my father called us "the Vassady gang."

It was a well-organized "gang." On Sunday outings we kids immediately lined up in a close column. My older brother and I led the file, followed by our two sisters, then the two smaller boys. Last but in firm control came our parents. Everybody had to participate in the household chores, and the law of rotation prevailed. Father was kept busy by his professional work, so Mother needed all the help she could get from her growing brood.

During World War I, when food became scarce in the cities, mother assumed the extra responsibility of accepting "boarders." These boarders were children of well-to-do gentlemen farmers who were sent to live in the city with a good family in order to further their education. Their parents in turn supplied our pantry with produce. These children were treated like us in every respect; they even participated in the household duties.

As a child I learned the blessings of teamwork. Decades later, when I became involved in organizing and administering the life of the church—not only on the local and national level but increasingly on the ecumenical level—remembering the value of this teamwork served me well.

3

MY TEEN YEARS
(1913–1920)

Three Vignettes

By the age of thirteen I was regarded as the family poet. Birthdays were regularly celebrated at the dinner table, and on each occasion it was expected that "the verse-monger of the family" should stand up and toast the feted person in rhymes and ditties. At sixteen, as "the poet of the school class," I also inundated my girlfriends with verses. But by the time I was eighteen I was objective enough to recognize that I could never develop into a bona fide poet. (Twelve years later, when I was thirty, my interest in poetry must have been one of the factors that prompted me to fall in love with a girl who, at the age of eighteen, was already a first-prize winner in a nationwide poetry contest.)

Ours was a bilingual family. We always had an Austrian "Fräulein" as governess in our house, and thus German became a second language for my siblings and me. This fluency was a great help to me in my later scientific research as well as in my work on the ecumenical frontier of the church.

I also received certain spiritual blessings from being a child of a mixed marriage. Till the end of her life my mother remained a devout Roman Catholic, and we children grew up with complete respect for her religion. On Sundays we went with our father to the early worship service at the Reformed church. But by half-past eleven we were present at the celebration of the mass in the Roman Catholic church. My older brother and I took pride in the fact that we thus pleased not only our mother but also God, the Father of all people, Roman Catholics and Protestants alike. But of course the real reason we so willingly attended the mass was that all our girlfriends were Roman Catholics, and walking them home after the mass made our "sacrifice" worthwhile. So "mixed marriage" and "mixed motives" enriched the diet of our Sundays and everydays.

All in all, my childhood was a pleasant one. Alas, the time soon came when a bitter experience disrupted the harmony.

An Introverted Teenager

My older brother and I were complete opposites. He was the handyman in the family; I was the unhandy one. He was the extravert; I was the introvert. Whenever he could, he went out to socialize with his friends, but I was inclined to withdraw. Nothing gave me more pleasure than reading poetry, fiction, and, when I was older, the great philosophers. Already at fifteen I began to read the German Idealists—Kant, Fichte, and Schelling.

Whether it was justified or not, I felt that neither my parents nor my schoolteachers were able to understand me. At home, one of six vocal children, I was rather reluctant to approach my parents with the kinds of things that were on my mind. And in school—for eight years I attended a *Gymnasium* (middle school) run by members of the Premonstratensian order—all my teachers were Roman Catholic priests. They were very able teachers but hardly concerned about the spiritual well-being of a Protestant pupil. At the same time, the instructors in my own faith—who took on an extra load by teaching students belonging to the Reformed Church on certain afternoons (quite often on Saturdays)—lacked both the time and the desire to help me with my personal questions and doubts.

For these reasons I drew a conclusion: I would have to work out my own religious convictions, my own philosophy. With a stubborn "I will do it all on my own" attitude, I became more and more of a loner who had but one confidant—his diary. (I started to keep a diary at the age of twelve and continued to do so for thirty years, until the end of World War II. Alas, during the war all my diaries were destroyed by the invading Russian army, a loss I have never ceased to mourn.)

Soon my interest turned toward metaphysics. For a while I stubbornly believed that I could construct an irrefutable proof for the existence of God. The result was, of course, complete frustration. In another of my adolescent stages, influenced by Schopenhauer, I began to question the meaningfulness of human life. The reality of death as our "prospective contingency" kept me in suspense. There were days and nights when suicide—"the invited death," as the poet Endre Ady called it—began to seem rather intriguing. And so, on the ebb and flow of introversion, I was drifting closer and closer to the abyss.

Two other factors contributed to my drifting: the untimely deaths of my two sisters.

My older sister died when I was only fourteen. I will never forget the conversation that my father and I had immediately after he had pronounced her dead. I turned to him and said, "Dad, let's open the window." When he asked me why, I replied, "So that Margaret's soul can find an easy access to heaven." At that time I was still thinking of the human soul as if it were a mist, a vapor.

I accepted Margaret's death without much difficulty. I simply took it for granted that her soul had ascended into heaven to live happily in the company of angels. And I took comfort in the fact that my younger sister, whom I loved dearly, was still with us.

But three years later, she died too, and I was shaken to the core. She had been precocious, sensitive. And besides my diary, she was my only earthly confidante. I simply could not accept her leaving me all alone in this world. Her passing away made me think of death as the most arbitrary and cruel enemy of mankind. Is it worthwhile to pursue anything in this life, I wondered, when we are totally at the mercy of this invisible and capricious enemy?

The March of Death

From the perspective of modern child psychology, it would seem to have been a most inappropriate place for that picture. But evidently my parents had no qualms about hanging it over my bed. Because of its placement, it was the last thing I saw before going to sleep and the first thing I saw when I woke up. It was a reproduction of the famous painting by a German artist called *The March of Death* (*Der Zug des Todes*).

The main character in this painting is the skeletal figure of Death. In one of his hands he holds a scythe ready for harvesting; in the other he holds a constantly ringing bell, the sound of which is a peremptory command to follow him. And those who hear the bell obey. A young hero of the battlefield, a bride in her wedding gown, an archbishop in his pontificals, a child torn from his mother's arms—all step into a solid column marching after Death. . . . From the roadside an old woman, crippled, pain-ridden, stretches her arms toward Death, pleading, "Take me! I have nothing to live for. I am a burden to others and to myself. End my miseries!" But Death indifferently passes her by. Her turn has not yet come.

"Maybe the hedonists were right," I thought. "Why not just 'eat, drink, and be merry' while we can?" Nihilism also began to encroach: "What's the use of working for any goal if we're to be snatched away before realizing it?"

Strangely enough, the cruel, senseless deaths of my sisters, instead of promoting such ideas, made me stop and look at the deeper message of the picture. I began to wonder if Death was really the dominant figure in that painting. It was domineering, yes. But wasn't the truly dominant authority Someone Else behind the scenes? A Mind with a plan beyond our understanding? Someone who had a purpose in letting Death take the child and leave the old woman behind? Someone high, inscrutable, a Sovereign Power, who said of himself,

"I am who I am"? The only thing that we know of him is that he seems to be in full control. God!? Are you there? Behind the marching throng, the cold, arrogant figure of Death, the canvas itself behind the behind? It was at that time that I read somewhere, "You would not have sought me, had you not been found by me." Could it be true? Had I sought him because he had already found me, though I had been all unaware?

These and similar thoughts began to occur to me more and more frequently because I had already had two encounters with him, the living God. The first was only an indirect encounter, but the second turned out to be direct and positive, grasping me in the very core of my unsettled teenage existence.

Two Encounters

Down through the centuries an interesting tradition developed in the life of the Reformed colleges and seminaries of Hungary. As part of their struggle for subsistence, they trained their students how to contact the constituency of the church and how to encourage the various congregations to support their education. On the so-called Great Holy Days (Christmas, Easter, and Pentecost), the colleges and seminaries usually sent out their best students as "legates" or "emissaries" to the congregations to relieve the local pastors of the arduous task of preaching four times within forty-eight hours. (In Hungary these great celebrations last two days, and two sermons are preached each day.) As recompense for the services of these "legates," each congregation contributed a certain amount of money for their schooling.

I was only fifteen when I was first assigned to be a "legate," and thus began my indoctrination in how to be a good one. I duly memorized the sermons written by my father, who taught me how to ascend the high pulpit in our church without falling on my face. With two other minister friends, he also tutored me in the art of offering a public prayer and delivering a sermon. In the end they were all very much pleased with my "performance," and when the Holy Days arrived, the congregation to whom I preached was equally pleased. "You certainly know how to speak," they said. "You'll be a great orator." And I returned home, elated by my success and gratified by the generous contribution in my pocket.

These "Holy Day excursions" undoubtedly helped me to overcome my introversion, but they also prompted certain questions. Did mere eloquence make one a good preacher? Was it enough to memorize sermons written by someone else and merely recite them from the pulpit? Was it right to say to the congregation "Hear the Word of God" when I, the speaker, had never before listened to the Word of God myself? But why didn't I listen to God? Why didn't I ever open the Bible and let God speak to me? In retrospect I can see how, through such questions, God began to approach me at least in an indirect way.

Then one day the real, the direct, the first and unforgettable encounter occurred. In 1918, at the end of the school year, my teacher in religion awarded me a book, the Hungarian translation of Harry Emerson Fosdick's *The Manhood of the Master*. In it Fosdick discussed the various traits of Jesus' personality and concluded each daily reading with appropriate Bible quotations and prayers. And that—especially the Scripture verses—had a tremendous impact upon me. For the first time in my life I was reading coherent parts of the Bible. I was amazed, thrilled, moved, enriched. "God speaks to me here," I wrote in the book's margin. And during my last two years in the Roman Catholic middle school, I became an almost regular reader of God's Word.

Now I began to apprehend that I was not alone. God was with me. The God of Judgment and the God of Mercy, the Father of us all. *Our* Father.

A Bitter Experience

One day during the period that our younger sister was terminally ill, my older brother and I came home and found our mother sobbing. She had just received an anonymous postcard that said, "God is punishing you because you let your two daughters belong to the Reformed Faith. Now your

21

second daughter is also condemned to die. But you still can do something for her and for yourself. The parish priest would be more than willing to help you. Just call on him."

After this happened, our father instructed us to watch for the mailman and intercept any more anonymous postcards that might be sent to our mother. No others came, but one day the parish priest himself showed up, "just for a friendly, comforting visit," he said. We ushered him into the sickroom, and although he kept insisting that we go out to play, we refused to leave him alone with our dying sister and distraught mother.

A few weeks later our sister was gone. And as the funeral procession was passing the Roman Catholic cathedral, its bells suddenly started to toll. The tolling clearly indicated that the Catholics were "reclaiming" the soul of a girl who should have belonged to their church but now was on her way to damnation. This was more than Mother could bear, and she fainted.

That same night I quietly resolved that in the future, should the opportunity arise, I would work for a better understanding between Roman Catholics and Protestants. Let the bitter experience of the present turn into a blessing for the future, I thought to myself.

As the years have gone by, God has indeed opened the doors of opportunity before me so that I could make the most of that resolution. He has helped me to become an ecumenical Christian.

The Boxcar Dwellers

In 1914, when World War I broke out, I was only eleven years old. Thus my teens were marred by the privations and struggles of an increasingly bloody and desperate war, and the end of it brought a devastating loss. With the peace treaty of Trianon, our historic thousand-year-old country was dismembered. It was parceled out like so many pieces of meat: the entire northern part of Hungary was given to the newly created country of Czechoslovakia, the southern part to Yugoslavia, and the eastern part, Transylvania, to Romania. And so by 1919 my hometown, Nagyvárad, was occupied by the Romanian army.

At that point my father was divested of his office as superintendent of education. But about a year later he was invited to "repatriate" and to continue to serve as superintendent in a mutilated Hungary, first in a smaller town, then (two years later) in Debrecen. Thus, in the middle of August 1920, we loaded our furniture into two boxcars, bade farewell to our old friends, and left the city of my youth. For ten days and nights we were boxcar dwellers, although we didn't travel more than sixty miles! After we crossed the newly created boundary between Romania and Hungary, we could breathe freely again, although our hearts were heavy.

Prior to all these events I had been trying to make up my mind about my career. My first choice was to become a middle-school teacher with a doctor's degree in philosophy (which at that time also included psychology). But my father advised me to study theology first and earn a preacher's diploma, then take another two years to get my teacher's diploma. Having two degrees, he explained, would greatly increase my chances of finding a position in a shrunken land burdened with job shortages. It was for such pragmatic reasons that I decided to register as a divinity student at the State University of Debrecen, located in the same city in which my father had earned all his degrees in the last decade of the nineteenth century.

But just before we left Nagyvárad, a friend of the family who heard of my decision threw a monkey wrench into my tidy plans. "Theology has lost its status as a science," he told me. "Higher criticism has dissected the Bible. Its authenticity is either questioned or denied. To speak about the authority of the Scriptures is nonsense. The sciences of religion [the psychology of religion, comparative religions, and the philosophy of religion] are an adequate substitute for theology. So you'd better change your mind now, or else you'll be bound to be terribly disappointed later."

That conversation with such a highly cultured, knowledgeable man meant added tension for me throughout the days and nights that we traveled in those boxcars. But I kept my dilemma from my parents. They had their own problems—why should I burden them with mine? With the seeds of doubt in my mind, I still clung to the idea of registering as a student of theology. "Let me find out the hard way who was right," I said to myself: "our friend, or Fosdick with his bold-faced quotations from Scripture. Why not give the divinity faculty in Debrecen a chance? After all, they must be experts. Surely they must know how to dissolve the doubts of their students."

Thus September found me in the city of Debrecen as a newly registered student of divinity. "From now on," said the dean to all newcomers, "you are regarded as candidates for the ministry of the church. A lifelong series of new opportunities and responsibilities is waiting for you. Make the most of them."

"I will do so, so help me God," was my sincere response.

4

STUDENT ON TWO CONTINENTS
(1920–1925)

Popular yet Disillusioned

It took only three months. By December I was the most popular yet at the same time the most disillusioned student on campus.

I was popular because of my versifying talent. My epigrams and dithyrambs began to be circulated, and they became known everywhere on campus. But in the midst of this visible popularity I carried the burden of an invisible disenchantment: I was greatly disappointed in our professors. They were just reading their pedantically prepared lectures to us students without offering us any opportunity to raise questions. "Higher criticism" and "rigid orthodoxy," though strange bedfellows, were lumped together and dumped on us in those mechanical lectures. The Bible was treated as merely a collection of historical documents, and God's dynamic Word was replaced by a closed system of thought about the so-called biblical message. "If this is 'theology,'" I said to myself, "I had better chuck the whole thing. This is a waste of time."

During Christmas vacation I felt compelled to shed my reticence and pour out my soul to my parents. They listened and responded sympathetically. "Son," said my father, "we want you to be content. So you had better change departments—switch to the liberal arts."

His total understanding surprised me. Considering how much he had wanted me to become a minister and how persuasive he had been in steering me toward theology, I had been sure he would oppose my quitting, and so I had steeled myself against all the arguments I had anticipated. But now his sympathetic reaction unsettled me and somehow changed my whole attitude. I became adamant about continuing my theological studies. Even if I had to grit my teeth, I would stick it out. As I look back on it, I realize what a good natural psychologist my father was.

So I remained a student of theology. Divine providence took care of the rest.

Rotating Preachers

Alas, my disappointment only deepened when I became acquainted with the preaching schedule of the ministers in Debrecen's downtown churches.

The first Sunday after matriculation, I went to worship in one of them. An old minister, highly acclaimed as the best in the city, was preaching. His text was Jeremiah 6:14: "They have healed the wound of my people lightly, saying, 'Peace, peace,' when there is no peace." I ate up every word, and I decided that I wanted to hear him again the following Sunday. That next Sabbath he was scheduled to preach for another downtown church, so I went there. To my astonishment, the text of his sermon was the same. Surely, I thought, he will preach a sermon that will be a sequel to the previous one. But no, it turned out to be exactly the same all over again: the same text, the same contents, the same delivery, the same gestures. Baffled, but certain that next time I would hear a different message, I followed him to the third church the next Sunday. Imagine my disappointment when once again I heard the same text and the same sermon. I tried hard to listen, but by this time I knew his words almost syllable by syllable. I sat there seething inside.

Soon I found out that the ministers of the four downtown Reformed churches resorted to the rotation method to make their task easier. On four consecutive Sundays each of them preached the same sermon in the four different churches. Since each of the churches was attended only by its own constituency, each congregation had the advantage of hearing four different preachers in the course of a month. If some among them didn't like one of the preachers, they simply skipped the worship service that day. I abhorred this method. I felt that the primary tasks of a minister, of any minister, were to proclaim the Word and to provide pastoral care for the members of the congregation. But how could he fulfill both requirements unless he preached a fresh sermon every Sunday to the same flock, whose chosen pastor he was?

After these disillusioning experiences, I lost all inclination to attend church services. Providentially, the election of a new minister a year later brought a refreshing change. A former theological professor from Transylvania, Dr. Emeric Révész, became the pastor of the old, traditional "Great Church" in the center of Debrecen. He immediately began to break down old habits. Though at first he was bound to accept the rotating system, he managed to preach a different sermon each Sunday. The people were electrified, and began to follow him, packing whatever sanctuary announced him as preacher. For me, a student of theology by compulsion, listening to his sermons was an immense blessing.

God Lands Me on My Feet

In 1909, John R. Mott, the leader of the Christian Students' Volunteer Movement, visited Hungary. His guide and interpreter, John Victor, the translator of Harry Emerson Fosdick's books, was himself a thought-provoking evangelist. Each year thereafter, John Victor invited the theological students of the seminaries in Hungary to attend the summer conference of the Evangelical Students' Federation at Tahi, near Budapest. In 1921 I was among the very few from Debrecen who responded. And it was at Tahi that the "theological student by compulsion" had his first personal encounter with Jesus Christ, his Lord and Savior.

John Victor and his fellow workers not only spoke the Gospel—they lived it. I was greatly impressed that our spiritual leaders, as talked-out and tired as they must have been by the end of the day, were still eager to help us pitch our tents, prepare our meals, and wash the dishes. They even served as watchmen during the night. They not only *believed* but also *served*. Words in deeds and deeds in words, testifying, sharing, and serving: that is the Gospel, and they embodied it.

And God had even more in store for me. One day we made a steamboat excursion on the Danube to the historic fortress at Visegrád. After climbing all the battlements of the fortress, we gathered to hear the address of an evangelist in that unique setting. Picture a mountainside sloping down to the deep, slowly rolling waters of the Danube, and only a rickety wooden railing separating a lot of tired, hungry young people from the precipice. Foolishly, we sat or leaned on that old rail during the address. What followed was bound to happen. The rotting wood gave way—precisely where I sat. As I tumbled backwards, I caught a sickening glimpse of the fast-approaching rocky bottom of the river. I tried to grab a protrusion of the mountain's face without success, but that one desperate lunge straightened my body, and I hit the river bottom in a vertical position, landing on my feet. My feet were injured, but not my head or back. Although I was in pain, I could smile into the worried faces leaning over me and assure my friends that I was all right.

For weeks after that fall, I was limping, but it was a happy limp. For now I knew that not I but God *had landed me on my feet*.

A Prizewinning Essay

I began my second year as a theological student with an enthusiasm that I had previously lacked. Getting acquainted with the sciences of religion now seemed a labor of love. I accepted a simple equation: theology = sciences of religion. Theology's true subject matter is not so much God but religion—religion as "a seed sown by God in the human soul" (Augustine), as an undeniable empirical fact. There is no need for metaphysical speculation or for a rigid, lifeless orthodoxy. Let us simply give full vent to our religious experiences and let them speak for themselves. The "religious man" (*homo religiosus*) should be the object of our investigation. Theology at its best: that is the sciences of religion.

Thus the announcement of a contest for the best essay critically appraising the various theories about the origin and nature of religion seemed custom-made for me. The professor of systematic theology, a rather remote scholar, was pleased but also somewhat amused that a babe in the woods of theology would venture to sink his milk teeth into this solid food. He had intended the challenge for his graduating class. "Do you read German?" he asked me. When I said yes, he gave me Nitzsch's *Dogmatik*, pointing out the pages that I should read. Soon I learned about Ernst Troeltsch, the head of the *Religionsgeschichtliche Schule* (School of Comparative Religion). So for my essay I used as a frame the division of the sciences of religion—religious psychology, religious epistemology, the metaphysics of religion, and the philosophy of the history of religion—that Troeltsch offered in one of his monumental books.

Preparing the essay entailed a lot of discomfort for me. World War I had recently ended, and Hungary faced not only a severe winter but also an acute shortage of coal and electricity. Our rooms in the dormitory were hardly heated at all—usually I had to wear my winter coat while working on the essay. And each night, at precisely eleven o'clock, the electricity was shut off, so I had to light at least four candles in order to continue my reading and writing. One night I was so absorbed in my work that I failed to notice that one of my candles had burned down to the tabletop.It scorched the linoleum inlay, and I had to pay for the repair. It was my first lesson that scholarly work can be costly in more than one way.

In the end my hard work paid off. My essay, three hundred pages long, won the prize, and also high praise from the whole faculty. Glowing with inner pride, I was inclined to believe that I had already become a full-fledged theologian.

Believing this was, of course, total self-delusion, but it took me many years to find that out.

A Decisive Meeting

When the German theologian Helmut Thielicke was asked to write a short autobiography, he entitled it *Begegnungen* ("Meetings" or "Encounters"). In its original German version, one of the most popular books of the Swiss theologian Emil Brunner bore the title *Wahrheit als Begegnung* (literally, "Truth as Encounter"); happily, in the English editions it was simplified to *The Divine-Human Encounter*.

None of us could live in a vacuum. Our lives consist of "meetings," "encounters," and "confrontations." Yet the kinds of meetings we have vary enormously. There are official and private meetings, everyday and once-in-a-lifetime meetings, casual and life-shaping meetings. The rare life-shaping encounter makes a deep impact and may radically change the direction and motivation of an entire life.

When, at that Christian students' conference, God in Christ accosted me for the first time, I returned home with all the blessings of a divine-human encounter. When I attended the conference a second time, God again had a unique experience in store for me, but this time in the form of a decisive meeting with a man whom I later liked to call "my American father."

One day an American church historian, James Isaac Good, visited our camp. We heard that he had crossed the Atlantic more than fifty times, and once he had even circled the globe—in the days before airplanes! His main interests were Christian missions and the history of the Reformed (Presbyterian) churches. He came to Hungary primarily because he was writing a book on the history of the Heidelberg Catechism, and he knew that the Reformed Church of Hungary used that catechism in depth and quite extensively.

Following Dr. Good's address to the conference, another theological student, Coloman Tóth from Pápa, and I were called in to meet him. With a warm, grandfatherly smile, he popped an unexpected question: "Would you like to study in America for two years?" We were speechless. Without waiting for us to recover our voices, he continued, "I would cover all your expenses."

First dumbfounded, then elated, we of course gratefully accepted his generous invitation. Soon we learned that he was a bachelor, a man of means, and a philanthropist. The only condition he laid down was that, after spending our two years in America, we should return to Hungary and make the best use of our American experience by sharing it with our native country and church.

This was long before the words *ecumenical* and *ecumenicity* had become common currency in the life of the churches of the world. In the person of James Isaac Good, God was already giving me not only an "American father" who knew that the best way for a Christian to live is to share with others, but a living example of an ecumenical Christian: one who shares his talent, his time, his treasure, even his smile with students young in heart, soul, and body, so that they might become well-prepared servants of the Lord of the World and the Head of the Church.

"It is simply unbelievable," I repeated again and again. Had I not been the one who sixteen months ago had wanted to throw in the towel and leave theology behind for good? And now God was opening up before me, the would-be quitter, such a wonderful opportunity. No wonder that from this time on divine providence and predestination increasingly became not only the guiding principles of my personal life but also the compelling themes in my theological outlook.

"Westward Ho!"

I could hardly wait to share the good news with my parents. When I told them about it, they were both happy and scared. They were proud of me, but at the same time they were hesitant to let me go so far away. (In those days America seemed a very remote country.) They finally agreed, although with reluctance, and in a few weeks I was ready to leave for the "New World."

"Westward ho!" was the rallying cry of the pioneers struggling across the American continent, an exclamation that

Coloman Tóth and I used again and again to cheer ourselves on. For at that time it was not so simple to get to the United States. Especially during the aftermath of World War I, one had to overcome dozens of bureaucratic hurdles, and to wait, sometimes for months, for steamer reservations.

At last, in the first days of September, Coloman and I left Hungary. It took us two days by train to reach Rotterdam. There we were held in quarantine for three more days. Our hair was cropped and our bodies were shaved. In the dull gray garb and Dutch wooden shoes we were given to wear, we looked like prison inmates. After this grooming we had to submit to an almost endless string of medical examinations. The whole procedure filled us with acute anxiety. What if they found one or both of us physically unfit to go to America? What a blow that would be!

On the fourth day, however, we were allowed to proceed to our point of departure. We crossed the English Channel by boat, then traveled by train to Liverpool. Once there, we had to wait three days for the arrival of our liner, and it took ten days to cross the Atlantic.

When we finally disembarked in New York, Dr. Good was there to welcome us with his grandfatherly smile. In two days he showed us as much as he could of the city. Then he escorted us to the Pennsylvania Railroad Station and put us on a train westward. Destination: Dayton, Ohio.

Two Years at Dayton

Fellow Students and Professors. My two years at Central Theological Seminary in Dayton were very rewarding. The seminary was small in size but high in quality. It belonged to the Reformed Church in the United States, also known as the German Reformed Church. Its students and professors were mostly of German and Swiss extraction, and the spirit and theology of the seminary reflected the German-Swiss Reformed traditions.

Coloman and I were the youngest members of what was called the middle class. We were "middlers" because we were following the academic traditions of Europe. There a student begins seminary training at the same time he begins his four years of college or university education—at about the age of eighteen. And I was not quite eighteen when I began my theological studies. In fact, in our senior year I was the youngest member of the entire student body, and for the next twenty-five years, whether I happened to be a student or a professor, I was always the "Benjamin" of my class or faculty. During that time I got used to the fact that my age always lagged behind my achievements.

Our seminary mates were eager to introduce us to everyday English and help us explore the intricate world of American slang. They enjoyed our Hungarian accent but found it hard to imitate: they admitted that they could scarcely manage the exact pronunciation of our names. When they tried to pronounce my last name in the proper Hungarian way, they were tempted to call me "Washday." And since washday in America traditionally used to be Monday, I was finally nicknamed "Béla Monday."

The professors were pragmatic in their teaching methods, informal and open in their approach. They encouraged us to express our doubts in the classroom and were ready to answer our questions. Needless to say, this was quite a change for me. Another pleasant change was the humor that prevailed within the boundaries of mutual respect. I will never forget one professor's tongue-in-cheek instruction in homiletics: "A good sermon is like a woman's skirt. It must be short enough to be interesting, and long enough to cover the subject." This may have sounded frivolous to me, but it proved to be most useful advice.

Psychology and Theology.   While studying in the United States I kept on doing more and more research in the field that I had become most interested in: religious psychology. The wealth of Anglo-American literature suddenly at my disposal inspired me. The works in the psychology of mysticism especially attracted my attention, and in the end I wrote my B.D. thesis on this subject.

Besides reading as much as I could, I also wanted to reap

the benefits of practical observation. For this reason I made "psychological excursions" to meeting places of various religious sects and cults on Sunday evenings. The Salvation Army welcomed my visits. The services of the kind of Pentecostals sometimes called "holy rollers" gave me excellent opportunities to observe firsthand the use of mass suggestion and hypnotism and the various stages of trance.

Once, while attending the worship service of a religious group that relied heavily on pressure tactics, I had a rather unpleasant experience. Upon entering the hall, I sat down in the last pew. Soon a man approached me, offered me a hymnal, and settled down on my right side. A minute later another man left his pew and came and sat on my left side. I felt nailed down when they started to work on me. "You must be saved today!" they entreated me. "Come, sit down in the front pew, the pew of the newly converted. We want to pray over you and praise the Lord for your conversion." I assured them that I was already saved, but that declaration fell upon deaf ears. Apparently only a conversion in their presence and to their special religious views would count in their eyes. When I naively disclosed that I was a theological student merely interested in observing their worship, they turned on me like hornets. "Get out of here! You are headed for hell!" they shouted, and threw me out.

Although religious psychology was my first love, I also became more and more attracted to theology. My particularly avid interest in the issue of predestination and free will became common knowledge in the seminary, and it elicited a lot of good-natured ribbing. The professors were aware of my interest too, of course, and one of them decided to tease me a bit himself. He was the professor of Old Testament, whom we had nicknamed "the rocking-chair theologian." He lectured sitting in a rocking chair, and the more involved he became in the class the more vehemently he rocked back and forth— hence the primary reason for the name. But the jest also applied because we found his theology, especially in the area of divine predestination, rather shaky.

He started each class by calling the roll. One morning, when he called the name of Mr. Tóth, my Hungarian friend, I responded, "He is not yet here, but he is coming." At that instant Coloman entered the classroom. When the professor called my name a moment later, I responded, "Here."

He looked at me teasingly: "*Will* he be here?"

"He *expects* to be here," I replied. The class began to smile.

"Of course," said the professor, "he is *predestined* to be here." Smiles turned to laughter.

For a second I was taken aback; then I retorted, "Certainly, it is *not of his free will* that he is here."

The class roared, and the professor's rocking intensified as he began his lecture with a strained smile. (I should mention here that my Old Testament professor and I remained good friends. A few years later I had the privilege of being his host and interpreter when he visited the various seminaries of the Reformed Church in Hungary. One day as we were riding together in a coach, he even reminded me of our great debate on predestination and free will. "We sure had a grand time in that classroom, didn't we?" he said, with an understanding smile on his face.)

I received my B.D. degree (*cum laude*) from the seminary in May 1924. Soon after that, in Cleveland, Ohio, I was ordained to the ministry in the Reformed Church of the United States.

God's gracious election and man's moral freedom: this antinomy was still very much on my mind when I chose Acts 9:15 as the text for my ordination sermon: "The Lord said to him [Ananias], 'Go, for he [Saul] is a chosen instrument of mine to carry my name before the Gentiles and kings and the sons of Israel.'" In my youthful zeal I boldly declared, "I too regard myself a chosen instrument of God," and I pledged that in my forthcoming ministry I was ready to testify to his mighty works.

A Very Welcome Book

I served my first pastorate during the summers of 1924 and 1925. I was charged by the classis to act as supply minister for three Hungarian Reformed congregations: one on the banks of the Niagara, one in Buffalo, and one in North Tonawanda, New York. That meant holding three services each Sunday in two languages (English and Hungarian), supervising three Sunday schools, and overseeing three women's guilds and three youth organizations—in addition to making regular visitations and offering personal counseling.

During these very busy summer months, I also reached another phase in my intellectual development. In 1917 Rudolf Otto's *Das Heilige* was published, and in the early twenties it was translated into English under the title *The Idea of the Holy*. I could not have asked for a better stimulus to keep alive in me both the psychologist and the theologian. Otto regarded history, psychology, and philosophy as "handmaidens of theology." He stressed the point that his line of inquiry in the book "was directed toward Christian theology and not towards religious history or the psychology of religion." Yet his book was primarily a historico-psychological work, a "phenomenology of religion." It reconfirmed my belief that the psychology of religion *must* be used as a stepping-stone to real theological scholarship.

According to Otto, the matrix of religious experience is located in the awareness of our creaturehood (*Kreaturgefühl*). This is coupled with a feeling of unworthiness when we compare ourselves with the Holy One and find our real worth in him. Terror and bliss, dread and awe (the *"mysterium tremendum et fascinans"*) are the main ingredients of our religious experiences. The Cross of Jesus is "the monogram of eternal mystery." Humility and exaltation are our simultaneous responses to the events of crucifixion and resurrection.

At that stage of my development, Otto's book fascinated me no end. However, I was not yet aware of certain temptations that man's sinfulness insinuates into even his religious experiences. Nor did I realize that in our Christian faith-experience nothing should be regarded as irrational, nonrational, or even antirational, as Otto assumed. God's revelation to us may transcend our rational apprehension, but it does not contradict it. Finally, I did not notice that Otto's assumption necessarily leads to a dualistic interpretation of science and religion, which is wrong. Theology should be treated as a science in its own right. It has its own method, which is appropriate to its subject matter, and this method should never be identified with any other scientific method, not even with that of religious psychology.

Squirrels, Fireflies, and Studies

It was during my second year in Dayton that I had received the telegram informing me of Dr. Good's sudden death. The news had hit me almost as hard as if my own father had passed away. Two days later I had gotten a letter that Dr. Good had written and mailed on the evening of his fatal heart attack. In it he told me that he had made the necessary arrangements for me to spend a third year in the United States at Princeton Theological Seminary. Thus, even after his death, his good deeds spoke loudly and tangibly about the wondrous works of God through one of his servants.

The academic year of 1924–25 at Princeton was particularly wonderful. Of all my student years it was the least disturbed, and intellectually as well as spiritually the most enriching. When I looked out through the windows of my apartment, I could see squirrels frolicking on the lawn. And when I took my evening walks among glittering fireflies, my ideas mimicked them, swarming in my head, prodding me to put them on paper. But these flashes of inspiration were like the fireflies' light: fascinating but short-lived, changeable and elusive. Even when I was able to capture some of them, I felt frustrated because they merely scratched the surface of my thoughts or warmed the bottom of my heart.

I began my days with devotional Bible-reading and prayer. The courses I took ("The Work of the Holy Spirit," "The Theology of the *Institutes*," "Nineteenth- and Twentieth-Century Theologies") all proved invaluable later. I also benefited greatly from classes I attended at the graduate school of the university (I took courses in advanced psychology, Greek philosophy, and ethics). My private reading opened up to me the world of American neorealism and pragmatism. In the meantime I was also joyfully preparing my thesis on divine predestination for Professor Gaspar Hodge.

My studies at Princeton clearly showed me the dividing

line between providence and predestination, and made me see why the first should be subordinated to the second. I saw that in the life, suffering, and crucifixion of Jesus Christ, divine predestination and man's responsible agency were working together in perfect harmony. Moral spontaneity, thankful obedience, courage, and perseverance are gifts owed to our gracious election in and through Jesus Christ.

Thus the theologian in me began to take shape—but by no means at the expense of my abiding interest in religious psychology. In the well-equipped libraries of Princeton I had a field day gathering data not only in English but also in French and German, thus fanning the flames of my first love. By the time I returned to Europe I was quite familiar with the Continental material I would need later for my doctoral dissertation on the history of religious psychology.

Visit to a Former Opium Den

When I was attending school at Princeton, I had even more opportunities to visit various churches and religious organizations, especially in Philadelphia and New York.

In Philadelphia I went to the meeting house of the Quakers, and I was deeply moved by the simplicity of their worship service. They waited for the Spirit in complete silence, and under his guidance some uttered short, sporadic testimonies. They all stressed the presence of the "inner light" and its transforming, guiding power.

In New York my favorite preacher was Harry Emerson Fosdick. In my adolescence his books had opened up a new world to my uninitiated mind. I had believed that everything he wrote was the truth and nothing but the truth. Now, however, I could listen to his preaching with more critical ears. At that time the fight between Fundamentalists and Modernists was raging, and many Fundamentalists considered Fosdick not only a Modernist but definitely a heretic. Responding to the question "Are you for Fosdick or against him?" meant instant labeling. Since I could discern elements of truth in both views, my sincere answer had to be both "yes" and "no."

One night while I was in New York I visited a former

Chinese theater and opium den in which a rescue mission was conducting its evangelistic work. During that visit all the conflicts between Fundamentalism and Modernism lost their relevance for me. It seemed so petty to quibble over theological fads when the actual salvation of lost people was at stake. Above the door of that former opium den was a sign that read, "Come in, brother. Christ is waiting here for you!" Underneath, in smaller letters, was printed this promise: "Whoever enters this building will be offered a cup of coffee and a piece of cake, and lodging for the night, should he need it."

The offer attracted a sorry group of people, a garden variety of vagrants, unemployed workers, winos, and drug abusers. In the auditorium all the methods of aggressive evangelism were applied, aimed to shake up and shock. But the audience was a hardened bunch of people who were difficult to reach. Each night, out of the many, only a few made a decision to start a new life, and even fewer kept their promise. The majority came just for that cup of coffee and piece of cake, listened quietly, and then disappeared into the lower regions of that building and lay down on the floor, using their worn-out jackets for pillows—if they had jackets at all.

Harry Emerson Fosdick or the rescue-mission evangelist: which of these two did a better job in the name of the Lord? Surely neither of them could have done the job of the other, and each of them was performing an important service. That night I gave thanks to the Lord for the work of both men.

That "Third Degree"

In Freemasonry "third degree" indicates the rank of a Master Mason. Badgering alleged criminals to wring a confession out of them is also called giving them the "third degree." In my case, however, this phrase had a third meaning.

As a farewell present, my fun-loving mates from the Bennham Club (one of the boarding houses for students) at Princeton Seminary conferred upon me the honorary degree of "M.P." It did not mean "Member of Parliament" or "Military Police" or even "Mental Patient." Since I had written my thesis at Dayton on the psychology of mysticism and my other thesis at Princeton on the doctrine of predestination, the Benn-hamites' "M.P." stood for "*Mystical Predestinarian*."

Therefore, on my homeward journey from America to Hungary in August 1925, I had in my pocket a B.D. from Dayton, a Th.M. from Princeton Seminary, and an honorary M.P. from the Bennham Club. I left with sadness because I loved what I left, but also with joy because I loved what I was returning to. My native country was waiting for me.

Of course, my parents were waiting for me at the railroad station in Debrecen. Their stare reflected how much I must have changed. When they had last seen me, I had still been in my teens; now I was an adult. On top of that, I was dressed like an American, I must have smiled like an American, and I also spoke Hungarian with a distinctly American accent. But all these proved to be temporary effects.

The lasting effects of my American experiences became relevant only later. When the deluge of history washed away all normalcy and tossed my life to and fro, the so-called American activism in European garb indeed came in handy. It not only helped me to keep my head above the waves, but also taught me to turn my classroom theology into action theology at times when deeds truly spoke louder than words. It also enabled me to feel at ease with and within churches other than my own, and to discern the benefits of their unity and diversity. Finally, it helped me to gratefully accept the fact that the church's often hazy ecumenical frontier was to be the dwelling place that God had prepared for me.

5

THE PSYCHOLOGIST TURNS
INTO A THEOLOGIAN
(1925–1934)

"The Infant Professor"

Emeric Révész was the pastor whom I had been going to hear—whose sermons had meant so much to me—just before I left for the United States. When, after my return, he asked me to be his assistant minister, I happily agreed. Within a few days I stood in the highly elevated pulpit of the Great Church of Debrecen ("highly" is used here both literally and figuratively). I had to preach in a mammoth sanctuary that seated several thousand. As soon as the people learned that I was to be the speaker, they began to flock to the church. The new voice, fresher and more dynamic than they were used to, attracted them.

But it turned out to be a short-lived ministry. A few weeks after I had been appointed to the post, the Reformed Theological Seminary at Pápa asked me to join their faculty as an assistant professor of philosophy and education. Thus I left Debrecen again.

It was a strange feeling—to be not yet twenty-three, yet

called to teach the prospective ministers of the church! Many of my students-to-be were older than I. No wonder that soon after my arrival I was nicknamed "the infant professor." But in a matter of months "the infant professor" became a very popular teacher. The students tried me—and liked me. By December they knew more about Anglo-American religious psychology than any other student body in Europe. Besides teaching, I also led Bible-study groups in which we had soul-searching conversations.

Whenever the bishop had to be absent, he asked me to supply his pulpit. Afterwards, my students and I always discussed my sermons, and we all profited greatly from these lively postmortems. Those were indeed very enriching years in my life.

Doctor Sacro-Sanctae Theologiae

Busy as I was at Pápa, I still found time to finish my doctoral dissertation, entitled *The History of Religious Psychology*. In April 1927 the University of Debrecen conferred upon me the doctor-of-divinity degree *summa cum laude*. I was given the title *Doctor Sacro-Sanctae Theologiae*, a Latin phrase that literally means "Doctor [or Teacher] of Most Sacred Divinity." This may sound too solemn and overly holy to the modern ear, but the phrase dates back to the Middle Ages.

My dissertation traced the origins of religious psychology back to the Scriptures, the Greek philosophers, and the Church Fathers, especially to Saint Augustine. Then it discussed in great detail the various trends (subjects and methods) of twentieth-century religious psychology: first the Anglo-American psychologists (those of the Clark School, Starbuck, James, Leuba, Pratt, Coe, Thouless), then the French (Ribot, Flournoy, Delacroix), and finally the German (Wundt, Österreich, Otto, Müller-Freienfels, Spranger, Freud, Girgensohn, and Gruehn). I was especially taken by the method of experimental self-observation as applied by Karl Girgensohn in Leipzig and later on by Werner Gruehn at the University of Berlin.

A Theology of Syntheses

In the meantime, I became increasingly torn between the presuppositions and methodologies of psychology and theology. In order to relieve this tension, I devoted a lot of time to studying the life and work of Karl Girgensohn (twenty-five years my senior), and ended up writing an entire book about him (published in 1928). I felt a certain kinship between us, particularly because he was interested in both psychology and theology, as I was. Furthermore, he was a theologian from one of the Baltic States, and we both felt we had a religious and cultural responsibility to the East as well as to the West.

The works of Girgensohn helped me to achieve a higher synthesis of psychology and theology. Like him, I too tried to construct a theological edifice by differentiating "dogmatics in the broadest sense of the word" from "dogmatics in the strictest sense of the word." I regarded the first as a vestibule leading to the second, to the sanctuary of that edifice. The vestibule was the seat of the various sciences of religion. In the sanctuary the Word of God and saving faith prevailed. We both held that one could enter the sanctuary only through the vestibule, the sciences of religion. Consequently, the more knowledge one accumulated in the vestibule, the better-equipped he became to appreciate the goods of the sanctuary.

At the time, I thought that this construct provided a magnificent view of the whole theological edifice. But it had inherent flaws because it had been constructed by one who still regarded the experience of faith as a one-way street—a street leading *from* man up *to* God, *through* the vestibule of the sciences of religion *to* the sanctuary of God's revelation—instead of letting God speak of himself to people whenever and wherever he wanted to, and open up the doors of his sanctuary even to those who had never heard of the sciences of religion.

At this stage of my intellectual development, a theology of syntheses was certainly helpful. But it still needed correction, which would come later, when further experiences had prepared me for it.

Student Evangelism

In the last years of his short life (he died suddenly in 1925 at the age of fifty), Karl Girgensohn reached the plateau of biblical realism, and I joined him there in both theory and practice. We both realized that the critical exegete must always take the position of a distant objective observer. But in so doing he reduces Scripture to an object for scholastic scrutiny. He usually fails to ask, "What if God wants to tell me something here and now through this ancient text that I am merely dissecting?"

In the instant in which this question is raised, the researcher and interpreter of the biblical text finds himself on the pneumatic (spiritual) level, where suddenly, with unstopped ears, he can hear the up-to-date, personal message in the two-thousand-year-old text. His analysis and exegesis turns into a tool for unearthing the Truth beneath the layers of truths. Pneumatic exegesis does not necessarily reject the results of a historico-critical appraisal. But it never uses them as standards for measuring God's Holy Word.

When this became clear to me, I suddenly saw the vital importance of in-depth biblical study, a Spirit-guided interpretation of the Scriptures. After my doctoral examination I began to travel from one student conference to the next. "Necessity was laid upon me" (as Paul said), and I had to share this new insight of mine with students and to demonstrate to them what real Bible study was meant to be.

These conferences were held in various parts of the country, usually in tranquil, picturesque settings. Traveling with the students on the train gave me a good opportunity to get to know them in a different way. It helped them to realize that their companion was not the lecturing professor they were used to but a brother who wanted to share what had been given to him. And sometimes during these conferences the Lord taught a good lesson to students and professor alike.

During the summer of 1927, for example, Hungary was plagued by a long-lasting drought. But the day we boarded the train in Budapest, dark clouds began to gather on the horizon. The students started to pray that there would be no rain, at least not for those two days we expected to spend in a small village. By the time we arrived in the village, however, it was raining, and it continued to rain. The next morning my hostess, a devout peasant woman, happily exclaimed, "Now we can be sure that these young men and women who came to our village are really *godly* people. For weeks we have been praying for rain in vain. Our crops were drying up. We were desperate. But now look—as soon as these angels arrived, God almighty immediately began to pour his blessing upon us."

I felt ashamed. I hoped that this good woman would never learn that those "angels of God" had prayed for exactly the opposite "blessing." I told the students what had happened, and then we talked a good deal about self-centeredness and selfishness in our prayer life. The rain kept on pouring nonstop throughout our stay, and we were cooped up as a result. Nevertheless, we reaped a bountiful spiritual harvest.

Critique of a Papal Encyclical

When the Life and Work movement and the Faith and Order movement held their first conferences (in 1925 and 1928 respectively), they also extended an invitation to the Roman Catholic Church. But the Vatican declined to send delegates either to Stockholm or to Lausanne. In January 1928 Pope Pius XI promulgated his encyclical *Mortalium Animos*, in which he not only reiterated that the Roman Catholic Church considers itself the only true, holy, and catholic church of Christ, but criticized all other churches for their participation in the two movements.

The National Federation of Reformed Ministers in Hungary asked me to give a critical review of the encyclical at its next conference. At that time I was only twenty-five years old. I agreed, regarding this as a way to begin fulfilling the pledge that I had made at the age of seventeen: that I would do my utmost to promote love and unity between Roman Catholics and Protestants. In my address I refuted point by point the accusations of the encyclical and emphasized that we Protestants are not "a-catholics" or "anti-catholics," only "a-Romans" and "anti-Romans." The greatest flaw of the encyclical was that it wanted to make all Christians "pan-Romans." On the other hand, the purpose of the conferences in Stockholm and Lausanne was to bear witness to the one holy catholic church and to serve the cause of Christian unity both in faith and in action. We Protestants stretched out our arms toward our Roman brethren firmly believing in the ultimate triumph of an "evangelical catholicity," in a visible consummation of Christian unity.

As is well known, since 1928 many promising things have happened and are happening in the realm of ecumenical Christianity. But in 1928 ecumenical unity was still considered a pipe dream. I am grateful to God that already in that early and shaky stage of ecumenicity, he had started me off to serve him on the ecumenical road.

Another Prizewinning Essay

Student evangelism and ecumenical dialogue: the emerging theologian in me had now been engaged in both. But the time for developing into a full-fledged theologian was yet to come. Something important hindered its arrival.

In the spring of 1928 a friend of mine from Zürich called my attention to an announcement made by the distinguished Kant Society in Germany: it was offering a prize for the best essay written on the topic "the psychology of faith." Each essayist was expected to give an analytical description of faith and all its related phenomena; and to state its definite role in religion, philosophy, and scientific investigation, in the life of the individual and in society. The most important condition was that all phenomena connected with faith should be analyzed without any philosophical or theological prejudice. Every essay was to be submitted in a sealed envelope bearing a code name and containing the name and address of the competitor, and was to be postmarked no later than December 31, 1929. The members of the jury were Paul Häberlin (Switzerland), Paul Tillich (Germany), and Edward Utitz (Germany).

The contest pricked my interest. I launched out on it by

spending the summer of 1928 in the libraries of Berlin and Leipzig. While in Berlin, I was offered the Chair of Systematic Theology at the Reformed Theological Seminary in Sárospatak, Hungary. This meant a new challenge, one that pointed definitely toward theology and away from psychology. But the move to Sárospatak and the preparation to assume the responsibilities of such a position were a drain on my time and energy, so I almost gave up the idea of writing the essay. Almost. But at the renewed prodding of friends I decided to work day and night to meet the challenge.

On December 27, 1929, I left for Berlin by train with an unfinished copy of the essay. I was racing against time, because I could complete the final pages only in Berlin. During the last two days of the year I did not sleep at all. But my dedication paid off: on the thirty-first of December, just before midnight, in a state of hopeful exhaustion, I mailed a copy of my essay to the Curatory of the University of Halle.

Seven months later, on a hot summer day, a registered letter waited on my desk. The secretary of the Kant Society was writing to inform me that I had won the essay contest. This meant not only a sizeable monetary award but also a kind of glory. Psychologists, philosophers, and theologians in Hungary sang my praises. The National Academy of Sciences voted to subsidize the publication of the essay. And the members of the divinity school of my alma mater assured me that at the first opportunity they wanted me to join the faculty there.

Amid all this jubilation, my mother, proud as she was of her son, also voiced her concern: "You are now a respected scholar, but I am afraid you may never get married!"

"But mother," I joked, "haven't you noticed that I am already married? In fact, I am a *bigamist*. You see, when I am at home, my typewriter is my wife. When I go out for a walk, I take my second wife, my umbrella, and as we walk together, usually a dialogue is going on between us. My best thoughts are born during those dialogues with my umbrella."

The offspring of my bigamy were two books that I called "the twins." Their names were *The Psychology of Faith* and *The Mystery of Faith*.

The Freedom Fight of the Theologian

The second of these books, *The Mystery of Faith*, was published in 1932, and it is still being used as a standard reference work in the theological seminaries of Hungary. This is how I happened to write it.

From 1930 onward, all external circumstances steered me away from psychology and toward theology. As holder of the Chair of Systematic Theology at Sárospatak, I was committed to plying theology. Then too, in the summer of 1931, as a delegate of the Hungarian YMCA, I made my second trip to America to attend the World Conference of the YMCA being held in Toronto and Cleveland. There my American friends urged me to speak about "dialectical theology," more popularly called "the theology of crisis" in the United States. In the early nineteen-thirties, of course, America was in a deep economic depression, and concern, anxiety, and despair had taken their toll. Millions of unemployed people needed a positive, spiritual message, an assurance that their critical situation could become beneficial if they were able to discern in it the opportunity for a turning point, a new beginning, initiated "from on high." So at that time the theology of crisis was a solace to many confused and despairing Americans.

A third external reason for my concentrating on theology was my own scholarly advancement. I knew that sooner or later my alma mater wanted to enlist my services. An invitation to fill the historic Chair of Systematic Theology at Debrecen was on the horizon. And so I decided to write an extensive monograph on the theology of faith.

I finished this book in 1931 in a matter of months, with amazing ease. *Something irresistible* prodded me along. In the preface to the book I called it "the freedom fight of the theologian in me." This freedom fight had actually started long ago, during my student years at Debrecen, Dayton, and Princeton. It had intensified during the years of my "infant professorship" at Pápa, and it had almost made me a split personality while I had worked on my essay on the psychology of faith. The fact that I had been forced to obey the condition established by the Kant Society—that the empirical study of the psychology of faith had to be divorced from any theological prejudice—had served as a good, pragmatic reason for *suppressing* the emerging theologian in me. And there is no doubt about it: while writing that essay, I thoroughly succeeded in doing just that.

But any act of suppression sooner or later breeds its counterpart, liberation. And so, on the first day of 1930, after I had dropped my prizewinning essay in the mail, I had made a resolution: for a stretch of time, I promised myself, I would read nothing but theological works—Barth, Brunner, Gogarten, Thurneysen, Bultmann, Kierkegaard, and so on. With their books as my daily diet, the pendulum had started to swing in the opposite direction. The psychologist in me did an about-face, began becoming a full-fledged theologian.

In this process I did not discard the sciences of religion; I merely dethroned them. They became what they were originally intended to be: "handmaidens of theology." The elevated place they had occupied was now taken over by God's revelation and its human concomitant, saving faith.

There was no getting away from it. The "twin sister" of *The Psychology of Faith* clamored to be born. And her name was called *The Mystery of Faith*.

The Mystery of Faith

My "twins" took quite different points of departure. While the first was an empirical descriptive treatise, the second was an exposition in which the theological perspective prevailed.

The Psychology of Faith concentrated upon man as a "Striving Self" ("I strive, therefore I am"); described his instinctive drives as well as his rational (spiritual) yearnings; and defined believing as an act in which the Striving Self completely participates. It discussed the various patterns of believing as well as their social and cultural implications. It concluded by stating that the act of faith is the most relevant cementing factor in both our interpersonal communications and our corporate life.

The Mystery of Faith, though its dominant perspective was theological, did not take God alone as its point of departure — that would have led to sheer speculation. Nor did it take man

49

alone as its point of departure, as *The Psychology of Faith* had done. Its point of departure had to be man under God, his Creator and Redeemer.

Our Creator intended us to live in his nearness, within the circle of his love. But our disobedience, our desire to be equal to him, shattered the circle and distorted it into an ellipse. The circle has one center; the ellipse, two foci. We displaced God as the only hub of our life and created another focus, our own beloved capital *I*. We demoted God to an abstract concept, a distant principle. Or perhaps, bigheartedly, we accepted him as an equal partner with whom we could enter into some kind of trade relationship. And so we lived in, through, and unto ourselves, far away from the center of light, warmth, and love, out on the periphery, in the shivering wasteland of our mighty independence.

But eventually we had our fill of it, and then we poor, deluded, self-made outcasts tried to return to God. The world's great religions are demonstrations of human attempts to bridge the gap. But they all failed. Something had to be done from the other side, from the original center. Our total crisis could be dissolved and solved only by God. For "God so loved the world that he gave his only Son. . . ." His hands nailed to the cross smashed our elliptical world; his outstretched arms embraced it, shaped it back into a circle with God as its only center. And now we find ourselves back again where we rightly belong. Who said that we cannot go home again? Yes, we can. Never on our own, though, but only by the transforming power of his love.

What is described here is not just a series of events that happened in the remote past, far back in history. It is our story, depicting our own individual past, present, and future. It is the continuous happening of the human situation, our personal drama played out on the stage of the here and now. We are the men and women who pushed God away in rebellious independence. Now each one of us can cry out every day, "Against thee, thee only, have I sinned, and done that which is evil in thy sight . . ." (Ps. 51:4). You and I are in a mess we created on our own, and now we desperately thrash around to try to extricate ourselves—but every movement only drives us deeper into it, helpless and despairing.

Then one blessed day it dawns on us that we cannot rescue ourselves without help. That is when we cry out with Paul, "Wretched man that I am! Who will deliver me from this body of death?" (Rom. 7:24). That is when something happens from the other side. And, dear reader, it happens to you and me. The everlasting arms reach out, embrace us, hold us, and take us home again.

God's saving grace, his endlessly repeated forgiveness, cannot be explained, only experienced. Our only and total response is faith, *saving* faith. It is our faith, *an event* pointing beyond itself to him who initiated it in us. And it is, through and through, an existential occurrence. Man's whole self, every dimension of his being, is mobilized by it. At the same time, it is also an act of responsible decision-making in which man is quite free to accept or reject the salvation offered him by God.

This faith has its ebb and flow. Yet it is eternally ours in our "mystical union with Christ." As long as we are here on earth, however, this faith never changes into "sight." It continues to do its work through repentance, gratitude, hope, love, and obedience. Paradoxically, it is both man's ever-fresh commitment and the gift of God's grace to him. In Augustine's words, "I see what I can do; I do not see whence I can do it—except that I see this far . . . it is of God."

Saving faith is and remains a mystery (1 Tim. 3:9).

The Nature and Place of Theology

In the early nineteen-thirties three of the essays I wrote dealt with these subjects. In the first I discussed the role of paradoxes in theological thought; in the other two I discussed the place of preaching and theology in the life of the church militant.

Paradoxes are an integral element of theology, the blood cells in its arteries. Each Christian doctrine is the expression of a faith experience, equally bitter and sweet. The bitterness is caused by our awareness that, try as we might, we cannot build a road leading to God. The sweetness is our sudden discovery that God has already built the road by revealing himself to us. This revealed and hidden God (*deus revelatus et absconditus*) speaks and acts in a mysterious way, transcending our common sense, doing the "strange things"—*paradoxa*—mentioned in Luke 5:26. And so our understanding of him can be expressed only in paradoxes.

Some of the chief paradoxes of Christian theology are these: Revelation is an event both disclosing and hiding the same one God. Faith is man's responsible response to God's revelation, yet it is also God's gracious gift to him. In the act of faith, man, being on the receiving end, is utterly passive; yet he is also totally involved and thus wholly active. Jesus Christ, the Word Incarnate, was a historic man who lived two thousand years ago, yet he is always contemporaneous with us, an ever-present companion. The Scriptures are historically conditioned books, yet it is the same one eternal God who speaks to us in and through these historical documents. The Triune God is Father, Son, and Holy Spirit, yet these three are the same one God. Divine providence assures us that nothing can happen without the will of God; at the same time, we know that many things occur that are against his will, and, in fact, we are challenged by God to resist and to overcome them. Finally, divine predestination and our free, responsible decisions together are the wellspring of our salvation.

If you are a believer and a theologian, you simply cannot detour around paradoxes. They may be stumbling blocks to the unbeliever, but to the believer they testify to a truth beyond our common understanding. They are the earmarks of genuine theology.

The sounding board of a theology, with all its paradoxes, is bound to be the church. The church's primary function is proclamation, the preaching of God's Word. It is an event in the form of direct communication. The purpose of a good sermon is not to impart human wisdom to its hearers, whether that wisdom comes from the preacher or from others, but to evoke in the hearers a decision-making process effecting their salvation. To this end the preacher must proclaim the whole God, both his judgment and his mercy. But he can hardly do this without constantly scrutinizing his choice of words in the light of sound theology. The preacher is like the driver of a car, theology is like the motor, and the Spirit of God is like the fuel for it. Without the Spirit's sparking presence, both driver and motor would be useless, and the car would stall. If preaching is the ministry of God's Word, theology should be defined as "ministry to the ministry of the Word of God" (*ministerium ministerii verbi divini*).

The "professional" theologian should also remain, till the end of his life, a preacher. Otherwise he might easily become "an abstraction walking on two legs." On the other hand, woe to the preacher (and also to his congregation!) who, on his commencement day or at any time during his pastorate, would say to himself, "Soul, [after so many years of study] you have ample goods laid up for many years; take your ease, eat, drink, be merry" (Luke 12:19).

Preaching and theology: both are functions of the church. Blessed is the church that has a leader who is both a real preacher and a real theologian.

My "Predestined Wife"

Now that the psychologist had turned into a theologian, and in his state of "bigamy" had been able to beget "the twins," it was high time for him to find a flesh-and-blood spouse, a helpmeet indispensable both in theology and in life. Again divine providence took care of it.

In the fall of 1932 I was asked to deliver a lecture on the "delicate" subject of predestination to the Protestant students of the University of Debrecen. I accepted the invitation and was welcomed by a huge audience. During the question-and-answer period, I was caught off guard when a coed took issue with what I had said.

"In your lecture," she stated without hesitation, "you have contradicted yourself. On the one hand you stressed that God is sovereign Lord, and his will is unconditioned. On the other hand, in attempting to explain the existence of sin, your reasoning was that it occurred because in his own inscrutable way God 'permitted,' 'tolerated' it. This is an apparent contradiction. If God is an all-powerful and always active Being, he cannot possibly tolerate sin. If, however, he passively lets the chips fall where they may, he cannot be a sovereign Lord."

I was taken aback. This was an astute question from a

very young, attractive, and apparently highly intelligent girl. Part of my mind was groping for an answer. This was a difficult task, particularly because the other part of my mind, together with my whole being, was completely electrified by the discovery I had just made—"Here she is, my wife-to-be!" It was love at first sight, overwhelming, irrevocable. I needed time to regain my balance, so I didn't answer her right away. Only after dealing with the other questions raised did I turn back to her.

"Now, young lady, the gist of your question is this: How can God be an always active sovereign Lord if he 'permits' sin to exist? For such 'permissiveness' reflects a passive behavior, indicating that he is not in complete control.

"What you say sounds logical, yet you are mistaken. Because what from our limited, human perspective looks as if it were only a passive attitude is actually a highly 'active' attitude of God. May I illustrate this?

"Let us assume that one day you should get married. And let us suppose that your spouse should turn out to be a bad-tempered, quarrelsome man. Also, let us imagine that, instead of lashing back at him, you would quietly tolerate his outbursts. I ask you, would such a response, or rather lack of response, on your part be a 'passive' or an 'active' attitude?"

"Of course," she shot back, "it would be a 'passive' attitude."

"Not so," said I. "For the act of self-restraint requires more inner strength than reciprocating anger for anger. In the same way, when God, omnipotent as he is, suffers sin to exist, he simply demonstrates an active, powerful self-control."

The girl remained persistent and left the room unconvinced.

I asked the president of the student body for the girl's name and address. He told me that she was Serena Nagy de Aldoboly, a freshman in the Liberal Arts Department. She was popular, respected, and talented, and she had just recently won first prize in a national poetry contest. Her mother, a widow, lived in that part of Romania that until World War I had belonged to Hungary, so Serena roomed in the sorority house.

The next day I wrote a letter to this interesting young lady, asking for an opportunity to continue our discussion on predestination. Her answer was brief: "I'll be glad to meet you in my uncle's study at the university." (It just so happened that her uncle was a popular professor in the divinity school.)

Thus it was that for a whole hour, in her uncle's presence, she and I continued our debate. Plato, Aristotle, the Apostle Paul, John Calvin—these and many other names buzzed in our conversation. At the sound of the bell she sprang up and left in a flash for one of her classes. I barely caught up with her in the corridor to ask my breathless, vital question: "Now tell me, when could I meet you again, but without your uncle?"

Two weeks later I asked her to be my wife, but she declined. I traveled to Romania to meet her mother, and I proposed again. Her mother liked me, but my beloved kept on balking. I continued wooing her. The more unattainable she seemed to be, the more I was fascinated by her. And I knew that this was not just a passing attraction. Only in her could I find my earthly fulfillment.

At that time I was considered the most eligible bachelor in the Reformed Church, and I was besieged by various invitations from families with girls of marriageable age. I constantly had to flee these ongoing attempts at matchmaking. But now here was a girl in flight from me: a strong, talented person who wanted to have a career of her own, not at all the type who was easily swept off her feet.

I wrote to Serena daily, and these letters finally eroded her resistance. One day her affirmative answer came in the form of a love poem. In it she confessed her love for me, yet she confessed it not directly to me but to God. A unique way, routed through the divine, of saying a human "yes" to another human. A perfect divine-human encounter, so often repeated in so many different ways in the years to come.

This happened more than fifty years ago. Serena is all that I expected her to be, and more. Time proved me right.

We were married in August 1933. She was barely twenty; I was nearing thirty-one. Soon her first book of poems was published, and I was appointed professor of systematic theology by my alma mater in Debrecen. Here again I was the youngest in the history of the church to fill that important and much-coveted chair. Our first child, Naomi, was born a year later. Life seemed to stretch before us like a straight, sunny road. Who would have dreamed at that time that within a few years our smooth road would be torn up, forcing us into perilous detours?

But let me close this chapter with a theological observation. Ever since we were married I have called Serena my "predestined wife." I fell head over heels in love with her because God's providence so ordered it. Yet I did it out of my own free will, and I was and still am more than happy to assume the responsibility for falling in love with such a precious child of God's providential care.

6

THE THEOLOGIAN IN ACTION
(1935–1944)

"A Servant to All"

In the following decade not only my alma mater and the synod of the Reformed Church of Hungary but also the entire church increasingly demanded my services. The once-introverted adolescent had long been forgotten. The fledgling theologian in me was now a full-feathered bird, and a clearly defined theological understanding charted my flight. But in my constant activity and growing status I tried never to forget the most important watchword: "by grace alone."

Each morning I dictated memoranda, letters, articles, and essays to three secretaries. By late afternoon everything was ready for my review or signature. But the real bulk of the work was done by volunteers, or, as I liked to call them, my "yoke-fellows," who were scattered throughout the country. They assisted me in every way, and wrote articles and essays for the various church magazines and journals I edited—all without remuneration. We were indeed all one in obeying thankfully and joyfully Christ's grand imperative: You "must work the works of him who sent me, while it is day; night comes, when no one can work" (John 9:4).

Ministry to Ministers

My work during these ten years was a fourfold ministry to the ministers of the church, both ordained and lay preachers.

My first responsibility was the training of prospective ministers at Debrecen. Besides serving as professor of systematic theology on the faculty of the divinity school, I also served twice as its dean. In addition, I was a member of the university council. For a few years I was also the principal of the Institute for Pastoral Training. This last office gave me the opportunity to participate in the legislative work of my church district and of the general synod.

In the nineteen-thirties the spiritual atmosphere as well as the scholastic standards of both the faculty and the institute were significantly improved. The students received the best possible theological education, and at the same time, their spiritual needs were also met. Many of the professors developed personal relationships with students, particularly through their Bible-study groups. Within the framework of the institute, with the principal serving as a senior pastor, the students organized their own "congregation" and elected from their own ranks "preaching and governing elders," "deacons," and other officials. The student congregation had its own "gazette," and held its chapel services, led by invited preachers, for all students attending the university. To serve as their guide in all these undertakings was a most rewarding experience.

My second way of serving ministers was primarily organizational in character, but it had strong educational implications as well. As general secretary of the National Federation of Reformed Ministers (which was two thousand strong), I organized and conducted the annual conferences and directed the in-service training program for ministers throughout the country.

My third line of work was editorial. I launched and edited a pastoral monthly, *Truth and Life*; served as editor for the weekly gazette of the federation; and was editor-in-chief of the quarterly *Theological Review*. For a year I even edited a Reformed daily paper. Hundreds of editorials, articles, and essays, both short and long, came from my pen for all these publications.

I took the greatest pleasure in my fourth job, in which I worked with ordained and lay ministers alike. In 1939 I launched (and for years directed) the *Coetus Theologorum Reformatorum* (the Workfellowship of Reformed Theologians). The *Coetus* was not just another formal organization. It reflected the spirit of a dynamic work-community on local, regional, and national levels. It did not treat theology as an esoteric science but demonstrated that it is the most personal and practical concern of every authentic Christian. In the life of this workfellowship the professional theologians served as working members, giving lectures, delivering addresses, leading discussions, and so forth; the lay theologians participated in all the proceedings of the local, regional, and national meetings of the *Coetus*.

The very reasonable annual dues paid by the members of the *Coetus* served also as a subscription fee for the basic *Handbooks in Theology* published annually by the Workfellowship. Before Hungary's total collapse at the end of World War II, five such books were published. Had the *Coetus* been able to continue its work uninterrupted, by this time more than forty volumes would serve as documents of the church's sound teaching. Alas, as it turned out, many postwar years had to elapse before at least some aspects of the objectives of the *Coetus* could be revived in Hungary.

"The Theology of the *Institutes*"

The year 1936 was the four-hundredth anniversary of the publication of the first edition of Calvin's *Institutes*. The Reformed Church of Hungary participated in this celebration by producing a new translation of it. I was asked to write an essay called "The Theology of the *Institutes*." In this 86-page treatise I identified five basic characteristics of Calvin's theology.

The first was what I called his "heavenly pragmatism."

This had nothing to do with a philosophical pragmatism, of course. Just like a coin, it had two sides: to glorify God and to work for the salvation and well-being of man.

Second, Calvin's theology was rooted in the ultimate reality of God's Word that accosts us in the Bible. The internal testimony of the eternal Spirit confirms this Word in our hearts and minds, in and through the act of saving faith. This puts us in a new relationship with ourselves and our era, with our church and our nation. The intransigent "realpolitik" of John Calvin was grounded in such a realistic faith.

Third, his theology was motivated by wholistic considerations. The whole man and the whole world are totally dependent on the whole God who is both a righteous Judge and a merciful Father. In such a theology, revelation embraces not only the Gospel but also the Law; faith and obedience become twins; and the demand that God alone be given the glory proves to be the controlling principle.

Fourth, Calvin's faith and theology also had an agnostic element. This had nothing to do with a philosophical agnosticism; it simply acknowledged that the revealed God still remains a hidden God. His judgments are inscrutable and his ways unsearchable. The finite mind is simply unable to grasp the Infinite.

The fifth and final trait of Calvin's theology was his penchant for speaking in antinomies. But his antinomies pointed beyond those of the philosophers. The matrix for Calvin's paradoxes was his own faith experience. These paradoxes not only safeguarded him from making an object out of God, but pointed to God as the absolute and gracious Subject who is in complete control of our lives.

The interwovenness and interplay of these five basic threads can be discerned everywhere in Calvin's theology. I kept them always in mind when working on my own theology.

The Reformed Church of Hungary as a whole, which certainly included me, closely adhered to the basic principles of Calvin's theology. But we did so without wearing blinders. We were not willing to identify the Reformed faith with any closed system of thought, even one called "Calvinistic." We always regarded the Living Word of God as our ultimate Basis and his Spirit as our ultimate Guide. After all, Luther never wanted to establish a Lutheran religion, nor Calvin a Calvinistic religion. And Karl Barth's daily prayer was "God, deliver me from the 'Barthians'!"

Barth's Lecture Tour in Hungary

During the summer of 1935 Serena and I toured Western Europe, meeting with ministers and theologians in Germany, France, and Switzerland. In Geneva we participated in one of the first ecumenical seminars conducted by Adolph Keller. But the most memorable events for us were our visits with Emil Brunner and Karl Barth.

We invited Karl Barth to make a lecture tour in Hungary, and he gladly accepted. When he asked what topics he should choose for his lectures, we suggested two. First, we proposed that he speak about the nature and mission of the church, using the title "National Church, Free Church, Confessing Church." He was more than happy to accept the challenge, especially since the Nazi government had just recently forced him to leave Germany, and he had much to share with us about the struggles of the Confessing Church there. For his second topic we suggested the doctrine of predestination. That surprised him. When he asked why we chose that subject, we explained that Hungary had been occupied by the Turks for 150 years in the sixteenth and seventeenth centuries. One of the tenets of Islam is fatalism, and the lasting influence of that long Turkish occupation can still be discerned in a hard-to-shed Hungarian tendency to interpret predestination in terms of fatalism. Given this explanation, Barth enthusiastically consented to speak on this second topic as well.

In the early fall of 1936 Barth and his secretary arrived in Debrecen. For three weeks, as we traveled in Hungary and Transylvania, I served as their guide and interpreter. During that time we visited five Reformed theological seminaries. Barth was received everywhere with great enthusiasm and respect. No other foreign theologian could have exerted so noticeable an impact upon Hungarian Protestantism as he did in those three weeks. At the end of the tour he told me, "From now on I will always feel a kinship with Hungarian Protestantism, and I will always be interested in whatever transpires in your church and nation." He kept his promise, as I shall explain later.

Barth's lectures in Hungary, especially the four talks he gave called "God's Gracious Election," represented significant advances even in his own theology. In a later volume of his *Church Dogmatics*, his more extensive reinterpretation of predestination was built upon the basic principles he laid down in these lectures.

This is not the place to give an in-depth appraisal of these events. But one occurrence should be described here because it symbolizes the kind of "Copernican revolution" so characteristic of his theology.

The Theological Seminary of the Reformed Church at Kolozsvár (in Transylvania) asked him to plant two Lombardy poplars on their campus. Those upward-reaching trees were to remind students and professors—indeed, the whole church—of the basic principle of Barth's theology: our sufficiency is from on high.

A Hungarian folk song, freely translated, goes something like this:

> Poplar trees, poplar trees,
> You can grow wondrous high.
> But not even at your tallest
> Could your tips reach the sky.

In other words, there is no straight way leading from man to God. But there is a way, *the* Way, descending to us vertically from on high. Strain as we might, we can never reach him on our own. All we can do is stretch out toward him, and he will then reach out to us wherever we are.

July 14, 1938

This day in my life has always remained memorable for more than one reason. First, because our long-awaited son, Béla, Jr., was born on that day. Second, because on that very same day I was almost nominated to be the bishop of the Transtibiscan Synod of the Reformed Church in Hungary, which had its headquarters in Debrecen. It would have set another record if I had been awarded that office at such a young age.

When the vacancy occurred, Professor Emeric Révész, my good friend and mentor, was approached to accept the nomination. His age and stature made him the logical choice for this important office. But his love for undisturbed scholarly work made the decision agonizingly difficult for him. He shared all the pros and cons with me in our private conversations.

He was asked to reach a decision by July 14. On the morning of that day, the seniors of the dioceses (the ministers of the presbyteries) came to see me. They wanted me to know that, should Professor Révész decline the offer, they would nominate me. But as I was discussing the situation with one of the seniors, Serena phoned me. It was time to take her to the maternity clinic. By the time our son was born, Professor Révész had decided to accept the nomination. The next day, his face showing traces of a sleepless night, he asked me to stand by him as one of his confidants and closest fellow-workers. And that is what I remained, even after I left Hungary for America.

July 14, 1938! Many things would have turned out very differently in my life if Emeric Révész had continued to resist nomination and I had been elected bishop. Instead of coming to the United States after World War II, I would have had to stay in Hungary and shoulder burdens of heretofore unknown magnitude. In 1948, for example, I would have been in charge of drafting a new agreement between the Communist government and the Reformed Church of Hungary. How far would I have gone in compromising or resisting? And would I even be alive today? Who knows?

"O the depth of the riches and wisdom and knowledge of God! How unsearchable are his judgments and how inscrutable his ways!" (Rom. 11:33).

A "World Assembly"

In August 1938, as secretary of the National Federation of Reformed Ministers, it was my task to organize and conduct in

Debrecen the federation's first conference, called "The First World Assembly of All Hungarians Adhering to the Reformed Faith." Many thousands came from all parts of the globe to attend. The Great Church in Debrecen was filled to capacity, and many had to listen to the proceedings outside in the park via a public address system.

The aims of the assembly were to testify to our common spiritual liberation by Jesus Christ, to confess our individual as well as national sins, and to express our thankfulness to God, who in all parts of the world took care of his children born as Magyars. Somehow we all felt that this world assembly was an eleventh-hour gathering—and we were right. A year later World War II was indeed upon us, and a similar assembly could never again materialize.

In connection with this assembly, I published a book entitled *Basic Questions in the Life of All Hungarians Confessing the Reformed Faith*. In it all the major objectives of our church were summed up in twelve points. The first and the last of these in particular will never lose their timeliness: (1) The nature and the mission of the church need to be rediscovered by each generation, lest it lose its vertical and dynamic identity; and (12) For all our works and achievements God alone should be praised.

Vital Issues

Out of the hundreds of addresses I delivered and essays I wrote during those ten years, I give here the gist only of those that later had an effect upon my theological deepening and development.

The Inspiration of the Scriptures. In this I identified myself with the view of dynamic inspiration, also called the reformation principle of the authority of Scripture. God speaks to us in and through the books of the Bible. First he revealed himself through the Holy Spirit to the patriarchs, prophets, and apostles. They, prompted by the Spirit, put God's revelation into writing. And as we, guided by the Spirit, respond to the written Word, the age-old Writ turns into the dynamic of God's self-disclosure, here and now, also for us.

Such a view points to the spiritual reality of the Scriptures and avoids twisting them into a code of laws and rigid casuistry. It does not regard biblical authors as skilled secretaries to whom God dictated memoranda in a mechanical way, but upholds the freedom of their personal decisions in witnessing to God's revelation. God is mighty enough not to be confounded or diminished by the human fallibility of those authors. And he knows that through the internal testimony of the Spirit his eternal message can come through loud, clear, and flawless, even via human errors.

This dynamic view of the inspiration of the Scriptures leads in turn to a dynamic interpretation of them. "The strange world of the Bible" (to use Barth's phrase) opens itself up to everyone who approaches it prayerfully and meditatively, saying, "Speak, Lord, for thy servant hears" (1 Sam. 3:10).

All this was said and published within the framework of a historic church, agitated in those years by all sorts of disputes about the authority of the Scriptures. Now I can see that already, then and there, God wanted to prepare me for another controversy about the same issue, which arose later in the United States.

"Continuous Reformation." God by his Word captivates us, and we serve as witnesses to his victory. But our serving and witnessing must be fueled by ever new and fresh commitments. Such commitments are events of a continuously ongoing reformation.

Alas, it is exactly here that we constantly fail, being fettered by idols. After we have crushed the old ones, new idols sprout in us. Some of them, in the guise of alluring modernity, are hardly detectable. It is difficult to differentiate between a wholesome patriotism and an uncritical worship of our nation. Greed and the lust for power create in us ever-new patterns and stages of idolatry. And there seems to be no end of various sorts of "isms" and cults. The newly formed pseudogods of pseudoreligions hold their sway, and like hydra heads must be continually chopped off by the two-edged sword of our witnessing *to* God's eternal Word and *against* the false philosophies and ideologies of our own—and every—age.

Writing about the need for an "always-ready-to-reform"

life-style became a recurring theme in my theological pilgrimage, especially later as I struggled on the ecumenical frontier for a church that would be truly evangelical, truly catholic, and truly *reformed*.

"The Church and the Churches." There is no doubt about it: my sad experience with overzealous Roman Catholic priests in my early youth greatly contributed to my keen interest in working for church unity. And as the years went by, it dawned upon me that there can be no reunited world without a reunited church.

In 1944–45 I developed this theme in "The Church and the Churches," an essay that wasn't published until 1946, after I had left Hungary. Ironically, it turned out to be my "theological swan-song," the last piece I wrote in my mother tongue and in my native country. Providentially, it summed up those principles that later guided me in my ecumenical work in the United States.

In the essay I differentiated between the Roman Catholic view of church unity and that of evangelical catholicity. The Roman Catholic view binds Christ's control to one visible institution with one visible head—the pope—and works to fulfill the principle of "one *fold* under one shepherd." Evangelical catholicity, on the other hand, continues to testify to the freedom and sovereignty of Christ over his body—that is, the one holy catholic church—and it prays and works primarily for the realization of "one *flock* under one shepherd" (cf. John 10:16).

The eventual realization of one flock will necessarily mean the realization of one fold. But it cannot happen in the reverse order. Naturally, Christ's ultimate victorious coming will involve much guiding of both the "one flock" and the "one fold." In the meantime, much prayer, much dialogue, and much cooperation will be needed to eliminate any sort of human triumphalism. But we can be sure that in the end the issue of "the church and the churches" will be resolved. For in Christ all things are possible. Let us, therefore, not try to conquer each other. But let us all allow ourselves to be conquered together by Christ alone.

Christus Victor: the fulfillment of church unity is possible only as *his* victory, not ours.

First Ecumenical Involvements

My first ecumenical involvement dates back to 1936. As a member of one of the preparatory committees of the Faith and Order movement, I spent two weeks in the palace of the bishop of Gloucester. Then in 1937, as a delegate of the Reformed Church of Hungary, I attended the conference of Life and Work in Oxford and the conference of Faith and Order in Edinburgh. My greatest disappointment at the Oxford conference was that the German Nazi government refused to grant exit permits to the church delegates from Germany, and thus I was not able to meet Dietrich Bonhoeffer, with whom I had been corresponding. On the other hand, at both conferences I was able to make good contacts with British and American church leaders and theologians. About a decade later, the friendships thus formed greatly enhanced the success of my American speaking tour.

At the Edinburgh conference I served as spokesman for the Reformed theologians of Europe. And at the end of this conference I was officially delegated to be a member of what was called "The Provisional Committee of the World Council of Churches While in Process of Formation." In January 1939 this committee held its first meeting at Saint-Germain, near Paris, under the able chairmanship of William Temple, who later became the archbishop of Canterbury. At that time we made the necessary preparations for the first assembly of the World Council of Churches, planned to be held in Amsterdam in 1940. But World War II temporarily quashed all our plans.

In the summer of 1939 Visser 't Hooft, the general secretary of the World Council, asked me to go to Geneva to serve on an important commission. Its mandate was to draft a memorandum to the heads of the Great Powers, asking them to avoid war by pursuing peaceful negotiations. How futile our efforts proved to be!

After the Geneva meeting I went to Grado, Italy, a resort on the Adriatic seashore. As my train pulled into the vine-covered station, I saw the smiling face of my expectant Serena—happily expecting her presently arriving husband as well as the arrival of our third child, Timea, to be born in November. She was standing there, filled with joy, with the Adriatic as a backdrop. The tune of "O Sole Mio" drifted from the town square, and a young couple started to dance. Everything seemed to be so right with the world, so peaceful, so unsinkable—like the *Titanic*. The whole picture belied my forebodings. I tried to hide them, but as I alighted from the train and Serena glanced at me, her smile quickly faded.

"What's the matter?" she asked. "Why are you so somber? Did something go wrong with the memorandum?"

"Nothing went wrong with the memorandum," I answered, "but there was a lot wrong with the Christian brothers who drafted it. So very wrong that I can see now that World War II is inevitable. We are at the very threshold.

"You see," I went on, "I was the only participant from Eastern Europe. I went to Geneva with high hopes. Two representatives from the United States were there—John Foster Dulles and Georgia Harkness—and it was so good to become personally acquainted with them. But my contacts with some of the other delegates were disconcerting.

"One day the two German representatives pulled me aside and said, 'Yesterday we saw you deeply involved in a long conversation with the French and British participants of the commission, and we didn't like that. Your country, Hungary, belongs to the living space [*Lebensraum*] of Germany. You had better stick with us.'

"The next day one of the French delegates cornered me with a similar warning: 'Yesterday I noticed that you spent a long period of time with the German participants. I ask you not to trust them. Your place is with us.'

"After that I tried to avoid prolonged contact with either the Germans or the French and the British. But if the representatives of the national churches—all brothers in Christ—could be so suspicious of each other while drafting a peace memorandum, then what in the world can we expect from the political leaders? May God have mercy upon us. This 'Christian' peacemaking effort has crushed my hopes."

Alas, I proved to be right. A few weeks later all hell broke loose. On September 1, 1939, Hitler attacked Poland, and the war irrevocably began. Yet our church kept on strengthening its friendship with the ecumenical leaders of other countries. I gradually withdrew from my work with the National Federation of Reformed Ministers so that I could devote more time to pursuing ecumenical objectives. Karl Barth, Visser 't Hooft, and I made preliminary preparations for launching the first ecumenical journal, to be entitled *Doctrina*. Karl Barth was to serve as editor-in-chief, Visser 't Hooft was to be general editor, and I was to have the periodical published in Hungary. But soon we had to give up all further planning.

In 1943 the Protestant churches of Hungary were still able to organize the Ecumenical Council of Churches in our country, and I was elected its first secretary. I was also asked to launch a theological quarterly in English, to be called *Theologia Hungarica*. And I was to draw up a plan, supported by the Genevan headquarters of the World Council of Churches, for an East European ecumenical institute to be established in Hungary. These were all magnificent plans, destined to remain truncated and to disintegrate in the turmoil of the war. A few months later Hungary was cut off from the West, and later on cut up into pieces.

"Under God's Mighty Hand"

During the first years of World War II, Hitler's army moved through Poland against Russia. For reasons of his own he bypassed Hungary. We hoped that somehow, by a miracle, we could remain neutral, uninvolved. But during the ensuing years we had to become increasingly aware of our economic, political, and military dependency on the Axis Powers. And slowly but surely a spiritual and political split manifested itself in the life of the nation.

There were those who blindly accepted the "new paganism" of national self-worship. Others became quite apprehensive about all the dangers inherent in Hitler's Nazism, and said so. But they were violently silenced, and a pro-Nazi government was formed. As it became increasingly obvious that we would be turned into a no-man's-land between two enemies, a battleground for Hitler's and Stalin's armies, defeatism and total despair shrouded Hungary.

Chauvinistic self-conceit on the one hand and national despair on the other: the church had to deal with both, and in so doing, it had to take a clear stand. But this was easier said than done. And since I was serving as editor for various church publications, the dilemma became acutely personal. Again and again, through the weeks, months, and years that followed, I had to decide how to answer the question, What does God expect me to do under such circumstances? In my editorials and essays I tried to represent a Christian philosophy of nationhood and to voice a theological appraisal of the nature and mission of my own nation and church. But to practice Christian honesty and objectivity in those months was indeed a dangerous game, or at least a futile one. Many times only an empty space represented my editorial. All or part of it was often deleted by the censor.

"Humble yourselves then under God's mighty hand, and he will lift you up in due time" (1 Pet. 5:6, NEB). During those trying months this verse motivated me in all I did. But before we could be lifted up by his mighty hand, we first had to be downtrodden. And we were about to be: the total collapse of our small thousand-year-old country was imminent.

7

STRUGGLING FOR SURVIVAL (1944–1946)

The Last Lecture

Important political and military events followed one after the other during the first half of 1944. Sections of the German army marched through Hungary twice: first toward the south, to the Balkans, to assure for themselves the safety of the Adriatic Sea; then back again toward the northeast, to resist the growing pressure of the Russian army.

In the meantime, the persecution of the Jews gained momentum. Many Christian families tried to hide some of their Jewish or Jewish-Christian friends in their cellars or attics. We too kept a young Jewish girl in hiding in our cellar, while at the same time we were forced to put one of our rooms at the disposal of a high-ranking soldier of the German army. The officer was most apologetic about the discomfort he was causing us. He was a friendly man who missed his family a great deal. Behind closed doors he was openly critical of Hitler and clearly saw his country's looming defeat. At the same time, he was a patriot and a soldier who followed orders regardless of the consequences.

On the morning of March 30, 1944, I was notified that two representatives of the German army would arrive shortly before noon to discuss with the university council their using the central building of the university as their temporary head-quarters. As a member of the council, I was required to be there.

At eleven o'clock I had a class to teach in dogmatics. As was my custom, I began it with Bible reading and a short prayer. Then I started lecturing on divine providence. Much as I tried to hide my emotions, my voice must have cracked as I emphasized the point that nothing happens by chance. Every-thing comes upon us from God's fatherly hand.

At exactly 11:50 A.M. I looked out the window and saw two high-ranking German officers approaching the building. I stopped lecturing and said to the surprised students, "May God, who in spite of all does care for us all, make it possible for us to continue our work." And then I left the classroom.

On that day and in that hour the continuity of my pro-fessorship in Hungary virtually ended. During the last two months of the spring semester we were hardly able to function as a school. Constant air raids repeatedly forced us to take refuge in the shelters. Then, during the first days of June, the serious bombardment of Debrecen began. One night, aiming to destroy the strategically important railroad station, the bombers missed their target, and numerous private homes, apartment houses, and a large Reformed church near the sta-tion were destroyed. Two whole streets were wiped out, and scores were killed, many of them fighting for their last breath in caved-in cellars.

It was high time to move my family out of Debrecen. So the next day, long before dawn, Serena and I woke our chil-dren and left our home. We inched our way through the rubble to the railroad station. After a seven-hour wait, we were finally able to board the train. We were on our way to our mountain, to the retreat we had built there, hoping for safety in that beautiful, remote spot. It was good logic, but logic soon flew out the window.

Cadence Tones

"Cadence Tones," or "The Last Chords:" that is what I called the meditations I published in my pastoral monthly during the late spring and summer months. The titles of these meditations indicated the seriousness of the situation: "Persecuted," "Seeing and Believing," "Between the Times," "Invasion," "What Is Written about Us?" The "chords" of a few of these pieces were particularly significant.

"Persecuted" was addressed especially to ministers, who in those fatal days were becoming more and more apprehensive. Rumor had it that they would be the first ones to be persecuted by the invading Red Army, so naturally many of them were wondering if they should stay with their people or flee. The text of the meditation furnished the answer: "All who desire to live a godly life in Christ Jesus will be persecuted" (2 Tim. 3:12). For Christ's sake I encouraged them to stay with their people.

"Seeing and Believing" acknowledged that in those troubled times, whatever we saw around us horrified us. Nations were rising against nations, kingdoms against kingdoms. Our former enemies had become allies, and our former allies had turned into enemies. As members of a small nation, we had become easy prey in a war that was not ours, of which we wanted no part. Yet we were helplessly tossed to and fro. No wonder that many of us tried to shut our eyes, as children do during a scary scene in the movies. But God wants us to grow up and dare to look into the face of scary things. Maturity means that we see such things yet continue to believe. Only the eyes of faith can discern "what God has prepared for those who love him" (1 Cor. 2:9).

At the end of the summer the last chord was struck. In "What Is Written about Us?" I reminded my readers that, up until the final moments in the life of Jesus, his disciples were still competing for first place. The Lord drew their attention to his own forthcoming suffering: "What is written about me has its fulfilment" (Luke 22:37). I closed this meditation with notes of comfort and encouragement. Our forthcoming sufferings, I assured my readers, would be under the guidance of the same divine hand that had achieved its mysterious work of redemption in and through the life, suffering, crucifixion, and resurrection of Jesus.

"No Lasting City"

What an uneasy summer that was! It was the last one we spent on our mountain, in our beloved vineyards. And the last one when we could use the possessive "ours" to describe whatever had been ours.

The only contact we had with the world was a small radio, and the news it broadcast was increasingly confusing and frightening. It was difficult to distinguish between bona fide news and mere propaganda designed to scare us. The only certainty looming before us was a nightmare turning into reality: our country was becoming a battlefield between the Germans and the Russians.

September was approaching, the time for me to resume my responsibilities as professor, principal, dean, and editor. Under the circumstances this was hardly possible. Nevertheless, Serena and I decided that the two of us should return to Debrecen to attend to whatever we should or could do; to make final arrangements, whatever those might be. In the meantime, my sporadic gall-bladder ache developed first into a continuous pain and then, just as we reached Debrecen, into full-blown agony.

Our stay in Debrecen was a mindless confusion. Three or four times a day the air-raid sirens drove us down into the shelters. By the third day I was lying in bed in acute pain, unable to move. I had but one desire: to get back to our vineyards and our children. I could see clearly that, pain or no pain, I could accomplish nothing more in Debrecen; no, not anymore. . . .

Serena spent a whole day running around in search of a taxi to take us to the railroad station. We were willing to pay anything, but that didn't matter: no cab was available. While she was away, our doorbell rang. I knew it must be my father, come to see us once more in this life. But I simply did not have the strength to get up and answer the door. I tried crawling, but I moved too slowly; my father waited for a while, then left. Pulling myself up to the nearest window, I watched his dejected, fading figure through my tears. I never saw him again. During the siege of Debrecen he disappeared, and his body was never found.

Serena finally managed to arrange for the horse-drawn carriage of the university to take us to the railroad station. There we learned that the train was twelve hours late. When, after many air-raid warnings, the train finally pulled out of Debrecen, I looked once more at our hometown, at the familiar buildings, many lying in ruins. Hebrews 13:14 started to hammer in my mind: *"Here we have no lasting city, but we seek the city which is to come."*

That was the most painful and—as it seemed to me at the time—the longest journey in my life. When we finally arrived at our summer home in the middle of the night, it was pouring rain, and the mud was ankle-deep. With heroic ingenuity and almost superhuman strength, Serena managed to drag me up the mountain slope. At last we were once again back in the surroundings so dear to us, praying to God for the extension of this period of grace. But gradually it sank in: we must get ready for a much longer and much more strenuous journey. For a journey that would make us refugees in our own country. . . .

The "Stalin Candles"

In those days our greatest problem was figuring out what would be the best place to meet the invading Russians. The ideal solution for us would have been to stay put in the vineyards. We were far from strategically important points, and there did not seem to be any impending danger of a large-scale battle developing in the vicinity. But this was not the only possible battle we had to consider. We were the most prominent people on that mountain, the family of the "squire," who owned the largest parcel of land on the mountainside. What kind of treatment could we expect from the invading Communist troops—we, the "bourgeois," the "landowners," and so supposedly "the enemies of the people"? The mounting evidence suggested that their arrival would turn our cool Shangri-la into a hellish place. Wouldn't it be wise, then, to go to the nearest city, Szatmár? It was a fairly small town, not likely to become a target—or so we thought.

Every evening Russian planes would cross the sky just above the mountains, then draw away toward farther destinations. But one night we suddenly saw the whole city of Szatmár flooded with light. What were called "Stalin candles" floated down in magnificent formations, descending upon the city and piercing it with sharp-shadowed glare. Into this quiet, eerie illumination burst the explosions. And from our mountain slope it seemed as if the whole town were going up in flames. The fires kept burning in the dead darkness, fading only in the beams of the rising sun.

Now we knew for sure that, should we need to face "the day of the Lord," "the day of darkness and of fire," we ought to do so in our own hometown, Debrecen. There we could at least say, "It was the Lord's will that we should die in the midst of our dear friends and fellow workers!"

When we reached this decision, we made all the necessary preparations. We loaded two wagons with food supplies, winter clothing, blankets, and chopped wood. We hired two coachmen with two pairs of horses. And we asked our loyal vinedressers to take care of the vineyards and to gather in the grapes when the time for harvest arrived.

Farewell to Our Mountain

On the day of our departure, late in the afternoon, I stole out into our vineyards by myself. I had to bid farewell to them without saying anything about it to anyone, not even to Serena. I was afraid it would literally break her heart if she came with me. We both loved that mountain dearly, she even more deeply than I. After all, she had been born there, and she was—body, heart, and soul—a "daughter of the mountains." All of her poetry, all of her life was brightened and colored by the images of vines and fruit trees. And in the mirror of her vivid imagination, I too had been captivated by the mountain of Halmi.

With tear-filled eyes I strolled along the familiar pathways and passed through the arbors and bowers. I carried on parting conversations with cherry, apple, and peach trees, listened to the twittering of the birds, and gazed after the quick-hopping rabbits. The vines were heavy with dense clusters of grapes basking in the caress of the setting sun. How I envied the sun, so eternally undisturbed in its course, no matter what happened on earth. It would rise again tomorrow and kiss the grapes, ripening them, swelling their bodies, readying them for the glorious occasion of harvest for the birth of the new wine. But we could not stay. And perhaps the "daughter of the mountains" would never return to greet these vines again with the rhymes of her poetry, to reach for them so lovingly with her slender fingers.

I tried to tear myself away. After all, reliving memories of the past can be more unbearable than the portentous realities of the future. And the human heart has its limits too.

Suddenly I heard it. No, not with my ears, though it was as if the whole mountain would have echoed it:

> I am the true vine, and my Father is the vinedresser.
> Every branch of mine that bears no fruit, he takes away,
> and every branch that does bear fruit he prunes, that it
> may bear more fruit. . . . Abide in me, and I in you. . . .
> I am the vine, you are the branches. He who abides in me,
> and I in him, he it is that bears much fruit, for apart from
> me you can do nothing.
>
> (John 15:1–5)

Not I but Someone Else straightened my stooped shoulders, lifted my chin, and put the spring back into my step. Suddenly I knew with absolute certainty what Paul meant when he said, "I can do all things in him who strengthens me." In him even the two-edged mysteries of divine providence find their ultimate meaning, and we begin to understand far beyond the capacity of our own understanding.

Looking for a Haven

Before we left, we gathered for a last Scripture reading, this time with the participation of our "extended family," our four vinedressers and their broods. The Scripture verse we chose was Psalm 37:5: "Commit your way to the Lord; trust in him, and he will act."

There is hardly anything more heartrending than seeing strong, weathered Hungarian peasants crying. Nothing could convey more dramatically to us that we had indeed "cast our bread upon the waters" (Eccl. 11:1).

Besides the two coachmen, there were eight people in our small caravan: Serena and I, her mother, the three children (at that time ten, six, and four years old), the governess, and a maid. We hoped that we would be able to reach Debrecen in two days and nights. But as we approached the city from the northeast, we learned that the Russian and German armies were waging a tank battle just southwest of the city. And so we had to look for another haven—quickly.

In seven days we covered only 280 kilometers. Whenever we became exhausted, we stopped in a village, looked for the parsonage, knocked on its door, and asked for shelter. Everywhere we were received with welcoming love. The pastors—some of them my former students—were all friends of mine. They accommodated us with zealous hospitality, and their wives never batted an eye at the prospect of suddenly having to feed ten extra hungry people.

Soon after our surprise arrival, we would inevitably hear the cackling of chickens running for dear life. We felt satisfied after we polished off those chicken-paprikash dinners. By the end of the third day, the children claimed they were tired of them, although their appetites never seemed to say so.

As we traveled we tried to avoid the main highways, which the German army used for strategic purposes; the country roads were our best bets. Ferries were also safer than bridges.

Dry humor is a Hungarian characteristic, the humor of the gallows something history has taught us. One of our coachmen was blessed with a special sense for it. As we were driving through the villages, people usually asked two questions: "Where did you come from?" and "Where are you going?" To the first query this coachman replied, "From Trouble-Village [*Bajlódról*]," and to the second, "To Pain-City [*Kinlódra*]." How right he was!

Along the way we had to scrap our plans to seek refuge in certain places. Remote villages would have been safe from bombardment, but we would have stood out like sore thumbs and no doubt would have been exposed to some "special treatment" by the invading army. The more we learned about the atrocities committed by the occupying forces, the more we saw the wisdom of remaining inconspicuous. And what better place for that than the capital city, with its two million inhabitants? Budapest seemed to be the best spot to hide. We also kindled the logical hope that "the Queen of the Danube" would be declared an open city, just as Paris and Rome had been. That would mean a takeover without any more destruction, bloodshed, and dehumanizing hardships perpetrated by an army required "to fight themselves through."

By the end of October we arrived in Budapest, exhausted but still hoping for the best. But our hopes were soon crushed. The Russian army surrounded the city, and the Germans, though they knew it was hopeless, made a strategic stronghold out of it, ready to fight to the bitter end. Unfortunately, the fate of the city was the least of their concerns. So what if thousands and thousands died, if artistic and architectural treasures of one thousand years were blown to smithereens? Who cared? The chic, elegant "Queen of the Danube" was turned into a city of agonies, and four months later looked like a tattered beggar-woman.

During the first two weeks we changed living quarters three times. One day I met a good friend of mine who immediately invited us to move in with his family. They had found a house in Buda, on the western bank of the Danube, which provided exceptionally good shelter. It surely sounded desirable.

Serena and I were on our way to look at the house, and in all likelihood to accept the invitation, when providence intervened. It was one of those luminous days of Indian summer, and there was a blessed lull between bombardments. We stopped at the "Fisherman's Bastion," a magnificent old fort that preserved the various architectural styles of successive eras. The Danube flowed underneath it, so quiet, so truly blue in the brilliant rays of the sun. It seemed totally absurd that all this beauty would be condemned to perish. "O God, spare our city. If it be possible, take this cup away. . . ."

Our wordless prayer was interrupted by the appearance of two high-ranking German army officers. They stopped nearby, with maps of Budapest in their hands. In rapid German, confident that no one could hear or understand them, they discussed the next strategic steps they ought to take. At one point one of them exclaimed, "Dann werden wir die Brücken sprengen!" ("Then we will blow up the bridges!") Just like that. So casually. So matter-of-factly.

Stunned and horrified, we decided at that moment not to move to Buda. "I'm not going to try to swim across the Danube in order to get back to our hometown when all this is over," I said to Serena. She agreed, and so we stayed in Pest. At the end of the siege we learned that the house we had almost moved into had received a direct hit, and everybody in it had been killed.

By the grace of God we survived the siege in the cellar shelter of the YMCA building. We took refuge there along with about sixty other people, some of them Jews and Jewish Christians who were hiding there.

Serving the Red Cross

As soon as they learned that I was staying in Budapest, the Relief Committee of the International Red Cross asked me to serve as its local chairman. Its purpose there, as everywhere, was to save as many lives as possible. There were several major difficulties to combat. For one thing, the long-drawn-out siege was depleting the food supply, and the number of people facing serious hunger increased daily. To alleviate the problem we organized public kitchens. In addition, the entire electrical and heating system of the capital had broken down, and many were suffering from the cold. In response, we made heated halls and large rooms available to those who were freezing, and we tried to secure as much wood, coal, and oil as we could.

The hospitals asked for our help; orphanages begged for our support. Many newborn babies died for lack of milk and medical supplies. We did all we could, but we were forced to watch with aching hearts as the needs grew and our potential for meeting them gradually dwindled.

As chairman of the committee I handed out hundreds of "Certificates of Protection" to Jews, Jewish Christians, and many others persecuted by the Arrow Cross Militia, a Fascist organization. These certificates, which stated that their holders were under the protection of the International Red Cross, were often of no practical help at all. But they did serve as placebos, psychological lifts that gave the recipients at least some illusion of security.

During the last weeks of the siege of Budapest, the Russians were fighting from street to street, from house to house, and they raped scores of girls and women. As the siege wore on, these victims multiplied, and they needed our physical assistance and spiritual comfort. This was the most dismal task of our mission.

There was, however, one particularly enriching aspect of the work of the Relief Committee: Roman Catholic priests, Protestant ministers, and secular social workers all participated in it. All of us felt that we belonged to the same "fellowship of suffering": we all faced the same predicament, and we all needed each other's comfort and help. Differences of denomination, race, and social standing (not to mention discrimination) were all relegated to the background. In fact, they simply disintegrated. Later, both in Europe and in America, I often thought, If only similar cooperation could prevail as enthusiastically among those who happen to live under so-called normal circumstances!

In those weeks and months I had no time to read theological books or any other books, of course. The urgency of saving as many lives as possible had exclusive priority. "Faith in action," or what I call "action theology," was the order of my days. Yet by the end of the siege, I felt that during that period without intellectual theology, *experiential* theology grew and deepened in me immeasurably.

Sinking Toward the "Kaput Level"

After living for a while on the sixth floor of the YMCA building, my family and I moved down into a supposedly safer corner room on the second floor. And there we spent the financially poorest yet spiritually richest Christmas Eve of our lives.

Our Christmas tree was a scraggly little pine branch that Serena had dug out from beneath ice and trampled snow. Of course there were no ornaments and no gifts whatsoever. The children not only took this in stride but decided to be the gift-givers. From old newspapers they cut out a "stable," a "manger," and a "star"; and with some glue, broken crayons, ingenuity, and lots of love, they decorated the "tree." Somehow they even managed to find a tiny candle, which made it perfect. And our spirits were perfect, too.

But just as we started to sing "Peace on Earth," all hell broke loose. As a special kind of "Christmas gift," the Russians launched an attack like none we had experienced before. The intensity of it made us move quickly down into the shelter. When we went upstairs the next morning to collect the rest of our belongings, we found a huge hole in the wall. Had we stayed in that room during the night, our whole family would have been wiped out. Once again, we survived.

On the last day of the year I conducted a worship service in the large chapel of the YMCA, located on the first floor. It was packed with worshipers, many of whom had daringly walked over from neighboring streets. My text was Psalm 90:12: "So teach us to number our days that we may get a heart of wisdom." I was halfway through the sermon when an air raid began and the shells started to whistle. I stopped and told the worshipers, "Whoever wishes to take shelter should do so immediately." Nobody moved. As the attack intensified, I repeated my warning, with the same result. I finished the sermon, then led the congregation in prayer. During the Lord's Supper the large chalice filled with wine and the heavy silver plates of bread trembled on the table as the foundations of the building shook. But we all felt that through our prayers the Holy Spirit shook our dwelling even more than the exploding bombs (cf. Acts 4:31).

As the weeks went by, we continued to sink toward the level of extinction. One of the German soldiers I met toward the end of the siege cried out, "Alles kaput!" ("All is lost, or finished"). The Germans certainly lost the war. But we who were refugees in our own capital city had to realize that we too were losing: at this point everything was near total collapse.

We began to run out of food. For two weeks our daily diet was some fast-dwindling rations of dried beans and dried peas. Meat seemed to belong to a never-never land. Then suddenly, in mid-January, we had the chance to sample a kind of meat we had never tasted before. Horses, fallen in battle, were lying frozen in their blood on the streets of Budapest; one of them lay right in front of our building. Serena and some other women, armed with big knives and a lot of stamina, dashed out and returned with large chunks of frozen horse-flesh. At first we almost choked on it.But when our revulsion subsided and our hunger increased, it tasted better and better.

We had been without electricity for a long time. We still had some candles, but the lack of oxygen inside our quarters nearly strangled the flame. Yet what enlightening Bible studies we had by the dying light of those candles! How much more we could see in the dimness that we had failed to see in the bright light of day! First of all, we got a good look at ourselves, so inclined to take everything for granted. Had it ever occurred to us before to say thanks for the daylight, for the breeze on our faces, for ever-fresh water (instead of that now rationed daily from a tub), for our privacy and bodily comfort? Innumerable small things that we had hardly noticed except in the most perfunctory way were now revealed to us as special gifts. Yes, we needed the darkness of the night to begin to appreciate what we had so lightly enjoyed.

In the meantime, the fight went on above our cellar, from street to street, from house to house, from floor to floor. A bloody, body-to-body struggle between the advancing Russians and the desperately trapped Germans.

January 16 and 17, 1945

At midnight the first Russian soldiers appeared in the door-way of our shelter. Their bright flashlights pierced the darkness. We just sat there, not knowing what the next second would bring. Their leader, a handsome lieutenant, said something in Russian that none of us understood. Then he asked in Romanian if there was anybody who spoke that language. Serena knew it, so she served as interpreter.

He was polite, assuring us of the Russians' goodwill. Their goal was to clean out the trapped Germans and their Hungarian Arrow Cross collaborators, he explained, not to harm any innocent civilians. But they had to regard every house as a potential hiding place for their enemies, and therefore they had to search every nook and cranny. His men did so in a professional, orderly way, and we sighed with relief.

Afterwards the lieutenant sat down. He seemed so exhausted and vulnerable. "You must be tired," said Serena. "But the war seems to be almost over. You can finish with Berlin, then go home and rest."

He looked up at her with a quizzical smile. "We would go home now, but not to rest. The war would not be finished merely by taking Berlin. Only after we took London, New York, Washington— only then would everything be over. We will not rest until that is done!"

We were stupefied. We simply could not believe what he had said. After all, the Russians were allies of the British and the Americans. They could never have gotten where they were without the military supplies and the food that America had sent. We told Serena that she must have misunderstood the lieutenant, but she had not. He reaffirmed that his country's ultimate goal was world domination.

"Our people know," he said, "that our present allies are our greatest enemies, and, cost what it may, we cannot stop until we can put the Red Star on the White House!"

We sat frozen in silent bewilderment. Of all the falling bombs, this was the deadliest.

"Early tomorrow morning," the lieutenant finally told us, "all the men in the shelter will have to report to an adjacent building for their new identification papers." Then he and his men left our shelter. Their actions were reassuringly professional—or so it seemed.

My March Changes to a Limp

Early the next morning, supervised by four Russian soldiers, the men from our shelter left to obtain those identification papers. At the last second, prompted by her love and her female intuition, Serena slipped into my pocket some biscuits and a small bottle of peach brandy (both treasured remnants of supplies from our mountain). "Why give me these?" I protested. "We'll be back in no time." But somehow she had sensed that the smooth-talking Russian lieutenant was lying.

When we reached the end of the street, we were ordered to line up in columns. Then the soldiers "relieved" us of our wristwatches, and made us march eastward. No identification papers were forthcoming, not at the next building nor at any building on street after street we passed. All that we got was the repeatedly barked command to march—why, where, and for how long, nobody knew. And we were kept marching in the bitter cold, nonstop, till nightfall.

That night they locked us up in an ice-cold warehouse. There was no room to sit or lie down, so we had to stand up, packed in like sardines. With those who were nearest to me, I shared the biscuits and the peach brandy. Each of us got only a few morsels and a few drops, but what a feast that was! How grateful we all were to Serena for her foresight!

The next day we had to march again. Miles followed dreary miles on the icy roads. By that time only our willpower kept us from falling down. At last we reached a railroad station and saw a train there with numerous empty boxcars. Are they waiting for us? we wondered. We had of course heard rumors about trains loaded with people and transported to Siberia or other bleak places in the vast expanse of the frozen unknown. Now it seemed that all those nightmares were about to become reality.

"Will I also disappear in the gray beyond? Must I accept this as my end? Am I kaput?" I asked myself. "No," shrieked something within me, "a thousand times *no!*" From on high a Higher Power began to move my mind and body: the adrenaline began to flow, my exhaustion strangely vanished, and willpower stronger than I had ever experienced before took hold of me. The words of Matthew 10:16 were my instruction: "Be wise as serpents and innocent as doves." What I needed now was the shrewdness of the serpent, and I got it. I misled the Russian guard, then crawled, ran, ducked, maneuvered— and escaped. Thus it was that I embarked on my desperate, dangerous journey toward the west again, back to Budapest, to my family. Picking my way through ruins and dead bodies, dodging stray bullets, hiding from the Russian patrols, I kept on going. But soon my "going" turned to limping. My shoes were torn, and my freezing, bleeding feet stuck to my ragged stockings. Each hour became an agonizing blur. Now and then I knocked on doors, never knowing what lay behind them.

The "liberated" city of Budapest was in the grip of terror. The disciplined occupying forces had departed and had been replaced by an unruly military mob drunk on victory, wine, and vodka. They celebrated by looting and raping; women left without men were their primary targets. Without restriction or supervision they did what they wanted, and did it to the nth degree. From fragments of descriptions offered by people fleeing, half-crazed, from the city, I pieced together what was going on, and I was terrified.

At last I reached the YMCA and fell through our shelter's door, to be embraced by my sobbing family. With my voice completely gone, I could only search Serena's face with my desperate eyes, but she "heard" my question and slowly shook her head: "No, it did not happen to me." Only later did she fully explain what a miraculous act of God had saved her from the greatest of all humiliations a woman can suffer.

Silver Lining

In Milton's *Paradise Regained*, Comus asks, "Was I deceived or did a sable cloud / Turn forth her silver lining on the night?" If you really believe that God is able and willing to bring forth good out of evil, you will be justified in saying, "Every cloud has a silver lining." And you will be looking for those shining edges around the dark clouds.

That's what we did during the last weeks we spent in the YMCA building. We looked eastward, to Debrecen. But mostly we began to look toward the neighboring villages and farms in the vicinity of Budapest. We badly needed fresh food supplies; for the past month we had not seen or tasted bread at all. Finally, by some small miracle, I managed to secure a loaf.

So there it was once more, a loaf of bread on our makeshift little table. Its texture was coarse, its color like mud. Since no mills were running, the grain had to be ground into flour by primitive manual methods. The product was raw and tough, but it contained the entire grain, and its nutritional value was undiminished, unadulterated by "refining." The children stared at the loaf in disbelief—not because it looked so pitifully inferior to what they used to eat, but because it was *bread*, "the staff of life." Bread—once more!

"Is this real?" "Can we touch it?" "Can we eat it?" What questions from little children who had been accustomed to sitting around a table laden with buns, cakes, and cookies! I broke the bread, and then we joined in saying the Lord's Prayer. By the time we got to "give us this day our daily bread," tears were streaming down our faces. "O Lord, thank you for giving us this bread, just the bread and just for today!" How we savored it, in awe and gratitude, so grateful for something we had always regarded as a nonessential side dish, something we had previously taken very much for granted.

Those post-siege weeks in Budapest were filled with both gratitude and grief. The immense destruction everywhere, the intense chaos around us, the increasing famine: all conspired to shroud the silver linings. Our main goal, of course, was to find a way back to Debrecen, but that looked like an impossible task.

And yet, once again, the right way out presented itself. The welfare department of the city proposed a child-saving project. Hundreds of children were to be sent to the various villages in the country, to be fed by the farming communities. The Russian military authorities cooperated with the plan, making some boxcars available to transport the children. The department asked me to be the official guide and supervisor of the train that would travel to Debrecen and the neighboring towns.

In just two weeks everything was organized. The early morning of March 13 was set as our date of departure. My family and I were assigned a boxcar and given permission to share its space with as many of our friends as we could accommodate. Of course, so many begged to go along and it was so hard to refuse the desperate requests that finally we ended up overcrowded. "Just be patient," I said to our children as they fidgeted on their too-narrow seats. "In a matter of hours we'll be in Debrecen."

Once Again a Boxcar Dweller

During this experience, memories of my boxcar dwelling in 1920 flooded back. Then my father had been in command; now I was the father, not only taking care of my own children but also assuming responsibility for hundreds of temporarily parentless children.

Our train with its precious cargo had been scheduled to leave in the early morning. But by late afternoon we were still stranded in Budapest because the locomotive granted us by the Russian commander had been seized for military purposes. After we finally got a replacement and were underway, the same thing happened at almost every large railroad station we passed. Again and again I had to get off our train to beg, cajole, and convince the local Russian military commandant—if I could find him at all—either to let us keep our locomotive or get us another one.

On one such occasion I must have been very convincing, because the train started to pull out sooner than I had expected. I barely managed to grasp hold and clamber onto the last car. Unaware of this, Serena thought that I had missed the train. It is hard to explain how, in those days and under those circumstances, missing a train was not just an annoyance. Many times it meant missing for good, never arriving, disappearing without a trace. The nightmare that Serena had just lived through in Budapest—believing that I had been deported to Siberia—descended upon her again in full force. When I rejoined my family at the next station, I found her racked by sobs.

By that time our train was twenty-four hours late. The children were shivering and hungry in those boxcars. I phoned the welfare department of the next city where we were to arrive in a few hours, and they promised to prepare a hot meal for the children. But this time we were stymied by a quick departure rather than a delay. Before the waiting women could ladle out the hot soup they had made, our train was ordered to leave. Oh, the bitter disappointment on the faces of those good women and those cold, hungry children!

By late evening of the second day we finally arrived in Debrecen. The first priority was to feed the children, and then to place them in the care of those good people who were waiting for them. For some unknown reason my family's boxcar was suddenly dispatched to a sidetrack on the outskirts of Debrecen. Thus we had to spend one more night and day in that cramped space before we were able to disembark and find some temporary living quarters. Ironically, what we found was one of the surgical rooms at the maternity clinic, on the same floor where two of our children had been born. There were no beds or mattresses there, but what a luxury it was to stretch out on the bare floor and, for the first time in 1945, to spend the night in a heated room.

It was now mid-March, but after a few false spring days winter decided to return with two feet of lasting snow. By that time we had learned to expect the unexpected, the haphazard. The rule was to have no rule at all.

Screening, Adjusting, but Not Wavering

The first of these three, "the screening," was done by local interparty committees. The second, "the adjusting," was something we had to do ourselves—in fact, it was something that had to be done by everyone who was attempting to survive in a country occupied by the Russians. And the third, "the not-wavering," meant "obeying God rather than men," even while the art of delicate compromise had to go on and on.

We wrestled with a dichotomy: constantly skirting yet never succumbing to a double standard.

I too was "screened" by an interparty committee. To my great surprise, it went smoothly; they simply approved my past behavior. My greatest "assets" were my anti-Nazi stand, as evidenced by those editorials that had been partly or wholly deleted by the censors; my generally democratic attitude toward the so-called proletariat; my chairing the Relief Committee of the International Red Cross during the siege of Budapest; and finally, my being instrumental in saving the lives of so many children by escorting that train to Debrecen.

"Adjusting" to the new situation was not so easy. During those weeks there was an anecdote making the rounds about two Hungarian friends who meet each other on the street. "What are you doing?" asks one of them. "Adjusting, and adjusting to adjusting," answers the other. I did the same thing, but I tried to submit my adjustments to psychological, moral, and theological considerations. After all, my whole psychology was built upon the principle that the "Striving Self," in trying to get its bearings, has to submit to certain moral and religious standards while making its own value judgments and decisions. In the case of a Christian, the ultimate standard is God's will. Should anything contrary be demanded or expected of him, there must be no compromising, no adjusting, no wavering at all. There are, of course, concrete situations in which the question "to adjust or not to adjust" can no longer be raised. One simply *must* adjust.

After we arrived in Debrecen we were snowed under by such "musts." First of all, we were forced to make adjustments on the material level. During our absence all of our personal belongings had been looted, and we found our house occupied by twenty Russian soldiers. We had to stay in my seminar rooms, located in the central building of the university. We were just a stone's throw away from our home, so with bated breath we watched what went on around the house. One day the Russians put our furniture in a pile and used it to start a bonfire. Antique pieces, treasured items from past generations, a unique hand-carved dining-room suite—all were burned before our eyes for no particular reason at all. We also had to reconcile ourselves to the fact that our vineyards, orchards, and other pieces of real estate were to be nationalized by the new Communist government of Hungary, Romania, and Czechoslovakia. Some of that land had been held by our families for centuries. Now we simply had to write it off as "lost" ("kaput!").

One day, as I was trying to put in order all the books scattered about in the library section of my seminar rooms, a Russian soldier appeared in the doorway. For a while he just watched me. Then suddenly he said, "Kultura kaput!" The expression on his face and his whole attitude seemed to ask, "Why do you care for those books? Culture is not going to save you!"

It was a strange coincidence that this soldier used exactly the same word that the German-Nazi soldier in Budapest had used. The coincidence filled me with disheartening questions. Should we really have only one common word in our European vocabulary, and should that word be *kaput*? Was everything truly lost? Hungary? Europe? The entire civilization? Should we be satisfied with a philosophy of despair? Or was there a way out of this chaos?

My answer was yes. But that way out could only be the one who said of himself, "I am the Way." The Way out of chaos and the Way into a life of repentance and renewal.

I had this revelation long before Jürgen Moltmann launched his "theology of hope." Then and there, sitting on a pile of scattered and tattered books, I knew that over against all sorts of philosophies of despair, I would have to proclaim a theology of hope. "Christ, the hope of glory, is in us" (cf. Col. 1:27): that is the church's message to a chaotic world.

Airlifted to the West

In September the Russian soldiers vacated our house, leaving it in indescribable condition. It took weeks of scrubbing, scraping, and patching to make it at all livable again. Finally, with some badly damaged secondhand furniture, we were able to return to our own place. How Serena created a lovely home out of that squalor and brokenness, I don't know. But she managed it.

At the same time, she and I were in the throes of making

the hardest decision of our married life. Both of us agreed that the reconstruction of the churches in Hungary could not be done without the assistance of Western (primarily American) churches. It seemed obvious that my urgent mandate was to go to the West, to serve there as the messenger of a downtrodden country and church. But we were cut off from the West for a few more months. It was not until late in the fall that a letter from Geneva could reach me. It was written by Samuel McCrea Cavert, the secretary of the Provisional Committee of the World Council of Churches. He invited me to attend the first postwar meeting of the committee, to be held in Geneva during the second half of February 1946. He stressed how important it was that I be there because I was the committee's only member from Eastern Europe. This letter enabled me to officially apply for a passport. I also needed to secure a Russian exit permit because we lived under Russian military occupation.

When I left my family to go to Geneva, food was still very scarce. Every day Serena had to walk five miles to a farm to bring back one liter of milk for the children. Public security measures were still barely operating, and inflation started its rapid upward spiral, making even such food as there was practically unobtainable because of its price. Under such circumstances it certainly was a hard and risky decision to leave my family.

By the end of December 1945, I lacked only two things for my trip: the necessary transportation and the Russian visa. The transportation problem was easily solved: the American Military Mission in Budapest promised me that, as soon as I was able to obtain the visa, they would transport me at least as far as Vienna. But securing the visa from the Russians was not so simple: it took four long weeks to get it. Their daily promises sounded like a broken record: "come tomorrow," they always said. It was like the Spanish *mañana*, each day a near yet indefinite postponement. Those weeks truly tested my perseverance. But I said to myself, "Béla, you are not supposed to get tired of the Russians. Let them get tired of you."

Finally, in the middle of February, just a few days before the Geneva meeting, I was granted the visa. I dashed to the headquarters of the American Military Mission, but none of the army officers was available. It was Saturday afternoon, the weekend! The GI at the desk told me where I could find his superior, so I rushed over there. I found the officer just as he was leaving his quarters. When I asked him for the promised transportation, he was very cooperative. But while he and I were discussing the details, a Russian military truck, driven at full speed and coming from an illegal direction, suddenly careened at us and hit us both. The officer was injured in the head, I in the back. My clothes were torn, my glasses were broken, and my lung was bleeding internally; I was rushed to a hospital.

Once the diagnosis established that after a few days I would be able to walk again, I decided not to inform Serena about the accident. I knew that, had she learned of it, she would have risked everything to join me in Budapest. And seeing my weak condition, she would have prevented me from leaving Hungary. At that time there still was no dependable and punctual mail service. So I arranged for a good friend to deliver my letter explaining what had happened, instructing him not to give it to Serena until the day of my departure.

Two memorable things happened while I was in the hospital.

The first was my hearing an interesting radio broadcast one morning. I heard the announcer say, "The first meeting of the Provisional Committee of the World Council of Churches after World War II opens today in Geneva. The Protestant churches of Hungary are represented at the meeting by Professor Béla Vassady, a member of the committee." That news shook me up. Instead of being in Geneva, I was still lying on that hospital bed in Budapest.

A day later, a young, sympathetic Communist secretary came to visit me and expressed the Russians' sincere regrets over the accident. We had a long conversation. To my great surprise, he tried to persuade me not to risk my trip to the West. "Don't you think," he asked, "that through that accident God wanted to tell you not to leave your family and your country?" It was ironic to hear a supposedly atheistic Communist referring to God and his "providential warning." But what if he was right?

As soon as he left the room, I opened my Bible to Romans 8 and focused my attention especially on verse 28: "*In everything* God works for good with those who love him, who are called according to his purpose." It only affirmed my original conviction that God had allowed that accident to happen not to make me give up my goal but to test me and to strengthen my faith. His test should steel my heart to fulfill my commitment. And so I decided that, as soon as I could walk again, I would proceed with my plans.

On February 27 I was able to board a small American military plane that usually commuted twice a week between Budapest and Vienna. This time it flew to Paris. There was room for only seven people on that plane. Six of them were GIs; I was the only civilian. The GIs, aware of my physical condition, wanted me to be as comfortable as possible on the hard bench that provided the only seating, so three of them stood for the entire trip to allow me more space. In a few hours we arrived in Paris, where for the first night I was put up in an American military hostel.

Sore in body but soaring in spirit, I could savor once more something I most needed: the feeling of freedom and security.

8

A MESSENGER: HIS MISSION
AND HIS MESSAGE
(1946–1947)

Emaciated yet Persevering

During the siege of Budapest and its aftermath I had lost about forty pounds, and my recovery from the accident was far from complete. Weak as a day-old kitten, I could barely walk. Climbing stairs was a particular ordeal, and in Paris I had to climb a lot of them.

My first day there I succeeded in dragging myself to the Ministry of Foreign Affairs, where I presented my passport and my French visa. There I was informed that I was the first Hungarian civilian to arrive legally in Paris since the end of World War II; my French visa was the very first one issued by their consular service in Hungary. After that, everything began to happen very fast, like action in a speeded-up film. I met the pastor of the American Church in Paris, Reverend Williams, who greeted me jubilantly and offered to help me in every way possible. Other key persons also lent a helping hand. Embassies opened their doors to me outside their normal operating hours. In a daze I realized that quite a few people knew about me, that I was a "cause célèbre," a sheep given up for lost and suddenly found.

But the greatest boost came from an American friend, Henry Smith Leiper, the secretary of the American Committee of the World Council of Churches, who stopped over in Paris. He immediately invited me to make a speaking tour in America. "You are a godsend," he told me. "We need your message in America. The World Council of Churches, our National Council, and all the American churches need you."

In a matter of hours my name was placed on the list of VIPs. That meant that it was put ahead of thousands of other people's names, and thus I was granted immediate passage to America. Was I the same person who not so long ago had had to walk daily to the Russian military headquarters and plead for a visa, only to be told, "Tomorrow, tomorrow"?

But before embarking upon my American mission, I had to make two other trips: to Switzerland and to Scotland.

Through Ecumenical Glasses

What a welcome I received in Geneva from the entire staff of the World Council of Churches! They were eager to hear my news about the multitude of damaged or destroyed churches in Hungary.

Visser 't Hooft informed me that a few days earlier he had gotten a wire from Serena asking where I was. She had not heard from me at all since I had left Hungary. For some reason my wires and letters to her from Paris had never arrived, and her concern and anxiety had mounted daily. (Later she told me that due to the spiraling inflation in Hungary, the single wire she had sent had cost her an amount equivalent to my month's salary.)

The staff members of the council inquired about my personal needs. I told them about the truck accident in Budapest and about my broken eyeglasses, and within hours they furnished me with a new pair of spectacles. Since the World Council of Churches was also known as the Ecumenical Council, I baptized them my "ecumenical glasses."

Besides providing optical benefits, the glasses symbolized something that became a source of inspiration for me.

All that had happened to me in the preceding months and years began to assume new meaning as I started to view those events through ecumenical glasses. I decided that my most urgent message must be that every Christian may not physically need corrective lenses, but spiritually speaking, every Christian needs a pair of ecumenical glasses. For there will be no peace, no justice, no reconciliation or unity on this earth unless we all learn to tackle the problems of the world not from a national or denominational perspective but from an ecumenical perspective.

"A Wide Door for Effective Work"

The Scottish Presbyterians were waiting for me with open arms. They were sorry that I had to make my visit with them much shorter than I had originally planned. Nevertheless, after briefly visiting London and Oxford, I was able to speak in various churches in Edinburgh and Glasgow, and to address the Presbytery of Edinburgh as well as the semi-annual meeting of the European Section of the World Alliance of Reformed Churches. A press conference and an encounter with members of the Scottish Church Theology Society made my visit to Scotland even more unforgettable.

From Scotland I hurried back to Paris, which had served as a springboard for my jaunts. Then, on April 8, 1946, I made my biggest leap, on a TWA plane, from Paris to New York. And I was able to report to Henry Smith Leiper's office on exactly the date he had suggested.

Paul once wrote from Ephesus to the Corinthians, "I will stay in Ephesus until Pentecost, for a wide door for effective work has opened to me, and there are many adversaries" (1 Cor. 16:8–9). In America God surely opened a wide door for effective work before me. To my great surprise, I met very few adversaries on my speaking tour. During those months and years the people of the United States were eager to overcome any further temptations toward isolationism. Everywhere I went I saw the yearning for the formation of the United Nations and also for the cooperation of all Christians in and through the World Council of Churches.

I was welcomed by the various national church bodies as

a member of the Provisional Committee of the World Council of Churches, as a secretary of the Ecumenical Council of the churches in Hungary, as a Continental theologian in my own right, and as a graduate of two American theological seminaries. But what touched me far more than the official greetings of the various church leaders was the warm, spontaneous welcome people gave me wherever I went.

My speaking tour had been well-planned by the New York office of the World Council. But it soon became obvious that I would need to stay longer than the six months originally granted me, so I had my visitor's visa renewed—twice. A broad range of churches wanted to hear me speak: Presbyterian and Reformed, Methodist and Baptist, Protestant Episcopalian and Congregational churches, as well as many smaller denominations. They all wished to hear the authentic reports of a man who had lived through World War II in his own country, and they all wanted to participate in supporting the work of reconstruction in the various churches of Europe. There were Sundays when I had to speak in three or even four churches. In November 1946 I spent seventeen nights on trains, enjoying the luxury of a sleeping car. The former boxcar dweller was now provided with all the comforts of a technically advanced country.

I was still very gaunt. A friend of mine remarked, "Your description of all the privations and destruction in your native land is indeed very effective. But you could easily save all those words. All you need to do is stand up and show yourself. One look at you drives home the message loud and clear." Everybody was eager to feed me, but often I choked on the food. Not for a moment had I lost sight of my family, and I knew that although the war was over, the famine they had to face had become even more severe since I had left. Everywhere I went, I distributed—mostly with the help of local women's societies—names and addresses of families in dire need. And soon hundreds of gift packages began their slow journey from America to Europe.

For many months my headquarters were the so-called "prophets' chambers" of Princeton Seminary and of Union Seminary in New York. During that time I taught courses at the seminaries in Princeton and Bloomfield, and I spoke in eastern Canada and in the northern and southeastern regions of the United States. During the winter of 1946–47, McCormick Seminary in Chicago served as my headquarters. Here I taught two courses, fulfilled speaking engagements in the midwestern states, served as an ambassador of the Florida Chain of Missions, and spoke in various churches in midwestern Canada. I spent the spring of 1947 in California, addressing large ecumenical gatherings and visiting almost all the seminaries on the West Coast.

I finished my American speaking tour during the summer of 1947. In sixteen months I had traveled more than one hundred thousand miles, delivered more than one thousand sermons, addresses, and lectures, and raised who knows how many hundreds of thousands of dollars to be conveyed to Europe's war-torn churches through various channels and agencies: the Church World Service, the National Association of Evangelicals, denominational relief committees, and others.

Staying on the Right Track

Throughout my entire trip, *chronos* and *kairos*, physical time and God's own timing, had been unalterably intertwined. I had known this, yet I had to relearn, again and again, that unless my constant running paradoxically also remained a constant limping along the path of God's Word, my mission, in the true sense of the word, would be derailed.

A fund-raising project is a tricky business, rife with temptations. The most prevalent is to regard collecting money, even if for the highest Christian purpose, as *the end*, while the basic commitment to proclaim the *Kerygma* (the Good News) is reduced to *a means*. The Gospel has a total claim to be preached for its own sake. Let the Lord do the rest—let him bring forth the fruits wherever and whenever they may ripen. Those fruits are not necessarily the opening of billfolds and checkbooks, but first and most of all the opening of eyes, minds, and hearts.

Having come from a devastated country, I was filled with heartrending stories, stories of empty stomachs and burned-out sanctuaries; of chaos, despair, and death; of a history gone completely "kaput." All these stories were effective and true, yet in their truth they were also one-sided. I had to describe the grief, which was real. But I also had to testify to the joy, equally real. Death? Yes. But also life, new life, growing vigorously in the improbable soil of rubbish. Burned-out homes? Yes. But also hearts burning in the flame of the Spirit. God's houses in ruins? Yes. But the invisible Temple still standing firm. It is bomb-proof, hell-proof. At its gateless portals, Death has been swallowed up in victory.

I came to this country representing a fellowship, the fellowship of suffering. For a basically untouched and affluent people I had to describe the needs and agonies the war had inflicted on us. But I was also able to share the good news: that many of those who belonged to that fellowship had gratefully experienced how God had turned their losses into gains, their physical privations into spiritual enrichment, their defeat into triumph.

Two Golden Bracelets

While I toured America as an ambassador of the fellowship of suffering, again and again I rejoiced to find here its integral counterpart, the fellowship of compassion. What a thrilling experience it was for me to be instrumental in the intertwining of these two fellowships! I could offer countless examples of this, but one is particularly memorable.

One morning I received a heartbreaking letter from Serena. "Yesterday," she wrote, "I had to sell the golden bracelet you gave me as a wedding present. It was an excruciating experience, like giving up part of you. But I had to do it, because in these times of runaway inflation gold is the only and ultimate source for obtaining food. I had to do it for the sake of our children."

That same evening I was scheduled to speak at the Biblical Seminary in New York City. I went there with a heavy heart, debating within myself: Should I or should I not mention the letter in my address? I decided against it. After all, it was my private problem. Why mix a personally poignant story in a talk meant to relate the needs of many? But what happened that night turned into a unique message in its own right.

After my speech, a coed and her fiancé came to see me. "Your address deeply moved us," she said. "We expect to get married soon, and my fiancé promised to give me a golden bracelet as a wedding present. But it would hurt me to accept such a gift now, when there are so many people starving on the other side of the world. So, instead of buying that bracelet for me, I asked him to give the money it would have cost him to you. Please, accept this from us and send it to your country, so that it can be used to alleviate at least some of the needs you have just talked about."

Her words left me speechless. Coincidence? No one in his right mind could call this just a coincidence. Now was the time to take Serena's letter from my pocket and translate it for them. When I did so, they in turn were speechless.

There were two golden bracelets in the picture: one had to be sold out of dire need; the other, out of compassion, would never be bought. There were two women involved: one an overburdened young mother, the other a happy young bride-to-be. And there were two continents involved: one in which destruction had taken its toll, the other untouched. Though there was an ocean between them, I saw two arms stretched out across the Atlantic, two hands tightly clasped over the churning waves of history. The hands of two women, neither of them wearing a golden bracelet.

What better demonstration of the truth that hatred undeniably has its spectacular achievements, yet despite that and above all else, there always was, is, and ever shall be that "one great fellowship of love throughout the whole wide earth."

The Bifocal View

To someone coming to the United States from a European country, it is startling, sometimes even bewildering, to see here the proliferation of so many denominations. It was a blessing for me to look at them through ecumenical glasses. Wherever I spoke, I told the members of the congregations that I was not interested in their denominational affiliation. My only concern was how they related to the one Head of the one holy catholic church, to Jesus Christ himself.

In the late summer of 1946 my physical vision started to deteriorate. Alas, the eye doctor had to prescribe a new pair of glasses—and they had to be bifocals. I felt like a storyteller who had lost his story. Now that I no longer wore the glasses originally given to me by the Ecumenical Council, how could I tell people that I was looking at them through my bona-fide ecumenical glasses? But then I became aware that the Lord had a good reason for taking those glasses away from me. For he wanted to make me see that the truly ecumenical view cannot be anything other than "bifocal"!

After all, the New Testament refers to the church both as a local congregation and as the church universal. Therefore the ecumenical perspective must always and everywhere be bifocal. On the one hand, it is through the lower lens of our ecumenical glasses that we can clearly see and tackle the problems of our local community. On the other hand, it is only through the upper lens of the same glasses that these problems can be viewed and appraised from the perspective of the church universal.

At my speaking engagements it quite often happened that I was introduced as the secretary of the *Economical* Council of the churches in Hungary. In those days people still had to be taught the etymological difference between *economics* and *ecumenics*. But this gave me another opportunity to point out that in the life of the church, especially when the church is fulfilling its redemptive mission, ecumenicity is the best possible economy, both locally and globally.

9

FAMILY REUNION IN AMERICA (1946–1947)

The Struggle Goes On in Hungary

The end of a war is never the end of it for the defeated. The bombs may stop falling, but that only means the beginning of a different kind of struggle, probably more bone-breaking and soul-wrenching than what the defeated had faced before. Formal peace treaties bring anything but peace; they only create a hydra. Its head is a multitude of problems. Cutting one off means the sprouting of two in its place—a seemingly no-win situation.

In Hungary, too, each day brought with it new problems in the life of nation, church, and family. The struggle continued on political, social, and economic levels. And it assumed spiritual dimensions as well.

While I was traveling in America, I got the red-carpet treatment as the postwar messenger from another continent. I was praised for my "heroic" achievements. But I knew that if anyone deserved to be called "heroic," it was Serena. For she remained with the children in the same devastated surroundings, facing that hydra, chopping off its daily-multiplying heads, all alone.

Before I had left her in Debrecen, she had slipped a note into my suitcase that I had discovered when I unpacked in Budapest. It read,

> No need to tell you how hard it is to let you go. My heart is breaking. Still, I know you must leave these ruins in order to build. I stay among them and set the same goal before me. My most ardent prayer is that while you are building far away, I might *upbuild* everything in me and around me. That would make you happy. And all I want from this life is to make you happy. You take with you my imperishable love.
>
> Your Serena

I carried this note in my wallet constantly. What a source of strength it was for me during our twenty-one-month-long separation!

The key word in her message was "upbuild," and she kept her promise to upbuild to the nth degree.

During our separation she sent me about 150 letters, each one about three typewritten pages long. She wrote these letters with cautious diplomacy, but even so, many of them bore the telltale signs of secret censorship. Yet she managed to give me the most moving and accurate picture of everything that was going on in the life of the family and the nation. She had to carry on the battle for three main goals: food, faith, and our reunion.

The Struggle for Sustenance

Serena's primary concern was to get food for the children. Hungary had always been known as the breadbasket of East-Central Europe. But during the war and its aftermath, that seemingly bottomless basket started to empty. Various factors contributed to this.

First of all, during the course of the war the country had been looted twice: first by the Germans in a systematic way and then by the Russians in an unsystematic way. In addition, during the war the farmlands had been turned into battlefields that could neither be plowed nor tilled. Compounding the problem was the lack of fuel, which rendered farm equipment idle. And the armies had driven away the horses, slaughtered the cattle. Unfortunately, you cannot milk a dead cow. Furthermore, all industrial production had come to a complete stop. And the total collapse of transportation had halted all trading. No exporting or importing was possible.

Inflation started to spiral rapidly. The main reason was that during the siege of Budapest, the German Nazis and their Hungarian collaborators had spirited all the gold bullion out of the national treasury and sent it to the West so that it would not fall into Russian hands. Since the monetary standard of the country depended upon that "exported" gold, it was no wonder that by July 1946 twenty-digit inflation plagued the nation. Hungarians had to learn to count first in terms of thousands, soon in terms of millions, then billions, and finally in terms of trillions of pengös. But not even these trillions were worth one penny on the foreign exchange.

Serena described all this graphically. Let me give just a few excerpts from her letters. On April 10 she wrote,

> Today I overheard the conversation of the children. They were fantasizing. No, not about having a new toy, but about how wonderful it would be to have meat again for supper, and sugar in the sugar bowl. I just gave them the last piece of chocolate you somehow got hold of in Budapest before leaving the country. I kept the chocolate pieces in various hiding places, and with careful rationing they lasted for many weeks. Now I told them there was no more. Still, they keep secretly hoping that maybe, just maybe, I stashed away some more, and one of these days I will surprise them again with a tiny chunk of chocolate. But I know there is none.

On May 15 her account was more grim: "Today two pounds of bacon cost two billions of pengös. I could not afford to buy it. I am happy if I can get for your monthly salary half a pound of salt, one cabbage, and the ration of our daily bread."

A letter she sent a few days later graphically illustrated the increasing economic lunacy in Hungary:

> Yesterday the government raised your monthly salary to five billions of pengös. I stuffed the money into a large basket, ran to the farmers' market, and bought two dozen

eggs for four billion pengös and one kilogram of flour for
half a billion pengös. Now I still have enough money to
purchase a stamp to mail this letter to you, provided they
did not raise its price since early morning. This is no joke
at all. The prices now change by the hour.

Even buying a daily newspaper was beyond the means of one
family. At first, three or four families of professors banded
together to order a paper. But soon even their pooled funds
were not enough. All sorts of small items were unaffordable.
In her letter of June 23 Serena wrote, "What would I give for a
typewriter ribbon! But what I need the most is a spool of
thread. Our clothes are going to pieces. I cannot even patch
them."

By the end of the inflation period, only the color of each
bill indicated its "worth." To put numbers on them became
superfluous. When money completely loses its buying power
like this, the only way to subsist is to resort to bartering.

Many of the farmers still had a hidden reserve of staple
foods that they were unwilling to sell for worthless money.
What they needed most were clothes and fabrics. Because
stores had also been either destroyed or looted, all they could
offer were broken racks and empty shelves.

Bartering actually means exchanging need for need. The
price always depends upon how desperate the need is, and
hunger can be the greatest of price-hikers. So Serena offered
pieces of our family's already decimated clothing supply for
food supplies. In our case, the shirts and underwear I had left
at home were the best possible candidates to be exchanged for
handground flour, homemade molasses to be used as a sugar
substitute, and sunflower seeds, pressed through obsolete
machines, for cooking oil.

Serena saw this desperate wheeling and dealing as another challenge. She wrote,

> You would have enjoyed seeing your wife yesterday
> with two of your shirts hanging on her two fingers, walk-
> ing back and forth at the market, becoming more and
> more expert in bargaining. I succeeded in not losing my
> temper when one of the vendors had the cheek to offer
> half a kilogram of stale bacon for your beautiful and ex-

pensive poplin shirt. Finally, because he liked the color of
the shirt (light blue!), he topped his offer with one kilogram of potatoes.

Some of these transactions amounted to fantastic Machiavelli-
an maneuvers. Serena commented wryly, "You know, it is
rather amusing when you exchange one thing for another one,
and then you exchange the newly acquired thing for a third
one, so that finally you can get hold of the fourth thing that
you need the most."

Finally, at the end of July, the stolen gold bullion was
brought back from the West, and the government was able to
introduce a new, reliable currency called the forint. Serena
reported, "Now we begin to feel a semblance of security again.
We *seem* to have a stable currency. But will it last? We have lost
our confidence in certainty and permanence. . . . "

The Struggle for Faith

What one most needed to survive in Hungary during those
months were a lot of stamina and a sturdy faith. Serena had
always had the first attribute. Now, during her period of being
alone while I was thousands of miles away, her rather traditional and intellectual faith underwent a dramatic metamorphosis. Into her keen and extensive knowledge of the
Bible and theology God's Spirit suddenly threw a spark, so
that almost overnight my bright yet aloof Serena turned into a
torch, spreading her flame all around.

After I had left Hungary, a great spiritual awakening had
begun, especially in the Reformed Church. And as so often
happens in times of crisis, the women were the first to be
sensitized, moved and ready to move. I use the word *awakening* deliberately here. I want to emphasize how different it is
from an easily sprouting but ephemeral revivalism. What happened in the Reformed Church of Hungary was a powerful
and lasting spiritual recovery, born amidst but rising above a
total national collapse and individual aimlessness. And Serena
became an integral part of it.

I fully realize that this book is supposed to be my theological autobiography, and what I now describe, strictly

speaking, did not happen to me. After all, I was thousands of miles away. Yet all that happened to Serena became so much a part of my own spiritual deepening and theological development, and was so helpful in keeping me on the right track in the fulfillment of my mission, that my "confessions" at this point would be incomplete if I omitted her story. I am sure that more excerpts from Serena's letters will enrich the reader almost as much as they enriched me.

During the summer of 1946 she wrote of Hungary's spiritual renewal:

> Nobody should tell me that the age of miracles has passed. What is happening here in these days is an unfolding miracle of the Holy Spirit. His presence has become a tangible reality for us. He started an awakening such as we never had before, at least not since the time of the Reformation. He organizes the rapidly growing Bible-study groups, and kindles the burning eagerness in the young and the old, among the peasants and in so-called "high society."
>
> Watching—or rather actively participating in—the pangs of "rebirth" of our old, traditional Reformed Church, in the renewal of her whole structure and institutions, takes my breath away. The whole church is moving, stirring, bubbling. This is gigantic.

In another letter she wrote,

> How good and wise our God is. He demolished in order to build something incomparably better. Everything we possessed is buried under the ruins: clothes, furniture, social conventions, a comfortable way of life. God's cruel mercy destroyed our idols, our old selves, and his wonder-working hand planted a novel, different LIFE on the ruins.

In this spiritual transformation Serena saw herself and her people emerging as winners through losing:

> What an experience this is: to see how—in the life of many—a theoretical Jesus turned into a personal Savior. The personal Savior turns into a cosmic Christ, the ultimate and absolute Lord of the whole universe, who never promised us safety but who did promise us *victory*. And

he gave it to us. Yes, downtrodden, ragged, and weak as we are, *we have that victory*.

This spiritual renewal was evident everywhere, as several excerpts from Serena's letters show:

> Today we had a bitterly cold, snowy morning. My four-mile walk to and from the farm was not very pleasant in that icy gale. But again I succeeded in bringing home that precious liter of milk for the children without falling on that slippery road.
>
> By 8:00 A.M. I was at the headquarters of the Communist Party to ask for permission to hold our Bible study. Somehow I am the one who always ends up doing this. Some of our friends worry whenever I enter that building. They say such a thing takes great courage. Why would it? It seems that I am being made never to be afraid. It is as simple as that.

. . . . .

> We started to wash at 5:00 A.M. It was hard to heat up the water with that wet wood. Yet by 5:00 P.M. we were able to hang out the clothes in the attic. Our fingers almost froze to the sheets. I was dead tired physically. But I felt as if I had wings when I left the house for our daily Bible-study meeting.
>
> Each of us took a Bible, a chunk of candle, and a piece of firewood. Since the family in whose house the meeting was held could heat only one room, we made a roaring fire in the other room, sat around the table, lit our candles, and opened our Bibles.
>
> Who comprised our group? Well, two professors, several students, one minister, our former mayor, two farmers, three factory workers, Count Bessenyey, a cleaning lady, and a janitor from the university, most of them with their spouses. One could hardly imagine a more mixed group, both socially and culturally. Mixed we were, but not mixed up. The miracle of the First Pentecost is happening again and again. We understand one another because we hear the Word speaking directly to us, and we share whatever it says to each of us individually.

. . . . .

We have just returned from a three-day evangelistic trip through the country. There were four of us: the bishop, our homiletics professor, the president of the Women's Society, and myself. We usually hold the meetings in basements, since the sanctuaries of the churches are damaged. The people are flocking, willing to sit there and listen for hours. And then they want to pray. What beautiful prayers I hear from people who had hardly any education. . . . They did not want to see us go. . . . They simply wanted more and more of the living water. . . .

. . . . .

Yesterday I spoke in my former high school to some 500 teenagers. We started at 2:00 P.M., and at 6:00 P.M. I was still with them, answering many questions. Afterwards I dashed homeward, knowing that my own children were waiting for me and the supper. The whole day was so beautiful and rewarding. But it totally drained me.

Glowing reports about Serena's work came to me from all quarters: from friends, colleagues, the bishops. At first I was overjoyed. While I was dashing from place to place in America as a speaker, I beheld my beloved, transformed from a poet into an evangelist, become a fellow pilgrim on the path of God's Word.

But soon my joy changed into anxiety. Besides having to continue the constant struggle for mere survival, she was increasingly snowed under by requests to organize Bible-study groups, to lead evangelistic conferences, to serve as a spiritual counselor. Eventually she was even asked to be the vice president of the Reformed Women's Association, which had half a million members. My wife was not only burning her candle at both ends; her whole being was burning in an all-consuming fire. So I started to worry about her health, and I wrote her to express my concern: "My constant prayer to the Holy Spirit is that he should now apply the brakes to you and *slow you down!*"

I knew how much she would need her strength for yet another struggle: clawing her way through all the bureaucratic red tape so that she and the children could leave the country and be reunited with me in the United States.

The Struggle for Reunion

In February 1947 Princeton Theological Seminary offered me a position as guest professor, and I accepted it for a two-year term. Though my original plan had been to return to Hungary at the end of my speaking tour, this invitation opened up an opportunity to bring my family to America. Two years would give them enough time to learn the language and get acquainted with this country and its people so dear to my heart. Yet it would not be so long an absence that we would be unable to pick up the threads of our life and our interrupted responsibilities when we returned to Hungary. Serena understood my reasoning and proceeded to gird herself for the tooth-and-nail battle that would be bound to precede a reunion in the United States. She had to face this siege all alone—and it lasted seven months.

Before she could do anything, however, I had to get my own status in the United States changed from that of "visitor" to that of "non-quota immigrant." To do this I had to leave the country, and then, upon approval, enter it again as an immigrant. The State Department gave me its full support. At their suggestion, I flew down to Haiti and within the day was back in Miami with an immigration visa in my passport. This lightning-quick change dumbfounded the immigration inspector. He had had his job for many years, he told me, but he had never seen such a quick turnabout before.

George Herbert's famous dictum dates back to the seventeenth century: "God's mill grinds slow, but sure." How true! Yet it is equally true that sometimes it grinds much faster than expected. Slow or fast, however, it does its grinding according to *God's* schedule. The important thing is that, in either case, we accept his timing. Such acceptance may not be easy, especially when that mill almost comes to a standstill with our very lives between its grinding stones.

Though Serena agreed with me that two years in America would be beneficial for the whole family, she made her decision with mixed emotions. On the one hand, our separation had become just as unbearable for her as it was for me, and thus our reunion was her uppermost desire. On the other hand, she knew the price she would have to pay for it.

First of all, she realized that she had become a highly appreciated spiritual leader in the church, and that she was badly needed. The news of her prospective departure created sadness beyond her expectations. Bishop Révész voiced his sorrow in a letter to me: "It is a tragic blow to our Reformed Women's Association that Serena must leave them just at a time when they need her the most." Second, the waves of war neurosis had reached their zenith during those very months, especially in Hungary. The tension between East and West had intensified to such a degree that there was good reason to fear that Serena and the children might be held as hostages in Hungary until my return. Finally, the bureaucracy's slowness in processing the family's immigration visa to America and their Russian exit permit kept Serena under constant strain until the last minute.

It was no wonder that by mid-August she broke down physically; she had an abnormally enlarged heart. (I only heard about this later, from others.) Her leaping down God's pathways, like mine, was becoming a limp. In those crucial final days she found her comfort and strength in Isaiah 40:30–31: "Even youth shall faint and be weary, and young men shall fall exhausted; but they who wait for the Lord shall renew their strength, they shall mount up with wings like eagles, they shall run and not be weary, they shall walk and not faint."

A Poignant Scene

At the time my family was arriving in America—in September 1947—airline scheduling was still uncertain. Planes sometimes arrived twenty to thirty hours later than expected. And they landed with no prior information as to which was which or where they were coming from.

On September 14 I stood in the sweltering heat on the balcony of the main terminal at La Guardia Airport. I saw yet another Pan American airplane landing, giving yet another promise that my family might be on it. Still uncertain, I watched it with bated breath, my eyes glued to its door, waiting for it to open. As soon as it did, I saw the first three passengers skip down the stairway. Even from that distance I knew for sure that those were my children. Soon their tall, slim mother appeared, trying to keep up with them. At that point something unforgettable happened.

In those days each landing plane was assigned a policeman who instructed the passengers to follow him to customs. Our three live-wire darlings, eager to get ahead of everyone, were right on his heels and for a while obediently followed him. But as they approached the building, our younger daughter, Timea, saw her daddy waving from the balcony.

With shouts of "Daddy, Daddy!" in Hungarian, she jumped out of the line, whizzed past the guardian of law and order, and ran toward her daddy in the Land of Freedom. The other two children followed suit. The officer began to run after them, shouting "Stop, stop!" in English, but he was totally ignored. Serena, running alongside the policeman and shouting "Stop, stop!" in Hungarian, went equally unheeded. Near pandemonium broke out, to the delight of the onlookers. This little scene poignantly illustrated to many the pain of separation as well as the joy of reunion for a loving family.

But not even this touching incident could bypass a lengthy customs inspection. The children had to fidget for one more hour before the gate opened and we could run into each other's arms. We clung to one another, weeping, in a tight, total embrace, quite oblivious to the harried passengers who were halting in their hurry, surrounding us in a circle, and sharing in our happiness with tear-filled eyes.

Later Béla, Jr., asked, "Why did those strangers laugh and cry with us?"

Before I could answer, Naomi said, "Because, you see, they are Americans!"

What a blessed first impression this was of the basic nature of this people. And, of all places, it happened in New York City.

10

TIME FOR A MOMENTOUS
DECISION (1947–1948)

Getting Adjusted to America

Nothing seemed to have changed at Princeton. Twenty-two years earlier, during the happy year I had spent on campus as a student, I had enjoyed watching the playful squirrels and the swarming fireflies—and they were still there. And yet there was a world of difference, for now it was not the daydreaming gaze of a solitary young man following their movements but the eyes of my three lively children. After twenty-one months of agonizing separation, we were together again on this lovely campus, so unchanged by time and untouched by the turmoils of another part of the world.

It would have been so tempting to write off the past years as a bad dream and to embrace our alluring present even for our future. But our commitment to return to Hungary in 1949 did not waver. For this reason we wanted to make the best use we could of the two years we expected to spend in the States.

The process of getting adjusted to America started on the day Serena and the children arrived. And, by and large, it proved to be remarkably smooth.

Our daughters made the transition easily. Naomi, who was thirteen, had no difficulty at all. She was enrolled in a scholastically demanding private school where her teachers soon discovered that she was much more advanced in Latin than her classmates. So they simply taught her English by translating from the Latin words. Timea, who was seven, was by nature a happy-go-lucky child. Her simple philosophy was that since she could not understand the school rules set down in English, she was not obliged to follow them. Her disarming charm helped her to get away with everything.

But Béla, Jr., who was nine at the time, was another story. A rather sensitive and timid little boy, he had a difficult time in the beginning. The first day of school was a terrible disappointment for him, and by noon his teacher brought him home crying. This was an unusual phenomenon because he regarded crying as a weakness unbecoming to males. When we asked him why he was crying, he answered, "The teacher said something in English to me, but I could not understand him. Then I said something in Hungarian to him, but he could not understand me. What on earth can I do with these people?"

This frustration was short-lived, however. A few days later the teacher reported to us that Béla had started to play football with his classmates. When we asked him if he still had some difficulty understanding them, he looked at us in amazement. "Difficulty? What difficulty?" And that was that.

Serena too had to make adjustments. Although, in addition to her mother tongue, she spoke three other languages, English was not among them. She had had time for only a few lessons before she and the children had left Hungary, and thus her knowledge of the language was very limited. But she had two things: determination and linguistic ability. And just two months after arriving in this country, she delivered her maiden speech in New York before the members of the national board of the Presbyterian Women's Association. Even though she spoke in very broken English, her message exuded something that captivated the audience. Katherine Parker, the president of the association, assured her, "We American women have a lot to learn from you. We badly need your message."

Indeed, in a few weeks invitations for speaking engagements started to pour in, and soon Serena was booked for speeches months in advance. In 1948 her first thank-offering service, entitled "Under God's Mighty Hand," was published by the Presbyterian Women's Association and used throughout the country. And as a result of the many contacts she made and with the financial aid of the Presbyterian Women of America, the Reformed Women's Work Center was established in 1948 in our hometown, Debrecen. And what blessed, vital work went on in and radiated from that center!

Situation Analyses

In 1948 I was asked to share with American Christians my analysis of the spiritual state of Christians in Hungary and also in Europe in general. I delivered my extensive report on the church situation in Hungary (entitled "Buffer or Bridge?") at the meeting of the Western Section of the World Alliance of Reformed (Presbyterian) Churches held early in 1948. "Buffer or Bridge?" subsequently appeared as an article in about ten European and American church magazines.

In this address I told my audience that ever since the Magyars had been converted to Christianity in the tenth century, they had filled the difficult position of being the easternmost outpost of Western Christian culture. Buffeted from both sides, they persistently clung to the West. Then, at the end of World War II, their country was pushed into the Soviet sphere of influence. But they dearly wished not to become a buffer state again between East and West. What they were striving for was to serve as a bridge between the two.

To that end, the primary goal of the Protestants in Hungary was (and is) a renewed, more penetrating, all-embracing proclamation of God's Word. They sought divine support to maintain a proper balance on a tightrope that was spiritual as well as political. They were relearning one of the most frequently forgotten, or misinterpreted, truths of the Gospel: slaves, whatever kind of enslavement binds them, can be freer than their "free masters." So strong is the liberating power of the Holy Spirit that one can soar even if nailed to a cross. This lofty, seemingly impossible concept turned into down-to-earth reality for the Hungarian Protestants in those years immediately following the war.

I surveyed the spiritual mood of Europeans in general in another essay, "The Theology of Hope for the Philosophies of Despair" (published in *Theology Today* in 1948). I explained that many Europeans who had almost hit the "kaput level" of existence embraced either an *agnostic-nihilistic* or a *fatalistic-quietistic* philosophy: "Man, you don't do the pushing, you are being pushed around . . . by an arbitrary power." Nevertheless, quite a few attempted to counterbalance these ideas with the "philosophies of human achievement." For instance, the so-called "new collectivism" (once Nazism, now in the form of a totalitarian Communism), as a newfangled secular religion, spread the delusion that by creating a classless society, it could rebuild everything.

The Gospel of Jesus Christ, because of its distinctively wholistic claim, always collides head-on with these philosophies. It makes a theological claim as well as an ethical claim. The first stresses God's all-pervasive grace; the second speaks of man's total response to it. United into one Gospel, they offer a hope beyond despair.

Preparations for Amsterdam

Because of the outbreak of World War II, it had not been possible to hold the First Assembly of the World Council of Churches in 1940 as planned. Finally, in August 1948, it was ready to convene in Amsterdam. Both Serena and I were appointed to attend it: she as a representative of the Reformed Women's Association of Hungary, and I as a delegate of our native church. Prior to that, the presidium of the church had also informed me of their intention to nominate me to represent the Reformed Church of Hungary on the Central Committee of the forthcoming World Council.

Serena and I were in the peculiar position of going to Amsterdam as representatives of a European church while residing in the United States and intending to return there for another year after the assembly. This strange situation notwithstanding, we left our children in the care of a fine Presbyterian family in Hanover, Indiana, and boarded the *S.S. Mauretania* on July 21, 1948.

By the late nineteen-forties the tension between East and West had begun to escalate again, and kept doing so by leaps and bounds. West Berlin was isolated by the Russian army, and for a while an American airlift provided the only access to the city. The situation was so shaky that many questioned the wisdom of holding the assembly at all.

Serena and I were particularly troubled by such thoughts. What if a new war broke out while the assembly was in session? Should that happen, all American citizens would immediately be transported back to the States. But what would happen to us, who were only temporary residents of the United States? Belonging to two countries meant belonging to neither but floating in between them in an uneasy limbo. Would we be stuck in Europe, with our children in America? What would be the fate of our family? Would we have to endure a new separation? But these were only hypothetical questions. Such "what if's" were overshadowed by a deeper, more definite and existential question: Should we follow our plan to return to Hungary in 1949?

The churches' situation in Hungary during the first half of 1948 became increasingly difficult. Under the pressure of a totalitarian government, prominent church leaders and many ministers were forced into retirement. As acting president of the church, my close friend Bishop Révész was given the mandate to draw up an agreement between the church and the totalitarian-atheist state. This was a mind-boggling task: to safeguard the freedom of the proclamation of God's Word and at the same time to satisfy the demands and ordinances of the modern Caesar.

Bishop Révész wrote me letters that kept me up-to-date on church events in Hungary. At one point he sounded very apprehensive about the possibility of the state's introducing a total censorship that would cut off any further contact between Hungarian churches and Western churches. Just before the Amsterdam assembly he thought that censorship might be imminent. Similar letters, written by a number of our friends in Hungary, made Serena and me increasingly apprehensive as well. Under such circumstances, would it be at all advisable for us to return to Hungary in 1949? Would we be able to work there freely and fruitfully? Both of us had delivered many public speeches in America, and though we had always avoided making political comments, our words could be twisted and held against us. Besides, we had been unable to control the media, who are notorious for seeking sensational headlines. If nothing else, the mere fact that we had lived and worked in the States for a few years would brand us as "Western sympathizers" and thus as undesirables. Certainly we would be shunned—or worse. All the signs indicated that a new Stalin-era purge was becoming increasingly rampant in Hungary.

Paris, Geneva, Baarn, Woodschoten, and Amsterdam

In Europe our official engagements started in Paris, then took us to Geneva, Baarn, Woodschoten, and Amsterdam, and then returned us to Paris. First we attended the meeting of the World Alliance of Reformed Churches in Geneva. From there Serena went to an ecumenical women's gathering in Baarn, the Netherlands, and I went to Woodschoten to participate in the work of one of the preparatory study commissions of the Amsterdam assembly. I also had to attend the last meeting of the Provisional Committee of the World Council of Churches, which was still in the process of formation. That commission shouldered tremendous responsibilities, since it had to make all the formal preparations for the forthcoming assembly. And World War II had certainly made our task even more complicated and difficult.

At the Assembly

Openness, Courage, and Patience.   Pages could be written about the Amsterdam assembly: its proceedings, findings, and decisions; the various expositions of its main theme, "Man's Disorder and God's Design," particularly Karl Barth's provocative address on this theme; John Foster Dulles' and Joseph Hromadka's crossing of swords on the increasingly sensitive ecumenical frontier between East and West; the conspicuous absence of the Roman Catholic Church and its unacceptable reasons for it; the growing interest of the laity in the ecumenical movement; the forward surge and thrust of the younger churches; and finally, the message of the assembly to all the churches of the world.

By and large, we were all pleased with the first united steps taken. At Amsterdam, we found one another; as churches we covenanted with each other; and we expressed our earnest desire to stay together.

Personally, I left Amsterdam having made one overriding decision: wherever the Lord wanted me to serve him, I would always regard that spot as an ecumenical frontier. Without becoming an "ecumaniac," I would work for church unity with openness, courage, and patience.

With *openness*! The times for defensive polemics are long past. As Christians we must all hang together, or else we will hang separately. It is utter hypocrisy to work for a reunited world and at the same time to bypass the task of organic reunification of all the churches. We need to heed Karl Barth's admonition: there is a "horrible plural" (*"eine schreckliche Pluralität"*) in the official name of our organization. We are still only a World Council of Chur*ch*es, but not yet the *one* holy catholic church. Jesus Christ has but *one bride*, but we make him a polygamist, a Bridegroom with many brides. Complete openness and ecumenical repentance: that is what we need the most.

But our openness must be coupled with *courage*. In itself, "courage to be" (Tillich) is not enough. Courage to be *ecumenical Christians* should be the order of our days. Chesterton once said, "Nothing is real unless it is local," and he was right. It requires no special courage to be ecumenical bureaucrats attending world assemblies, but it certainly takes dedication and daring to work as grass-roots ecumenists in our own hometowns.

The third ecumenical requirement is *patience*. It took two thousand years to beget, or rather misbeget, our disunited churches. Thus it would be utterly unrealistic to expect that through some miraculous conception a reunification could be born overnight. It is of paramount importance for us to learn that the reuniting of our fragmented churches can never be achieved by human ingenuity. Any self-reliant attempt to undertake it as a human task would fall flat. Hard as it is, we must harness our fidgety ambitions and let the Lord build the house. The only thing we ought to do and can do is to accept the less glamorous job of unassumingly and obediently lending our hands to the Master Builder. To carry for him the tools, the mortar, the bricks. To move at his command and to be still at his command. In other words, "to wait upon the Lord," and *be patient.*

That Inevitable "Must." Happy were those who could soak up the unique happenings and ideas of the First Assembly in complete peace of mind. Unfortunately, Serena and I were not among them. While we diligently participated in all the proceedings of the assembly and contributed to it wherever we were needed, we were heavily laden with the burden of our great personal problem.

Wherever we went, Hungarian refugees approached us, pleading with us to help them find a way to America. In many instances we succeeded, especially when theological students and ministers were involved. But whatever they were (or rather, used to be), they were united by one common denominator: fear. They were saturated with it. It clung to them, even in the atmosphere of the free West. They telephoned us under assumed names, trying to explain in a sort of code language who they were. They asked us to meet them secretly, preferably after dark, at a place they designated, in complete privacy. But despite all these precautions, they were nervous during our meetings. Their eyes kept darting around; they were constantly glancing over their shoulders; they kept putting a warning finger to their lips at any sound of footsteps or rustle of leaves. The more innocent a bystander looked, the more convinced they were that he was a watchdog of the Hungarian secret police.

These meetings brought back to us the sour air of insecurity, suspicion, repression, and fear. Trying to get rid of that smell was like trying to freshen clothes stored in mothballs. No matter how much you air them, the odor lingers. By this time our family had lived together in America for almost an entire year. But we still vividly remembered that it had taken months for Serena to overcome the habit of leaning out the window and looking around to make sure that no one was listening to our conversation. Now, meeting these desperate, frightened people, it hit us again: To what kind of atmosphere would we return a year from now? To a country where freedom was packed in the mothballs of fear? Fear—penetrating, pervasive, far-reaching?

Partly for emotional reasons and partly for practical reasons, settling the question of whether or not we would return to Hungary became a must. True, we had one more year to stay in America, but we couldn't wait until the last minute to make up our minds.

When I had accepted the invitation to teach at Princeton Seminary, I had made it clear to everyone, both in America and in Hungary, that I would be there for only two years. My "old chair" in Debrecen, the Chair of Systematic Theology, was waiting for me, and I felt committed to reoccupy it in 1949. Consequently, Princeton Seminary had already offered its Chair of Systematic Theology to someone else for a term beginning that year. This meant that if I did not return to Hungary, within a year I would be without a job. It seemed wise, then, to start looking for something else right away. But what Serena and I needed to do first was to share our inner turmoil with our dearest and most trusted friends.

Meeting Old Friends. The first old friend we met was Karl Barth. He greeted us with a warm embrace and childlike joy. For us, too, it suddenly seemed like only yesterday that Serena and I (in 1936) had anticipated his arrival in Debrecen and had accompanied him on that unforgettable lecture tour in Hungary. In the light of later events, that tour turned out to be history-making, for it established a very close relationship between him and the Hungarian Reformed Church. That is why, under the new political circumstances after World War II, the leaders of the church repeatedly turned to him for a theological appraisal of the situation. Thus it was that just a few months before the Amsterdam assembly, he had visited Hungary again. He talked to us in detail about the problems he had discussed with church leaders there. By the time we met the members of the Hungarian delegation, we already had a clear picture and an in-depth evaluation of the entire Hungarian situation.

Barth was deeply concerned about our possible return to Hungary. He told us that because of the growing tension between East and West, the simple fact that we had spent the past few years in America—even though we had done so for good and justifiable reasons—would work against us. He emphasized that he did not want to make up our minds for us, but he felt it necessary to point out all the difficulties and handicaps we would have to face should we return to our native country.

After talking with Barth we met the Hungarian delegation and had heart-to-heart conversations with our most trusted friends among them. These talks increasingly convinced Serena and me that, because of growing anti-American sentiment, returning to Hungary would be mindless folly. Rumors were floating around that our names were already on the political blacklist. Whether or not that was true could never, of course, be established. But the rumors themselves would have been enough to render us completely inactive if we had returned.

Wrestling with the Lord. As the assembly was drawing to a close, Serena and I again had one of those nights: a night of desperate soul-searching, clamoring prayer, and flowing tears. We held each other in a tight embrace as we gave up our former dreams and plans. It was like chopping chunks of flesh from our bodies without anesthesia. My hope for founding an ecumenical institute in Debrecen and for directing all ecumenical work from Hungary, surrounded by my former students, coworkers, and friends, had to be written off. Serena too felt profoundly robbed and devastated. How she longed to go back to her downtrodden but spiritually vibrant sisters who so badly needed her leadership and special gifts! Now all these yearnings seemed to be quelled. We struggled with God, who in crushing our dreams appeared like a stranger. Just like Jacob at Peniel, we fought with that stranger until dawn. We were hurting; oh, how we were hurting. . . .

Then dawn came, and with it the blessing. For it dawned upon us that we had to deal with this unavoidable question precisely when we were participating in a unique ecumenical event. Much as we had thought we knew about it, *we still had to learn what ecumenicity really is!* God put us in this position in order to bring a strange-sounding concept down from the ivory tower and hammer it into a household word. If we were to keep on preaching that God's church is one, let it then become a precious, vivid reality first in our own lives! Now we saw clearly that, hand in hand, we could limp along the path of God's Word wherever on this globe that path might lead us. Wherever he put us, our home would be in him. And whatever the geographical location and denominational ties of our forthcoming church would be, always and everywhere we would remain members of the one body, his holy catholic church.

The Call to Fuller Seminary

It is amazing how quickly news can travel through the grapevine. Soon after Serena and I returned to Princeton, just as I was sending out letters to schools and friends to make them aware of my availability, a letter arrived from Harold J. Ockenga, president of Fuller Theological Seminary in Pasadena, California, and pastor of Park Street Congregational Church in Boston, Massachusetts. Without much ado he inquired whether I would be interested in serving as Professor of Biblical Theology at Fuller beginning in September 1949. He invited me to visit him in Boston and to go to Pasadena for a get-acquainted session with the faculty. And so I did. The visit went well: both sides were favorably impressed, and no controversial issues reared their heads. And in December 1948, just a few months after those agonizing days and nights Serena and I had spent in Amsterdam, I received the final appointment from Fuller Seminary.

This seminary had been founded about three years earlier by Charles Fuller, the well-known evangelist, and it was growing rapidly. The size of its student body competed with that of Princeton's, and it paid its professors better than any other seminary in America. All this looked very promising indeed. But what attracted Serena and me the most were the spiritual and intellectual goals of this new institution.

In his letter to me Ockenga had stressed that Fuller Seminary wanted to be an "evangelical and evangelistic school." Serena and I responded to this very positively. The full name of our native church is the Evangelical Reformed Church in Hungary, meaning a church that is constantly in the process of being re-formed according to the Evangel (Gospel) of Jesus Christ. We praised the Lord for opening before us the same kind of evangelical and evangelistic work in America that we had intended to do in Hungary after our return there. Even the fact that many of our friends called Fuller Seminary a Fundamentalist institution did not evoke in us any uneasiness or suspicion. In our vocabulary this meant that Fuller was a school training ministers to work on the only valid fundament, the Word of God. That was the very foundation of our vocation, too. What else could we have wanted?

Ockenga had also informed me that the seminary expected its professors to write and publish major theological works. This also was very much to my taste. Despite the many distractions during my two years at Princeton, my time there had been quite fruitful, even in terms of research. I had been able to compile a bibliography on Calvin; to revise for English translation my Hungarian essay entitled *The Main Traits of Calvin's Theology* (published in 1951 by Eerdmans); and—what I had enjoyed the most—to work on five lectures entitled "The Ecumenical Christian." I had first delivered these lectures in 1949 during the Sprunt Lecture Week at Union Theological Seminary in Richmond, Virginia, and I had plans to expand them into a major book on the same topic. They summed up the basic principles of my developing ecumenical theology.

The Ecumenical Christian

The "ecumenical perspective," in the Christian sense of the phrase, means something more than just "thinking in terms of Mankind" (Bertrand Russell). While "Mankind" is a given fact, so also is mankind's universal corruption. Therefore "Man," even if written with a capital M, simply cannot transcend his (or her) own self. Yet Christ did and does exactly that for us. He was sinless, and only with the help of his Spirit can we "rise above ourselves" (Calvin). With his guidance we can become truly ecumenical Christians by partaking in a *fourfold* act of "moving beyond":

(1) *The ecumenical Christian lives and moves and has his being beyond optimism and pessimism.* His faith in Christ's liberating power enables him to pronounce a judgment upon all sorts of utopian thinking, upon any self-reliant optimism. Likewise, it enables him to triumph over the varied manifestations of despair and frustrating pessimism.

(2) *The ecumenical Christian lives and moves and has his being beyond quietism and activism.* At Stockholm in 1925, and at the Life and Work Conference in Oxford and the Faith and Order Conference in Edinburgh in 1937, the tensions and mutual misunderstandings between the "activism" of American Christianity and the "eschatological quietism" of certain strata of Continental Christendom were bafflingly strong and deep. Even after the Amsterdam assembly, Reinhold Niebuhr felt it necessary to charge Karl Barth with defeatism and quietistic idleness simply because the latter had dared to admonish the assembly that "the final root and ground of all human disorder" is "the dreadful, godless, ridiculous opinion that man is the true Atlas who is destined to bear the dome of heaven on his shoulders." Therefore, he had noted, even Christians need to be reminded not to identify "God's design" with "some Christian Marshall Plan."

In any authentic Christian faith, "quietude" and "activity" are inseparable. But a healthy church, both as a worshiping and as a witnessing community of ecumenical Christians, must avoid a one-sided emphasis on either to the detriment of the other.

(3) *The ecumenical Christian lives and moves and has his being beyond "nationalism" and "internationalism."* He fights against any biased admiration of one's own nation, even if that fight makes him suffer. But he also cautions against identifying ecumenism with international organizations that may easily lend themselves to greedy power-politics.

As the society of ecumenical Christians, the church can never let itself become an instrument either of the status quo or of a demonic social revolution. It must constantly keep pointing beyond any national or international self-interest to the ecumenical man called Jesus Christ, the Prince of Peace and the King of kings.

(4) *The ecumenical Christian lives and moves and has his being beyond denominationalism and interdenominationalism.* He is a man who is conscious that the True Church is one; who realizes that denominationalism (worship of one's own denomination) can manifest itself not only in unconscious parochialism or provincialism but also in a judgmental, self-centered, even aggressive confessionalism that often leads to religious persecution and inquisitions. The ecumenical Christian rises above all these without identifying himself on the other hand with what is called "interdenominationalism." The basic characteristic of the latter is either doctrinal indifference or a sheerly activistic organizational interpretation of the reunion of various churches. Such "broad-mindedness" usually leads to shallow pragmatism.

The ecumenical Christian knows that no single denomination is big enough for the whole Gospel. Therefore he is never willing to use the confessional standards of his own group as ultimate benchmarks but gauges everything by the written Word of God. He is thankful to everyone whose insight into Scripture penetrates deeper than his own, and he is always ready to be *re-formed* "in the Lord."

I closed this series of lectures by summarizing the dynamic characteristics of the ecumenical Christian. His creative insight, creative daring, and creative tension, if entwined around the Cross of Christ, become the one "divining rod" in his search for truth, unity, and holiness. In this way ecumenical theology, ecumenical fellowship, and an ecumenical sense of responsibility gradually grow to maturity.

My American career as a theologian—which started in Princeton, then continued in Pasadena, Dubuque, and Lancaster, and went on, even after my retirement, in Ann Arbor and Grand Rapids—has been constantly inspired by the desire to exemplify these three characteristics. I regarded and still regard it my bounden duty never to lose sight of any of them.

11

BOTH EVANGELICAL AND ECUMENICAL (1949–1951)

At First Everything Looks Bright

In the summer of 1949 we said good-bye to Princeton and with a hope-filled "Westward ho!" embarked on a three-week cross-country drive to Pasadena.

Both Serena and I were quite inexperienced drivers at this point, and our recently purchased secondhand Chrysler was sturdy but old. Yet in our optimistic ignorance we had no qualms whatsoever about undertaking the long journey. The three-thousand-mile distance, the maze of highways and by-ways, the old car packed to the roof with fidgety kids and towering packages—all this could not daunt us.

But our realistic God forestalled our harebrained plans and provided us with a good, reliable driver in the person of John R. Bodo, a graduate student at Princeton Seminary. We jestingly called him "our ecumenical chauffeur," but as our trip unfolded we realized how invaluable he was to us. Because of his skill and guidance, we were able to see places that otherwise we never would have dared to visit: the highest peak of Yellowstone Park, for example, and the Grand Canyon.

That journey left an indelible imprint on us all, especially the children. Surely no one born in this country could be struck as strongly as we were by its vastness, grandeur, beauty, and bounty, by its busyness and its peace. The children never stopped marveling that we entered one state after the other without needing to show passports or stop for customs inspections. Such freedom of movement was blissfully amazing to people who thus far in their lives had hardly been able to take two steps without undergoing some kind of inspection, interrogation, and suspicious supervision. Strange how sometimes a name can hit home, as it did when Béla, Jr., exclaimed, "But these States are really, really *United!*" Suddenly this official name became filled to the brim with life and meaning.

When we first got to Pasadena, everything looked very bright, both literally and figuratively. No cloud appeared in the blue sky, and we were warmly received by the Fullers as well as the faculty. We yearned for a settled life, and under seemingly good auspices we looked for and then bought a darling little house surrounded by roses, azaleas, and palm trees. We had hardly any money for a down payment, but by securing a second mortgage we were able to sleep once again under a roof that we could call our own. We thanked the good Lord for such fortune.

At the seminary I met an enthusiastic, receptive student body. Besides being a professor of biblical theology, I was also made a professor of ecumenics. At first President Ockenga seemed to be receptive to my suggestion that Fuller Seminary not call itself "interdenominational" or "nondenominational." I thought it would be more appropriate if we regarded it as definitely an "ecumenical seminary" that trained young men and women for ministry in the one holy catholic church— even if that church was regrettably broken up into so many denominations.

At that time the Presbyterian members of the faculty were in the process of transferring their memberships from their former presbyteries to the Los Angeles Presbytery, and I was asked to do the same. Nothing could have pleased me more.

In August the acting dean of the seminary asked me to point out certain things in my application to the presbytery. He wrote, "Set forth your education and your record of service in Hungary as a minister of the Reformed faith. Be sure to include your service at Princeton Seminary, your participation in the World Council of Churches, and the various ecumenical activities in which you have been engaged." And so I did. I also incorporated this statement into my application:

> Fuller Seminary is a nondenominational institution. As the members of the faculty and of the student body belong to various Protestant churches, there is here given to me an opportunity to spread the spirit of evangelical Catholicity (or I could also call it the spirit of a wholesome biblical and practical ecumenicity) since I have been appointed to the Chair of Biblical Theology and Ecumenics. . . . And so I am offering here almost the same courses that I have been teaching as a guest professor in Princeton Theological Seminary. . . .

Alas, by the end of September I had become utterly disappointed in both the presbytery and the seminary faculty. And these two disappointments were destined to run parallel courses.

Two Disappointing Series of Events

In a nutshell, here is what happened. The committee responsible for admitting applicants into the presbytery informed me that, much as they would love to have me as a member, they would have to refuse my request. The reason given was that my request put them on the horns of a dilemma: should they allow me to become a member, they would be expected to do the same in the cases of other faculty members with possibly divisive attitudes. They even alluded to something that at the time seemed unbelievable. They suggested that my appointment to Fuller Seminary may have been prompted by an ulterior motive. Because of my background and ecumenical work, the presbytery could not refuse to accept me, and once they had granted me admission, the "less desirable" members of the faculty would find an easy ride into the presbytery on my coattails.

Extremely disappointed, I asked the committee simply to table my formal application. Later events proved that, under the circumstances, I did the best possible thing.

The scene of the second series of disappointing events was the campus of Fuller Seminary. One day in September I noticed that the fall issue of *Religion in Life* was changing hands rather rapidly among my colleagues. Their attention was focused on an article I had written entitled "Through Ecumenical Glasses." Soon I received a phone call from the acting dean. He informed me that it was not in the best interests of the seminary for me to imply in anything I wrote that I was "sold on the World Council of Churches." He also pointed out that in my article I had failed to mention that in the World Council there were "apostate churches" unfit for authentic Christians to associate with.

About two weeks later the newly arrived dean rushed into my study, brandishing the October issue of *The Christian Beacon* and shouting, "We are all in trouble!" When I asked him why, he said it was because the editorial "Caught in the Middle" by separatist Carl McIntire attacked Charles Fuller and Harold J. Ockenga for having hired a man "who writes in highest praise of the modernistic ecumenical movement." A second article, "World Council Praised by Fuller Seminary Professor," denounced me for stressing that the ideas of "one church" and "one world" organically belong together.

I rapidly scanned the articles, handed the paper back to the dean, and said, "Hallelujah!"

"What do you mean?" he asked me, dumbfounded. "Don't these accusations scare you?"

"Every sober-minded Christian will regard McIntire's attacks as the best of recommendations on my behalf," I answered coolly.

But gradually it was dawning on me that my days as a professor at Fuller were bound to be numbered.

In response to McIntire's articles the faculty drafted a statement (which, however, has never been made public) declaring that because the World Council of Churches did not show a concern for the evangelical convictions of its member churches, Fuller Seminary could not endorse it. The faculty also decided that each member should avoid any hint of approval of the World Council in his teaching ministry. I regarded all this not only as an expression of their negativistic isolationism but also as a curtailment of my right to academic freedom.

What bothered me most was the ethical inconsistency of the faculty. Earlier the acting dean had officially asked me to stress in my application to the presbytery my intensive participation in the work of the World Council from its very beginning. But now the faculty clearly wanted to go public with an anti–World Council statement, and so expected me to turn completely around and, with no spiritual or ethical qualms, declare that I too opposed the Council.

Those Inerrant Autographs

The waves caused by the debate on the World Council of Churches had hardly abated when the faculty, pressed by its extreme Fundamentalist members, placed on its immediate agenda the drafting of a statement of faith for the seminary. It was declared that, should the statement be adopted by a majority vote of the faculty and approved by the trustees, all professors would have to subscribe to it without any mental reservations. Should anyone be unwilling to comply, he must be prepared to leave the institution voluntarily.

One article, the one on Scripture, was unacceptable to me. It read, "The books which form the canon of the Old and New Testaments as originally given are plenarily inspired and free from all error in the whole and in the part. These books constitute the written Word of God, the only infallible rule of faith and practice." I found this statement objectionable because it is my conviction that we can and should believe in the inspiration and authority of the Scriptures even if we do not have the "originally given" autographs at our disposal. It is needless to state that they are "free from all error in the whole and in the part" because the Holy Spirit uses the present text as an authentic source for our salvation.

God's written Word is not a handbook in history or cosmology, not a timetable, not a compendium or a collection of historical data, not a paper pope offering us *ex cathedra* pronouncements and commandments, not a comprehensive theological system of propositional truths. Jesus never attempted to sum up his teachings in a theological textbook. Strange as it seems, he managed to save the world without first becoming a theological professor. And even today the Holy Spirit confirms God's message in our hearts and minds by transforming the written words into an ever-fresh and living Word. In this alone should we anchor our faith. The Reformation principle of Scripture is sufficient for our faith and practice: there is a "mutual bond" (Calvin) between God's Word and the work of the Holy Spirit, and that bond does not need to be fortified by any assumption about the inerrancy of the original autographs.

I knew, of course, that all my arguments would be futile. The ears of extreme and uncharitable Fundamentalists are stuffed with the wax of doctrinaire self-righteousness, especially once they make the principle of "literal inerrancy" a controlling norm for their own faith. Some of the faculty of Fuller Seminary at that time seemed to be such men. Others who did not entirely agree with them took refuge in well-camouflaged mental reservations.

Once it became clear to everyone that I was not willing to give way to their concerted action, the dean called the faculty members to an "important meeting." There he asked us to kneel and implore God to show us "the light," a way out of the dead end we had reached. Everyone prayed long and hard, but while they were speaking to God, I sensed that many of them were trying to work on *me*. At the end of that prayer period, remembering Ephesians 4:15, I too uttered a few words: "Lord, help me to speak the truth always in the Spirit of love."

The "Hellhole Church"

Much as Serena and I trusted in God's gracious guidance in those trying weeks, we still would have felt lonely without a human ally. We found solace in Eugene C. Blake's friendship.

At that time he happened to be the pastor of Pasadena Presbyterian Church. (Later he became the stated clerk of the

General Assembly of the Presbyterian Church, and after that the general secretary of the World Council of Churches.) We had become friends in 1948 in Geneva, during the meeting of the World Alliance of Reformed Churches. At that time he had said that he would be happy to welcome us to Pasadena if we were ever there. When the unexpected turn of events led us to Pasadena, our family joyfully joined his church.

When we first arrived, the faculty wives regarded Serena as a bird of their own feather. But once our family joined the Pasadena Presbyterian Church, she immediately fell from their good graces. In fact, she was told that the church she had joined was a "hellhole church" and that by joining it she had committed a "spiritual crime." For these women her witness to Christ and his Gospel had lost its authenticity and power. We were stunned that differences of opinion could drive Christians into such a state of animosity. We had to learn that the ecumenical frontier upon which we had so eagerly antici- pated working had turned out to be a battlefield, and we were caught in the crossfire.

Reactions of the Student Body

Long before the official decision and formal announcement that I was leaving the seminary, the student body could sense that "something was rotten in the state of Denmark." But the more they ferreted out the reasons for my impending depar- ture, the more those who wished to keep me on the faculty increased in number. Among other things, they intended to present a petition on my behalf to the faculty and the board. Some of them went so far as to tell me that, should I have to leave, they would go also. The loyalty of some of them was quite overwhelming, a balm for my bruised spirit and ego. At the same time, it was also surprising. After all, Fuller Seminary was a conservative institution that attracted young people with a similar penchant for conservatism. They came from strictly conservative backgrounds and intended to pursue their studies in the same tradition. How did it happen that many of them suddenly became "turncoats" for the sake of a new professor who was branded "liberal" by the extreme fundamentalists?

One of them offered this explanation: "Dr. Vassady, we held a number of discussions about you and your teaching. Our conclusion was that your faith has not only great depth but also a kind of breadth we never saw before, an outreach uncramped by manmade boundaries. Through your witness we met a God who indeed loves *the world*, not just a selected segment of it. You started us off on a road to new horizons. We sense that to be deprived of the knowledge you impart would be a loss, one probably greater than we can fathom in our present state of scholarly and spiritual search. In short, we feel that we badly need you."

It was obvious that the slightest encouragement from me would have created an upheaval, a divisiveness, the very kind of thing I opposed in my teaching. After all, causing splits was the favored weapon of the extreme Fundamentalists, and I didn't want to use it. So I calmed the students, explaining that their rocking the boat on my behalf would be contrary to my own theological stance. I had come to Fuller with a spirit of ecumenical openness, I pointed out, and my intention was to keep limping along the road that they too had learned to appreciate in such a short time, a road on which—no matter what—love, courage, and patience prevail. With some reluctance, they finally accepted my objections.

Of course, every coin has two sides. Besides that fairly large segment of the student body that was so gallantly ready to go out on a limb for my sake, there were a number of students who eagerly jumped on the bandwagon of the extreme Fundamentalist faculty members. To garner special favor, they hastened to report my so-called "liberal" remarks. There they were, sitting in my classroom, all ears, busily preparing questions fashioned to trip and trap me. Their purpose was so transparent that soon it amused me more than it disturbed me.

Their testings were mainly designed to prove my lack of belief in the authority of the Bible. On one occasion they asked me if I believed in the miracle of the floating axe referred to in 2 Kings 6:6. I answered, "It seems you regard this as a great and important miracle, one of the awesome wonders performed by God. Do you?" When they responded affirmatively, I said, "Frankly, I never speculated about this incident, which in my opinion is insignificant. After all, God, who created nature and all its laws, is omnipotent, so he can suspend any of those laws if he so wishes. Why should a possible reversal of the law of gravity preoccupy my attention when I fully and firmly believe in an incomparably greater miracle, in something truly shaking, shocking, shattering. . . ."

You could have heard a pin drop in the classroom when I opened my Bible and started to read John 3:16: "For God so loved the world that he gave his only Son . . ."

"You see," I continued, "for those who do not believe, this is the most unbelievable, impossible, dumbfounding miracle—nothing short of absurd. But it happens to be the anchor of my faith. Any more questions?"

My query was greeted by silence.

"Then," I said, "let us continue with our New Testament lesson for today." Providentially, it happened to be the parable of the Good Samaritan, a story that irresistibly prompted me to ask the class a few pertinent questions of my own.

"Had you found a half-dead Nazi soldier on that roadside, would you have done for him what the Good Samaritan did for his enemy?"

The answer was a definite "Yes."

"And what if he had been a Russian Communist soldier? Would you still have done the same thing for him?"

Again the answer was a resounding "Yes."

"But had you found out that the beaten-up man was a well-known American liberal theologian, would you still have been willing to help him?"

A few belligerent "Nos" could not be drowned out by the still-overwhelming "Yes."

And I replied, "It's not easy to do two things at the same time—on the one hand, motivated by love and compassion, to help a German Nazi soldier or a Russian Communist soldier; and on the other hand, prompted by the same love and compassion, to allow to bleed to death a God-fearing but—heaven help him—'liberal' theologian."

And thus passed the academic year of 1950–51. At the end of that year I said good-bye to my students. The farewell was moving and poignant, but the tears cried had no taste of defeat. The students' parting gift to me was a handsome silver-trimmed briefcase, which I used for many years as I continued my travels on the ecumenical road.

Looking for Another Job

My family and I had gone to Pasadena with high hopes. It had seemed that after all our losses and wanderings, we had at last found a haven, a steady job and a secure home. But it turned out to be another *Titanic*. We had hardly embarked when the ship started to tilt, and we had to do something in order to stay afloat.

It was not at all easy to find another vacant chair of theology, but I had help. My good friends all over the country were on the lookout for positions I might fill. And the president of Fuller Seminary gave me a good letter of recommendation that ended on this positive note: "Dr. Béla Vassady's departure is not due to any difficulty of personality or any deficiency in teaching ability or any lack of profound scholarship. The administration and the faculty of Fuller Theological Seminary hold him in the very highest esteem even though on some matters of conviction in Christian theology and polity we have basic differences."

The first positive news came in June 1951. The Lancaster Theological Seminary of the Evangelical and Reformed Church in Pennsylvania invited me to fill their Swander Chair of Systematic Theology beginning in September 1952, when the professor currently occupying the position was scheduled to retire. Of course this was good news, but it meant that I had to look for an interim position for the academic year of 1951–52. And finding such a short-term job proved to be even more difficult than finding a permanent one.

Meanwhile, the "For Sale" sign in front of our house was again a reminder that "here we have no lasting city." How many times we had to learn that in the span of two short decades! We became experts in feeling at home with homelessness. Still, since we had just recently lost all our estates for political reasons in our native land, losing this house for religious reasons seemed ludicrous, and it was heartbreaking.

The house was mortgaged to the hilt; the furniture and appliances in it, recently purchased, still had to be paid for in monthly installments.

When I received my last paycheck from Fuller during the first days of August 1951, my family and I still had no idea where the next one would be coming from, or whether it would come at all. Yet I do not recall that any one of us was in a dither about the future. Without expecting any miracle or visitation by an angel, we knew, in a very matter-of-fact way, that the Lord would provide. He always did, always does, and always will. In fact, just after getting that final paycheck, I received a phone call from the president of Dubuque University in Iowa. He invited me to serve for one year as guest professor of philosophy there, and as guest lecturer in ecumenics at the Presbyterian seminary connected with the university. God again proved that his mills are surely grinding, always according to *his* timing.

At the end of August, having sold our house, we left Pasadena for Dubuque. And there we found a school in which we were allowed to breathe freely once again, unhampered by any sort of totalitarian demands.

Thirty Years Later: A Perspective

After our return to the East, our friends often asked us how we could have decided to go to Fuller, thus exposing ourselves to the Fundamentalists. Our answer was that, even though we had heard about their strictness, we had never thought that it could assume the proportions of such an uncharitable attitude. It must have been God's purpose to expose us to totalitarian demands in the name of "religion" in America after we had encountered the totalitarian claims of both Nazism and Communism in Europe. Evidently this was his way to better equip us to serve him in American Christendom.

In 1949, before we had left Princeton for Pasadena, John A. Mackay, the president of Princeton Seminary, had told me, "Béla, with your ecumenical disposition and perspective, you will have a real mission to fulfill at Fuller Theological Seminary." How right he was! And although at that time my mission there seemed to have failed, it was certainly not in vain, as subsequent events showed.

During the sixties those professors at Fuller who had fought for a belief in the total inerrancy of Scripture either retired or took positions elsewhere. And so in 1972 the faculty finally succeeded in rewriting its statement of faith. But they paid a price for doing so: in 1976 they were attacked by Harold Lindsell, who in 1949 had been one of my most ardent adversaries. In his book, *The Battle for the Bible*, Lindsell devoted fifteen pages to describing what he called "The Strange Case of Fuller Theological Seminary." He began his critical review by touching upon "The Case of Béla Vassady."

Fuller Seminary accepted Lindsell's challenge, and in the same year the faculty published a special issue of its *Theology, News and Notes* under the comprehensive title "The Authority of Scripture at Fuller." In it they published again the revised version of the seminary's statement of faith.

The two paragraphs on revelation and Scripture in this second statement reflect the same ideas that I had represented in 1949 when I spoke out against the text of the first statement. No reference is made now to "originally given" autographs. Instead of basing their testimony on a human assumption of inerrancy, the faculty members point to the Holy Spirit, who makes Jesus Christ known to us through sacred Scripture. All in all, in these two paragraphs the teachings about an ongoing, "savingly spoken" self-disclosure of God and about the dynamics of the inspiration of the entire Scripture are objectively and graphically defined. And that was all I had wanted to see some thirty years earlier in the first statement—nothing more, nothing less.

When, in 1949, the faculty had quite unexpectedly placed the drafting of the first statement of faith on its agenda, I had wondered if the whole procedure might be a well-disguised, concerted action against me. But I had rejected this notion, assuring myself that such a thing could never happen in the fellowship of a Christian theological faculty.

Yet that is exactly what had happened, although I didn't know it until a quarter of a century later. In the above-mentioned issue of the seminary's theological bulletin, in an article called "Life Under Tension—Fuller Theological Seminary and 'The Battle for the Bible,'" my earlier suspicion was verified. In the article one of my former colleagues wrote frankly,

> Dr. Fuller usually kept his hands off the operation of the Seminary, and many times said simply, "You men are the educators; you run the Seminary." But in this case [i.e., in the case of my connection with the World Council of Churches], he was losing financial support with almost every mail he received. He appealed to the faculty by stating pointedly, "You'll have to get rid of Dr. Vassady." The obvious approach, it appeared, was to draw up a doctrinal statement worded in such a way that he couldn't or wouldn't sign it (p. 7).

In other words, Dr. Fuller had wanted the members of the faculty to serve as executors of his commanding will. Some of them had obeyed happily, others grudgingly—but all had obeyed. Expediency and concern for money had triumphed over honesty of faith and action; and the end had justified the means.

In the same article there appeared this recollection:

> The Statement of Faith was adopted, and we all were asked to sign it. Béla Vassady refused, and was most "disappointed" with me because I was willing to sign it. I had already made the decision to cast my lot with Fuller Seminary, and I felt that there was nothing to be gained by refusing to sign the Statement. There were others on the faculty who were as aware of the problems as I was . . . (p. 8).

I disagreed. My conviction was (and still is) that much could have been gained by refusing to sign the statement. First of all, those who had signed grudgingly could have been free of mental reservations and uneasy consciences if they had not committed themselves. Second, had several others besides me refused to sign, the extreme members of the faculty would have thought twice before making the decision that they had made in my solitary case. And subsequent decades of tension in the life of Fuller Seminary could have been avoided.

But I was gratified to see that even Harold Lindsell developed and voiced a certain respect for my "openness" and "courage." In *The Battle for the Bible* he wrote, "Béla Vassady could not honestly sign that part of the statement of faith. He was a man of great integrity and was not in the least bit disposed to sign the statement tongue in cheek."

When I read that, I could not help recalling an anecdote about Karl Barth. He was once told that Pope Pius had declared on a certain occasion, "Since Thomas Aquinas, the Christian Church has never had such a great theologian as Karl Barth." According to the story, Barth's response was a hearty laugh and the quip, "The pope must be right. After all, he is infallible."

Ultimately, despite all the sad memories, I was (and still am) thankful to God for my experiences at Fuller. Had I been asked at that time to deliver public lectures on the ecumenical Christian, I would have added a fifth thesis to the first four I had elaborated in my Sprunt Lectures: *The ecumenical Christian lives and moves and has his being beyond Fundamentalism and Modernism.* At the time of my retirement in 1973, Eugene Blake wrote in his letter of greetings to me, "You and your dear wife have made it clear, sometimes in the midst of controversy, that one could and should be both evangelical and ecumenical. Nothing is more needed in all our churches today."

Evangelical and ecumenical! Even at Fuller Serena and I tried to be both: vertically evangelical and horizontally ecumenical; discerning and obeying the revealed Truth in its exclusivity while living in the inclusiveness of *agape*-love.

And I am more than happy to remark here that today's Fuller Seminary seems to be ready and willing to limp along with me on the evangelical and also on the ecumenical road in a *koinonia* of openness, courage, and patience. Only so can we approach the Kingdom of God, which is already here in the midst of us yet still to come, as both a hurting and a healing reality—the one thing supremely worth living for.

12

AN EXPANDING INAUGURAL ADDRESS (1951–1952)

Through Iowa to Pennsylvania

We felt very much at home in Iowa. In many ways the farmers there reminded us of the farmers in our native country—sober, steadfast, honest, clean, and orderly. In fact, many of the students enrolled in the University of Dubuque and its theological seminary were children of these Iowa farmers. They were unsophisticated, honest seekers with many questions. But they didn't ask barbed questions; they were not driven to prove their preconceived ideas but were simply eager to clarify matters of their own faith, their relationship to God and to the world. One could sense a well-balanced grassroots ecumenicity in their midst.

Serena and I were kept quite busy. We were both flooded with requests to speak at various places. While at Dubuque, I worked for a week with an evangelizing team in Evansville, Indiana. At Lancaster Theological Seminary, where I was about to occupy the Chair of Systematic Theology, I delivered the Swander Lectures on Ecumenism. Since that institution belonged to the Evangelical and Reformed Church, I was officially received into that denomination as an ordained minister by the Iowa Synod in Burlington. It was also in Iowa that Serena and I became citizens of the United States of America. The officiating judge was very gracious. In his speech he congratulated *America* for being able to naturalize us as her new citizens.

A few weeks after this event we had to leave Dubuque. I was fifty when we arrived in Lancaster, and by the grace of God, I was able to serve there twenty-one years altogether. We spent a longer period of time there, in the so-called Garden Spot of America, than we spent anywhere else during our earthly pilgrimage.

Lancaster Theological Seminary

Lancaster Theological Seminary was founded in 1825. Originally it belonged to the German Reformed Church, as its first and largest seminary. After the merger of that church with the Evangelical Synod of North America, the seminary primarily served the Evangelical and Reformed Church. By the time I got to Lancaster, the Evangelical and Reformed Church was already in the process of merging with the Congregational Christian Churches to form what is now called the United Church of Christ.

At that time the spirit of this seminary was molded especially by two influences. On the one hand, the "cultural Protestantism" of Germany, as it had developed during the second half of the nineteenth and the first two decades of the twentieth century, shaped its life and thinking. On the other hand, the Mercersburg Movement, initiated by John Williamson Nevin and Philip Schaff, exerted a wholesome influence on some of the professors. The Mercersburg Movement was primarily a liturgical movement, and its sound ecumenical principles had just been rediscovered in those years when discussions of the eventual merger were proceeding in the church.

The man who was instrumental in focusing attention on these ecumenical principles was George W. Richards, a church historian who for a while was president of the seminary. He was one of the first American theologians to respond favorably to the dialectical theology of Karl Barth. He was also the one who arranged for Emil Brunner to be invited to Lancaster to deliver the Swander Lectures on the topic "The Theology of Crisis." Richards' pioneering participation and leadership in the ecumenical movement were much-respected throughout Europe.

I recall a conversation that took place during the Faith and Order Conference held in 1937 in Edinburgh. At that time the adjective *ecumenical* and the noun *ecumenicity* had just begun to pop up in theological discussions, although some greeted the terms with certain reservations. Many regarded their usage as strange, artificial, and trendy. Thus one of the professors, a Scot, had remarked, "*Ecumenicity* is a cacophonous word." He was promptly rebuked by George Richards. "I think *cacophonous* is a far more cacophonous word than *ecumenicity*," he asserted. "To him who knows its original meaning in Greek, it sounds quite euphonious." (The Greek word *oikos* means "house" or "home"; *oikoumené* means "the whole inhabited earth.")

George Richards was one of those who recommended me for the Swander Chair of Systematic Theology. And after I delivered my inaugural address on the main theme of the forthcoming Second Assembly of the World Council of Churches, he expressed his joy that, in and through my work as a professor, the principles of evangelical and reformed Catholicity would continue to prevail in the life of the seminary.

"Christ Jesus: Our Hope"

For many years I had not had time to write elaborate theological discourses. So it was no wonder that now, as I started to work on my inaugural address, it expanded so rapidly that in the end I could deliver only one-fifth of it. Even in its printed form it had to be abbreviated. (It appeared in the *Bulletin of Lancaster Theological Seminary* of 1953.)

I made the best use of Tillich's method, which "correlates

questions and answers, situation and message, human existence and divine manifestations," but in the context of a witnessing theology (Barth), so that the elements of the truth in
the first were subordinated to the basic standards of the second. And so all my earlier psychological findings could be
mobilized in the service of a theology that was rooted and
grounded in the Word of God.

Man's Five Basic Questions.   I began my inaugural address by
analyzing the human psychological situation. The strivings of
man, I explained, are conditioned by the social, historical, and
future contingencies of his own and his fellowmen's lives, and
also determined by God the Creator, Sustainer, and Redeemer. Thus man is impelled to raise four basic questions:
"Who am I?"; "Where do I come from?"; "Where am I
going?"; and "Who is my fellowman?" All of these are asked
in the context of a fifth question, "Who is God?" This betrays
that man is "incurably religious" (Sabatier), or, as the Old
Testament teaches, that he was created in the image of God.

The Insecure and the Cocksure Man.   But a sound theological
anthropology must also stress that this image has been invert-
ed by the Fall. For man the sinner revolted in defiance against
his Creator and tried to make himself equal with God. And so
the "incurably religious" man developed a split personality,
both insecure and cocksure.

On the one hand, man the sinner is still bound to God;
otherwise, he would not be constantly fleeing from him. On
the other hand, rather than admit that there is in him an insecure or fugitive self, he is goaded by his vanity and pride to
believe that he can fight and conquer God by strutting as
"master of his fate" and "captain of his soul." He behaves as a
perpetual idol-forger whose self-reliant creativeness produces
ever-new objects of his own devising. And so, by a joint compulsion of his insecure and cocksure selves, he becomes more
and more entangled in a web of self-deceiving answers.

The survey of history teaches us that the self-reliance of
the cocksure man inevitably degenerates into the insecurity of

the disillusioned and frustrated man. And though the age of futility is then followed by an age of overconfidence, one does not have to wait long to see the metamorphosis, once again, of the cocksure man into a timidly fleeing "cockroach man." Just look at the creator of the atomic bomb! How he tries to hide himself from the devastating effects of his own creation! Will he succeed at least as much as does a cockroach that hides within the cracks of a wall? Man the sinner is undeniably caught up in a self-inflicted vicious circle. Saint Anselm was right: we have not considered how great a burden sin is. And there is no escape from our sinful state.

Behold the Answer!   But despite the fact that there is no human way out, there is still a divine way in, a breaking-through this vicious circle. This occurred in redemptive history, the central event of which is the incarnation, crucifixion, and resurrection of Christ Jesus. He gives to our fivefold human quest the ultimate answers by being himself *the* answer. God's grand indicative, his Gospel, has but one dynamic core: the crucified and risen Lord, our ultimate succor.

This crucified and risen Lord must be proclaimed to the insecure/cocksure man of all ages. Indeed, it was the same insecure/cocksure man in Judas, in Pilate, in the scribes and the Herodians, in the Sadducees and the Pharisees, in the whole Sanhedrin—and in you and me!—who really crucified him. But in a most incomprehensible way, the perpetrators of this atrocious act were the instruments of a gracious and almighty God who chose this way to make known to the whole world his self-giving and forgiving love.

Redemptive Apprehension.   God's redemptive history did not come to an end with Jesus Christ's resurrection, of course. It is still going on, as we respond to him in the act of saving faith (or redemptive apprehension). This cumulative act—through thankfulness (redemptive recollection), through repentance (redemptive self-assessment), through self-giving love and service (redemptive reintegration), and through hope (redemptive expectancy)—always culminates in our obedience to God (redemptive self-identification with Christ).

The Hope for the World. In the final section of my address I spelled out, in terms of redemptive expectancy, the main traits of the church's hope, which is also the only Hope for the world. And I also offered certain admonishments to the two extreme wings of American Protestantism, both Modernists and Fundamentalists.

The Modernists, I explained, are inclined to equate the Gospel of Hope with their own political, social, and economic programs. They tend to identify their own present earthly security with ultimate security, their temporary peace of mind with the peace of God that passes all understanding, and their own achievements with the will of God. At the same time, they fail to see that with their self-propelled activism and optimistic progressivism, they are simply trying to compensate for their own insecurity. They do not even notice that during the whole procedure they are fleeing from the ultimate judgment of the eschatological Christ, and consequently also fleeing from the continuous judgment of their contemporaneous Lord.

The opposite extreme is represented by the partisans of apocalypse, the threateners of doom, and their auguring fellow-travelers. They tend to change their eschatology into specific predictions, and, using their pulpits like information desks, they try to distribute perpetually revised timetables announcing the arrival of the millennial kingdom. They often start out on whistle-stop campaigns, delivering emotional messages filled with private revelations or with arbitrarily combined elements of ancient prophecies. In certain contemporary events of secular and ecclesiastical history they are prone to discern not only "the signs of the times" but also the final fulfillment of Old or New Testament prophecies.

Such a belief in the imminent apocalypse and the calculated millennium is again but another version of the flight of the insecure man—in this case finding shelter in a piously disguised cocksureness. He is simply withdrawing from the world by taking refuge in a safety-first Gospel. He is dodging his present responsibilities by awaiting, with holy idleness and sanctimonious conceit, the imminent victory of the Lord. He prefers to walk in separation, to live in isolation, and his reaction patterns are often loaded with the dynamite of partisanship and divisiveness.

The church's message of hope should overcome all extremes. Christ Jesus, our Hope, committed us to break into this world with tokens of his judgment and also of his mercy. We are not to identify ourselves either with the despair of the insecure man or with the foolish optimism of the cocksure man. Rather, we are to proclaim the message of true hope that aims to turn the world right side up, and to hold it together in him who is our eternal Hope.

Thus my inaugural address at Lancaster laid the foundations for my forthcoming theological work in the United States. But all of it was really a continuation of the work of the psychologist long since turned theologian, who in many ways was indebted to the psychologists and theologians of both Europe and America.

13

LIVING IN FELLOWSHIP
(1952–1973)
. . .WITH STUDENTS
AND COLLEAGUES

Are We *Koinonia*-Conscious?

In the late nineteen-fifties, during a chapel talk, I asked myself and the entire seminary community, "Am *I*, are *you*, are *we* really *koinonia*-conscious?" This is one of our basic life-and-death questions, and will always remain so. (I published this chapel talk, slightly revised, in a 1965 issue of *Theology and Life*.)

The Greek word *koinonia* is so rich in content that the Revised Standard Version of the New Testament uses six different words to do justice to all its connotations: *fellowship* (1 John 1:4), *communion* and *participation* (1 Cor. 10:16), *sharing* (1 Pet. 4:13), *partnership* (Phil. 4:15; 2 Cor. 8:23), and *contribution* (Rom. 12:13, 15:26; 2 Cor. 8:4). True Christian *koinonia* is fresh and spontaneous, always moves on the level of gracious relationship, and exudes self-transcending and expanding power. These characteristics turn a worshiping community into a witnessing community, a gathered church into a scattered one— scattered yet held together by an inner cohesiveness.

Throughout my twenty-one years in Lancaster, I tried to

practice this *koinonia*, to live in fellowship with my students and colleagues, with ministers and church members. And this became a bonding power in my married life as well.

Three Times Yours

Whenever I met a newly arrived junior student in the seminary, my first question would be, "Are you *existentially* involved?" He or she would usually look at me with a bewildered expression, groping for an appropriate answer. Then I would explain what the word *existential* means for those who decide to serve God. It means that Jesus Christ needs people who not only pay him lip service but who give a "whole-soul" response to his gospel and are totally involved in doing his business. The notes I wrote to these students I usually closed with the words "Existentially yours." By that time they all knew I meant that I was totally one with them in Christ's service. My notes to "middlers" closed with the words "Ecumenically yours," reminding them that in their work they would have to overcome any warped perspective of provincialism or parochialism. And my memos to seniors ended with the words "Eschatologically yours." This called to their attention that the Christ who comes to us and speaks to us every day will meet us also at the end. Therefore, let us rejoice in hope.

Three times yours—existentially, ecumenically, and eschatologically! By the end of their seminary training, my students clearly saw that their professor was a pilgrim theologian whose main objective was to win them as fellow travelers on God's path.

Classroom Fellowship

I entwined the elective courses I offered around my two basic courses, "The Ecumenical Christian and the Church" and "The Ecumenical Christian and the World." Invariably I began my class periods with a short prayer: "Bless us, O Lord, in our fellowship, and guide us by your Word and Spirit." I would lecture for about forty minutes, then devote ten minutes to questions and answers. The most visceral questions came from those students who had chosen to enter the seminary at a later stage in their lives, after they had worked for a while and had been unable to find satisfaction in other callings. Many of them left very lucrative positions, feeling compelled to seek something more spiritually fulfilling.

Work Fellowship

As the years went on, the elective courses I taught were transformed into seminar fellowships. During the nineteen-sixties and especially during the last years of my professorship, two of my seminar courses were among the most popular ones.

One of them was the Bonhoeffer seminar, in which I portrayed Bonhoeffer as a Christian, a prophet, a theologian, an ecumenist, and a martyr. Eberhard Bethge's definitive biography, *Dietrich Bonhoeffer: Man of Vision, Man of Courage*, served as our basic textbook. The students were delighted that their professor knew personally many church leaders and theologians mentioned in the text, and could make even more real for them what it meant to be a Christian when Nazism was at its zenith, as well as during the onslaught of another totalitarian political system: Communism. In the other popular seminar course, "Faith: Generic and Christian," I explored the first two pet subjects of my theological career. In this class I enjoyed demonstrating how my two loves, psychology and theology, could come to terms with each other to work for the same cause.

In-depth Bible Study

The formation of a student Bible-study group should always be a spontaneous affair. If organized at the command of the faculty, it may easily turn into an exercise in futility. What the professor should do is sow the seed quietly and then patiently wait for its germination. When this occurs—and with proper "watering" it usually does—the students themselves will feel the urge to form a group in order to share their understanding of Scripture. After a period of exchanging their rather rudimentary knowledge of the Bible, in all likelihood they will invite a professor—and the professor's wife, if she should share the same interest—to participate in their venture. A caring professor and his wife always react positively to such an invitation. They attend the meetings and, without taking over the leadership of the group, give helpful hints and guidance. Because the students' spouses are also present, such occasions can grow into truly enriching *koinonia* within the seminary community.

Soon some of the students' wives might become eager to form a study group of their own, and they will turn to the professor's wife for leadership. Serena, in fact, was repeatedly asked to provide such assistance. She taught many groups of young women, and she rejoiced in their spiritual growth, watching some of them develop into enthusiastic and knowledgeable leaders themselves. Even today she corresponds with some of the most devoted former members of these groups, who later became (and still are) effective Bible-study leaders for their respective congregations.

Theological Table Talks

Occasionally Serena and I invited groups of students and their wives to our home to sit down around our family table to talk about certain contemporary theological or socio-ethical issues. The topics were usually suggested by the students and were announced in advance. On the evening of the discussion one or more of them would introduce the topic, and then we would discuss it in detail. We encouraged complete freedom of opinion. Finally we would summarize our findings and draw various conclusions. Afterwards we would have refreshments, eagerly consuming the Hungarian pastries that Serena had prepared. We called such occasions "theological table talks"; they reminded us of the *Tischreden* Martin Luther had once initiated.

At least one of these table talks deserves to be described here, because it transformed us, quite unexpectedly, into a social-action group.

The topic for our discussion was "Little Rock and the Rock of Ages." It so happened that our "ecumenical student" from Ghana was also present. When he saw how distressed we all were as we discussed shameful cases of racial discrimination, he opened up and shared his personal grievance with us. He had recently gone to the barbershop across from the seminary and sat down with the other students to wait his turn for a haircut. But soon one of the barbers told him that he was waiting in vain because that barbershop didn't serve black people. The student had left the shop and kept his hurt feelings to himself, but now he felt he could speak to us about it. We immediately knew that merely to commiserate about what had happened was not enough. Something more had to be done.

The next day a delegation of theological students went to the barbershop and told its owner that all the students on the college and the seminary campuses would be encouraged to boycott his shop unless he changed his mind and offered his services not only to our much-loved "ecumenical student" but also to any other black man. The barber apologized and complied.

This was a small case in which God clearly demonstrated to us that he can use something like "theological table talk" to promote the great cause of social justice.

Seminar Abroad

During the first half of the nineteen-sixties, the seminary introduced a unique course, the seminar abroad. Its purpose was to help students become acquainted with other countries, with their various churches, and with the religious, social, and political issues they faced. In other words, the goal was to broaden the students' horizons, let them draw their own comparisons, and thus help them overcome their hidden temptations to provincialism and narrow-minded denominationalism.

In 1966 I had the privilege of conducting this seminar abroad in West Germany (in Frankfurt and Heidelberg), in Italy (in the Waldensian Valley, Florence, Rome, and Pompeii), and in Switzerland (in Geneva and Zürich). The local church councils were very cooperative. In addition, we were greatly helped by the World Alliance of Reformed Churches in

Germany, the World Council of Churches in Geneva, and the Waldensian Church in Italy, as well as the secretariat of the Vatican for Promoting Church Unity. The highlights of our tour in Italy were being granted an audience with Pope Paul and being guests of the Waldensian Theological Seminary. Alas, Serena was not able to accompany us (at that time she was visiting countries and churches in Africa); however, Béla, Jr., by this time a Ph.D. candidate in history, did serve as my secretary.

This seminar abroad gave me an opportunity to travel with forty-two students for five weeks. We all enjoyed the special blessings of *koinonia* offered by traveling together.

Ecumenical Seminars

During the second half of the sixties, under the influence of the ecumenical assemblies as well as Vatican II, seven Protestant seminaries and two Roman Catholic seminaries in eastern Pennsylvania were able to organize interseminary or "ecumenical" seminars. The participating schools incorporated these unique seminars into their own curricula. I was asked to serve as the dean of these seminars for the 1968–69 academic year.

The format was quite simple. For an entire semester we met once a week at Valley Forge. Each seminary selected four students, to be accompanied by one faculty member, to attend. We took care to give Roman Catholic and Protestant viewpoints equal representation. It was interesting to observe that quite often during the discussions the dividing lines did not necessarily follow denominational lines.

At the end of the course each group reported the findings and conclusions to the students of their own seminary. In this way the impact of these ecumenical seminars could be felt in the life of all the participating schools.

The Presidency of Robert V. Moss

When I joined the faculty of Lancaster Theological Seminary, its members were already slowly but surely breaking through the limited horizons of Pennsylvania Dutch provincialism and parochialism. Increasingly they expressed interest in an ecumenical orientation. During my first years at the seminary the most conspicuous ecumenical leap was made by the youngest member of the faculty, Robert V. Moss. He and I had adjoining offices, and so we often exchanged ideas and dreamed together about a more scholarly and ecumenical future for our seminary.

A few years after I joined the faculty he became president of the seminary. He was aware that I had done my utmost in recommending him for the position. I had asked the nominating committee not to dismiss him simply because he was quite young for the position. I told them that in Hungary my church and alma mater had dared to elect me for leading positions traditionally given only to older men. The committee listened to me and never had to regret it.

Robert Moss was a sound New Testament scholar and an excellent administrator. He knew how to enlist his colleagues to work for him and with him. He asked me to do what I used to do in my native country: to further the cause of continuing education by accepting the deanship of the summer school for ministers and by launching a new pastoral and theological quarterly. He and I represented our seminary on theological committees to prepare the merger between the Evangelical and Reformed Church and the Congregational Churches, which finally led to the formation of the United Church of Christ. And both of us contributed to the drafting of the statement of faith for the new church body. Those were indeed the most enjoyable years I spent at the seminary.

A Roman Catholic on the Faculty

Under Robert Moss's guidance, Lancaster Theological Seminary was one of the first Protestant seminaries—if not the first—to dare to welcome into its faculty a Roman Catholic theologian, W. J. Walsh, S.J. He was a great asset to our faculty both spiritually and ecumenically.

During my last years on the campus, the students usually chose two seminars for their elective courses. One of them was

Walsh's seminar on spiritual theology, and the other one was mine on Bonhoeffer, whose spirituality intrigued Walsh tremendously. And so we cherished each other's company and theology. To the best of my knowledge, he never tried to proselytize any of our students. This was another reason why his Christ-filled ministry meant so much to us all.

14

LIVING IN FELLOWSHIP
(1952–1973)
. . .WITH MINISTERS
AND CHURCH MEMBERS

Retreats and Conferences

The most natural way for me to live in fellowship with ministers developed through my attending their retreats and conferences and lecturing to and discussing with them vitally important issues of their ministry. They wanted me to talk to them on topics such as the art of sermon preparation, the role of Scripture in preaching, the proper interpretation of the Lord's Supper and its celebration, authority and freedom in the life of the Christian and the church, and how to resist the temptations of the "Gospel of Success." Most of these lectures were published in various quarterlies such as *Theology Today* and *Theology and Life*. Later I also incorporated some of them into my books.

Summer School for Ministers

I was able to strengthen and deepen my fellowship with ministers while serving as dean of their summer school, which Lancaster Seminary started in 1959. About forty pastors enrolled for five weeks each summer. We offered them courses in biblical studies, theology, pastoral counseling, and the sociology of the parish. We secured the best available professor for each course. For instance, Thomas F. Torrance, professor of theology, came all the way from Edinburgh, Scotland. The school was subsidized by various agencies of the church and to a degree even by local congregations, which gladly granted their pastors a sabbatical leave so that they might attend.

Theology and Life

Beginning in February 1958 I was able to launch *Theology and Life*, a pastoral and theological quarterly. To me it was the American counterpart of *Truth and Life*, which I had started twenty-five years earlier in Hungary. Neither of these was intended to be a highly technical publication written only for professional theologians. The new quarterly's motto was "Life Without Theology Is Blind." It was theological in its undergirding but thoroughly practical in its concerns. And while evangelical and reformed in its theological approach, it was thoroughly ecumenical in spirit. Its editorial goal was expressed by a quotation from Saint Augustine wedded to a dictum of John Wesley: "I take the whole Christ for my Savior; the whole Bible for my staff; the whole Church for my fellowship; the whole world for my parish." Many promising young theologians saw their first essays published in this quarterly.

Theology and Life turned out to be the only periodical that published full series of articles in preparation for the Eighteenth and Nineteenth General Councils of the World Alliance of Reformed Churches (held in Sao Paolo in 1959 and in Frankfurt in 1964) and for the Third Assembly of the World Council of Churches (held in New Delhi in 1961). It also discussed in a series of articles the basic objectives of the Consultation on Church Union (COCU), held in 1963 and 1964, and appraised the significance of Vatican Council II, held in 1963–65.

A Widening Circle

During the sixties, due to the growing interest in ecumenicity, more and more church bodies and congregations demanded me as a lecturer or keynote speaker. What surprised me the most was that the circle of interest widened to such an extent that even associations and conferences of Roman Catholic priests called for my services. In 1965 my book *Christ's Church: Evangelical, Catholic and Reformed* was published, and it served as the basis for my discussions with them. They were deeply interested in my interpretation of evangelical catholicity, and in many ways expressed their desire for reformation and renewal in the Roman Catholic Church. But creative tension always pervaded the air when we discussed the church as "the people of God" versus the church as a hierarchically governed institution.

In the late sixties the triple problem of revelation, Scripture, and tradition was the central theme for discussion at a conference of theological professors from eastern Pennsylvania. A young, very outspoken Roman Catholic priest and I were the two lecturers. I was prepared for a sharp debate, but his views on the teaching office of the church were so similar to the Protestant understanding that I could welcome him heartily among those who believe in evangelical catholicity. At the same time, I privately expressed concern that his views might cause him a great deal of trouble in his own diocese. Indeed, a few months later we heard that that is exactly what happened. Because of geographical distance, I could not follow the subsequent turn of events in his life. Maybe he had to stop "theologizing" so that he could remain a priest. For I hardly believe there are others in the Roman Catholic Church besides Hans Küng who could remain priests even though they were denied the privilege of teaching as spokesman of their church.

The "Hit-and-Run Preacher"

There is a general tendency to identify the church per se with its ministers and other professional workers. But the truth is that only five percent of the church consists of ecclesiastical personnel; ninety-five percent of it is laity. A significant proportion of my ministry has always been concerned with the latter.

Since, as a theological professor, I was not tied to any one local congregation, I could preach in many churches. But because I was both teacher and preacher, I became a so-called "hit-and-run preacher." After a church service I was often told, "You did 'hit' us with God's Word. We wish you could stay longer. But we understand that you must 'run' back to do your teaching at the seminary."

"To be or not to be a hit-and-run preacher" was a question I had to wrestle with again and again. The status has both advantages and disadvantages. Its real advantage is that it enables one to meet a larger segment of the people of God than can those who are bound to the same congregation on Sundays and weekdays. The disadvantage is that it deprives one of the opportunity to develop personal relationships with parishioners. One's ecumenical service may thrive in extensity but it will have to wither in intensity.

This lack of relationships with parishioners bothered me more and more, and it finally prompted me to decide to serve a congregation regularly. Thus for two years, from 1968 through 1969, I was supply pastor in a bilingual (English and Hungarian) church in Phoenixville, Pennsylvania. And from 1970 to 1973 I served in another bilingual church, North Mutchmore Presbyterian Church, in northern Philadelphia. It gave me special pleasure and satisfaction to preach expository sermons on the same biblical text in two languages for congregations of different backgrounds.

"His Servant People"

The World Alliance of Reformed Churches held its Eighteenth General Council in the summer of 1959 in Sao Paolo, Brazil. "The Servant Lord and His Servant People" was its central theme. The topics were the service of theology, the service of the church, the service of the Christian, and the service of the state.

A few months before the council met, I organized a study group of twenty-four men and women from the local Reformed and Presbyterian traditions in Lancaster who represented various walks of life and age levels. Our purpose was to discuss the central theme and the subtopics of the forthcoming meeting of the alliance. I wanted to encourage the candid input of "grass-roots" people unhampered by the authority of any official pronouncements. At the end of the study series, I summarized the findings of the group and sent the report to Geneva. The secretary of the theological department of the alliance greatly appreciated the report. "Had the same thing been done in other congregations too," he wrote, "what a blessing that would be to the forthcoming Council of our Alliance." During the Sao Paolo conference the findings of the Lancaster group were often referred to in various sectional discussions.

The Sao Paolo conference exerted quite an impact upon Reformed and Presbyterian churches throughout the world, even in countries belonging to the Communist sphere. In Hungary, for example, the idea of the servant church ("his servant people") became increasingly popular, chiefly because of its strong social implications. It became so popular, in fact, that a few years ago a Marxist ideologue chose "the servant theology of the servant people" as the subject for his doctoral dissertation. This dissertation was later discussed by Marxist philosophers and Christian theologians in a prearranged dialogue.

Lay School of Theology

At Lancaster we all felt that the summer school for ministers, though very much needed and beneficial, was only one side of the picture. If we really meant what we proclaimed—that theology is an integral part of every human life, not only of the lives of clergy and professional theologians—then we had to provide something for laypersons too. Thus the seminary undertook its second pioneering effort by developing its Lay School of Theology.

We usually had forty to fifty lay participants, members of churches in many places. Interest in the school was so great that some of those who signed up had to be put on the waiting list for another term. Those who came were eager and enthusiastic, even ready to burn the midnight oil in order to finish their daily "homework."

After so many years of teaching only those men and women who wanted to be "professionals," it gave me special delight to teach these people. They made me newly aware of how the words *lay* and *laity* have become distorted in common usage. The suggestion is that, in spiritual matters, those who belong to the laity are somehow of a lesser breed and necessarily more ignorant than the clergy—yet in the true sense of the word, they are the *laos*, the people of God, the Body of Christ. They are not just one ingredient of the church; they *are* the church.

When I left for Sao Paolo in August 1959, I had just finished overseeing the end of the term of the summer school for ministers and teaching in the Lay School of Theology. My cup overflowed with gratitude. After all, from these local schools I was now on my way to a global school of the same sort.

15

LIVING IN FELLOWSHIP
(1952–1973)
. . . WITH SERENA

The "Twin Theologian"

After the 1959 session of the summer school for ministers, Thomas Torrance sent me a thank-you note in which he wrote,

> It was a great joy to meet your wife—what a charming, cultured and intelligent lady she is! There are twin-theologians in your family—and that is as it should be, for man and woman together reflect the glory of God, and that applies to their theological activity as well!

In Serena, God gave me not only a wife but also a twin theologian, a helpmeet indispensable both in theology and in life. And since her life, work, and theology became completely interwoven with my own, my theological autobiography would not be whole without my repeated references to her.

After our return to the East, Serena was again able to renew her ties with the women leaders of the various historic church bodies in America. In two years (1952–54) she grew by leaps and bounds into a full-fledged, authentic Bible interpreter, with special zest and zeal for an evangelism that wrestles for each and every soul.

God has blessed her with a fourfold capacity. Two of the four gifts are indigenous traits of her natural intelligence, but the third and fourth are special characteristics given to her by the Holy Spirit.

First of all, she has an affinity for history. To her the history of mankind, and so also that "strange World of the Bible" (to use Karl Barth's phrase), is not just a mass of data. She senses the inner coherence of the whole. Second, she has the ability to discern the various connotations of every word and idiom in several languages. Third—and here we enter the realm of added gifts—her approach to the Bible is always wholistic, never merely atomistic. She has been given the capacity to perceive God's dynamic presence and eternal message in the human words of the biblical text. And fourth, she also has the gift of being able to make one suddenly become awake to and aware of a self-disclosing God.

This fourfold capacity has enabled Serena to offer her interpretation of God's Word in a way that has greatly affected her hearers. Her impact is described in this excerpt from a letter written in 1956 by an individual who had attended a conference where she spoke:

> Mrs. Vassady is like a masseuse who probes and massages and then suddenly administers some sharp slaps to a soft, flabby surface. Then with a quick, smoothing gesture she wipes the sting away, although a salubrious tingle remains. I don't suppose she'd like such a description of herself, and it is a very *physical* figure of speech to use on one who is and looks so ethereally spiritual. Anyway, I love her!

From Coast to Coast

As the years passed, Serena became a much-sought-after public speaker from coast to coast. Sometimes in failing health but always with an unfailing spirit, she delivered countless talks, devotional series, assembly addresses, and expository lectures on the various books of the Bible. Church magazines asked her for articles. Upon the request of the United Presbyterian Women's Federation, she prepared a second Thank Offering and Praise Service called "My Heart I Offer to Thee," used by local associations not only in the United States but also in Brazil.

Yet nearest to her heart was the service she rendered to her own church in Lancaster. John Gordon, the deeply committed pastor of the First Presbyterian Church, used a unique method for kindling the spirit of *koinonia*. He built the sermons he preached on Sundays upon Bible passages discussed during the preceding weeks in well-organized Bible-study groups. He asked Serena to prepare the guidelines for these studies so that they could be distributed a week before he preached the sermon tackling the same topics. Sometimes Serena had to stay up until the wee hours of the night to prepare those guidelines, but she was happy to do it. For God let her see and taste the fruits of her sacrifice.

Under John Gordon's leadership, that large church became a beehive of Bible-study groups, and the Sunday services, especially the sermons, turned into events of avid interest. All the participants in the study groups were eager to find out what other points and nuances the preacher would extract from the verses they had so diligently discussed and debated during the past week. When Reverend Gordon delivered his sermon, one could sense the sparks of personal involvement, an electric current racing from pew to pew.

Looking in Every Direction

In 1955 the committee for the World Day of Prayer asked Serena to prepare the service for 1957. They wanted her to voice the burning issues and the spiritual yearnings as well as the unquenchable, vibrant faith of persevering Christians living in Eastern Europe under very trying circumstances. This was a magnificent but delicate assignment. To write a service without being influenced by any sort of politics was not at all easy in those years. But Serena was determined and eager to do it. She knew that in preparing this service she would have to look again, more keenly than ever before, toward the East, but also in every other direction. For whatever she wrote would have to speak for Christians in all the countries of the world, would have to be written so that all Christians could identify with it.

By September 1956 Serena had finished the manuscript, and the editorial board of the committee had approved it and sent it to the publisher. It was about this time that something totally unexpected happened. At the end of October the uprising in Hungary against the totalitarian Communist government began, only to be crushed by a ruthless Russian intervention. The world stood by, watched, commiserated. But, short of waging a new war, what could it do? And so the entire episode turned out to be just another "Hungarian tragedy."

In November the secretary of the committee wrote to Serena, "We all deeply feel that our committee was guided by the Holy Spirit to ask you to write this service, which speaks so poignantly for those behind the Iron Curtain. What a meaningful experience this will be for Christians in all corners of the globe!" She proved to be a good prophet.

"Who Shall Separate Us?"

The service Serena had composed was based on Romans 8:31–32. Entitled "Who Shall Separate Us?" it was the work of a poet, a biblical scholar, an aching Hungarian, and an ecumenical Christian.

Serena received more than forty invitations to speak on March 8, 1957, the World Day of Prayer. Church councils in many states and in larger cities (such as Washington, D.C., New York, and Chicago) wanted her as their speaker. But we decided, amid all the flurry, that she would stay in Pennsylvania and give Lancaster first priority. There she spoke twice in the morning to many hundreds of people. Then in the late afternoon we drove to Philadelphia, where she spoke to a huge union service. I was deeply touched and my heart was filled with pride and gratitude when, at the end of the procession of the many ministers of Philadelphia, all wearing their colorful robes, I saw walk in the only woman, my own wife, the twin theologian, the author of that day's service.

"There she goes," I whispered to myself. "She marches on where I like best to see her—on the ecumenical frontier."

Tender Loving Care

It happened so abruptly: my unscheduled trip to the Land of Enforced Darkness!

In March 1960 I was working at the Ecumenical Institute of Heidelberg, Germany, doing research for my forthcoming book, *Light Against Darkness*. One day as I sat studying, black spots began to swarm all around me. Within a few hours I was flat on my back, blindfolded, in the eye clinic of the university, with a detached retina in my right eye.

Doctors there operated on my eye, and for five weeks after the surgery I had to lie motionless with bandages on both eyes, my head wedged between two sandbags. I could neither see nor move, but I could still talk. Thus I managed to dictate to Serena the rest of the chapter I had been working on, the one on gratitude. And after my eye was pronounced healed, I said to Serena, "With an eye regained, one is more apt to look at everything with an attitude of gratitude."

But two weeks later darkness fell again upon the same eye. An even larger rupture of the retina meant that there was virtually no hope for the success of another operation. The only sensible thing seemed to be to give up my right eye. In tears and prayer one evening I revised my former statement: "With only one eye left, one is even more moved to look at everything with an attitude of gratitude."

Fortunately, after this night of acceptance came a dawn of new hope. A good friend from America told Serena and me about a new technique that had been successfully used in cases similar to mine. Two days later we flew to Boston, and at the eye clinic there additional surgery was performed on my right eye. I regained twenty-five percent of my vision in that eye— not much, but how much better than nothing! Ever since then, part of my daily prayer has been "Lord, that I might (continue to) see!"

This series of events enriched me tremendously. It made me much better able to understand why the Apostle Paul dared to refer to the relationship between husband and wife when he spoke about "the great mystery" that binds Christ and the church together. For without Serena's tender loving care I could hardly have triumphed over the physical and spiritual agonies of those weeks. Once again she served as the faithful recorder of my thoughts. Because of my eye I had to dictate the rest of *Light Against Darkness* to her, and because of her sacrificial cooperation, I was able to meet the agreed-upon deadline for completion of the manuscript.

"Did You See? She Kissed Me!"

In 1962 he finally did it. As soon as he retired in Basel, Karl Barth came to the United States and lectured on evangelical theology in Chicago and Princeton. Serena and I went to Princeton to hear his closing lecture. James McCord, the president of Princeton Seminary, was aware of our close friendship with Barth, and he arranged for us to meet Barth privately in a small room, ahead of the long receiving line. But McCord's announcing our name to Barth brought no flicker of recognition. Of course, our dear European brother was quite unfamiliar with the American way of pronouncing our name. "These are your old friends from Hungary," continued Jim. In the dimly lit room Barth's eyes suddenly lit up with sparkles of memories, and he exclaimed in German, "Ach, die sind ja doch die Fassadys" ("Oh, these of course are the Vassadys"). Naturally he pronounced our name in the German way.

Seeing the happy, childlike excitement on his aged face was too much for Serena, whose reactions have always been dictated by her heart. She simply threw her arms around him and kissed him on the cheek. The world's greatest theologian, as he has often been called, did not know what to do. Finally, still somewhat awestruck, he turned to James McCord and exclaimed, "She likes me—she kissed me! Did you see? She kissed me!" In these few words was the whole man—his openness, his childlikeness, and his humility.

"The Ecumenical Couple"

Serena and I were dubbed "the ecumenical couple," and with good reason. Serena belonged to the Presbyterian Church, and I, as an ordained minister, was a member of the United Church of Christ. It often happened that our respective churches sent us as delegates to the same global church assemblies. In this way, though we differed in denominational status, we could serve the same cause together and share our experiences. In Nairobi in 1970, we were deeply touched by two former "ecumenical students" of mine: at that time, one was the associate minister of the local Presbyterian church, and the other was a professor at the nearby Presbyterian college. In their own lovely way, according to the custom of their people, they called us "Mama and Papa Vassady."

Though part of an ecumenical couple, Serena was also an ecumenical individual. In Frankfurt in 1964, at the special meeting of the women's section of the World Alliance of Reformed Churches, she delivered the address on the main theme, "Come, Creator Spirit." For seven years she also served as a member of COEMAR (the Commission on Ecumenical Mission and Relations of the United Presbyterian Church). And in 1966 she participated in the first Christian Causeways, a missionary journey of American Protestant churchwomen to various countries and churches of Africa. She was also given the special assignment of representing the United Presbyterian Church at the Diamond Jubilee Celebration of the Presbyterian Church in South Africa.

For many years she was also a delegate to the annual meetings of the Western Section of the World Alliance. Interestingly enough, her membership in that section began just when my term expired, and so, between 1946 and 1973, for more than twenty-five years, either one or both of "the ecumenical couple" could serve the alliance in one way or another as delegates of their respective churches.

Finally, in 1964, after almost twenty years, God opened yet another door before "the ecumenical couple"—the door to their native country.

16

ON THE ECUMENICAL FRONTIER
(1954–1956):
EVANSTON
AND ITS AFTERMATH

That "One Great Fellowship"

In Amsterdam, when Serena and I had to make that agonizing decision not to return to our native land, we also reaffirmed our vows that, wherever God led us, we would work for his one holy catholic church. Later on, our dismal experiences in Pasadena only served to remind us that the word *denomination* cannot be found anywhere in the New Testament. The word closest to it is *schisma*, meaning "division" or "dissension." As the years passed, the Roman Catholic Church began to call us Protestants "separated brethren." Alas, whether Roman Catholic, Orthodox, or Protestant, we are all separated, yet, by the grace of God, brethren nevertheless. We all belong to that "one great fellowship of love." At the same time, it is true that we are split into a wide variety of denominations. The dividing line between our own and other denominations, like the division between the upper and lower lenses of bifocals, blurs certain areas of our vision. In fact, it can play havoc with our sense of perspective and cause us to stumble. It is by no means an easy task to learn to look at our own denomination and to see it with unbiased clarity.

Once, while touring America, the great Japanese evangelist Kagawa quipped, "We Japanese Christians are not interested in your *damnations*—I mean to say, *denominations*." Now, should we call the maze of our denominations a damnation? Indeed we should, if we have been using our own denominational affiliation as blinder of rationalization through which we see only what we wish to see. It is so easy to paraphrase "My country, right or wrong" as "My denomination, right or wrong"!

At the Amsterdam assembly William Robinson stressed, "We have come here in order that our denominations die—not die out, but die!" Meaning to die with Christ so that we may be raised with him. And he was right—our denominations should not die out. Their historic heritage and their enriching cross-pollination deepen our understanding and widen our horizons. But this can happen only if denominations are willing to say with Paul, and truly mean it, "While we live we are always being given up to death for Jesus' sake, so that the life of Jesus may be manifested in our mortal flesh" (2 Cor. 4:11). Only this kind of dying (and living) can turn our denominations ("damnations") into blessings.

The Evanston Assembly

In Amsterdam I had been a delegate of the Reformed Church of Hungary. Now, at the Second Assembly, I belonged to the delegation of the Evangelical and Reformed Church of the United States. Naturally, I was especially interested in the pronouncements of the assembly in regard to the ongoing cold war between the East and the West. Hamlet's question "To be or not to be?" was now paraphrased as "To co-exist or to co-nonexist?" And it was the assembly's mandate to give an answer. A tall order indeed.

At the Amsterdam assembly the churches' pledge was "We intend to *stay* together." The Evanston assembly declared, "We intend to *march* and to *grow* together." In our international relations, identifying ourselves with others and making common cause with them loomed as vitally important. Bishop John Peter's statement caught the attention of the assembly: "We [the Hungarian delegation] came from the other side of the world, *but not from another side of the church!*" Indeed, the one holy catholic church cannot have any or many sides. It is the same church—everywhere.

The assembly urged all the nations to participate in peaceful competition leading to growing cooperation, with the ultimate goal of reconciliation. The articles I wrote after this assembly endeavored to support the same line of thinking. In one of them (published in *The Christian Century* in February 1955), I stressed the need for a *responsible* co-existence.

Responsible Co-existence

The tragedy of mankind in our days is that our spiritual growth lags so far behind our technological advancement. The "ABC" weapons (*a*tomic, *b*acteriological, *c*hemical) are in the hands of "man the sinner." This means that they can get out of hand—not only by technical accident but also by moral failure—and effect global suicide.

Under such circumstances, the much-touted concept of "peaceful co-existence" degenerates into a political slogan, an empty phrase. It is sheer hypocrisy to shout "Let us peacefully co-exist!" at the top of our lungs while the arms race goes on and on. What both sides badly need is not only a politically provided commitment but first and foremost a spiritually undergirded commitment to a mutual, responsible co-existence. It is the church's mission to render this spiritual undergirding. As Dag Hammarskjöld reminded the assembly, "The churches have the power to show men and women the strength that follows from the courage to meet others with trust."

Beachhead Church and Bridge Church

How can the church display the power that Hammarskjöld talked about? Only by serving the world as both a *beachhead* and a *bridge*, an idea I explored in "Beach-Head or Bridge?" in a 1955 issue of *Christianity and Crisis*.

The nature of the church in its relationship to the world can best be described by two paradoxes: (1) the church is *in* but *not of* the world, and (2) it is both *against* the world and *for* the world. These two paradoxes oblige the church to be both a beachhead and a bridge.

The beachhead church bears witness to the exclusiveness of Christian truth. Its mission is that of the prophetic critic, a ministry of "holy maladjustment." It ceaselessly challenges the conscience of society by confronting it with God's judgment. And it does not shrink from turning the world upside down.

On the other hand, the bridge church testifies to the inclusiveness of Christian love. As a fellowship of forgiven and forgiving sinners, it proclaims the good news, offering God's saving pardon to those who are ready to accept it. By so doing, it keeps turning the world right side up, and thus holds it together.

But how can the same church manage to be both a beachhead and a bridge? Certainly not by its own strength and skillful maneuvers, but by God's power alone. Where Christ is in control, there the church continues to resist the temptation to become the spiritual satellite of any political power bloc. It does not blend uncritically into current social fads, nor does it remain an idler in the complacent company of the status quo. Neither a Sovietized nor a Westernized self-righteousness could abrogate the power of our crucified and risen Lord. He will remain *Christus Victor*, the Head of the church that he not only commands but also empowers to be both a beachhead and a bridge.

173

17

ON THE ECUMENICAL FRONTIER (1956–1957): THE REVOLT IN HUNGARY

Prophetic Criticism—Quenched?

Two opposing factions emerged with increasing definition during the late forties and early fifties in the Reformed Church of Hungary. One was represented by the leaders who believed that cooperation with the totalitarian government was in the best interest of the church's survival. Therefore they avoided any criticism of the government, even at the risk of giving the impression that they were its "spiritual satellites." The other party for a while assumed a policy of passive resistance toward both the government and the leaders of the church. However, after Stalin's death, when the chill political climate began to warm and the short shackles were replaced by a long leash, they became quite vocal. Their underground circulars reached even the United States.

Both groups claimed that they were serving the cause of the Gospel in Hungary, and they both endeavored to maintain their contacts with sister churches abroad. So in the first half of 1956, during this hopeful period of liberalization, the Central

Committee of the World Council of Churches was able to meet in Hungary.

The fact that this meeting could be held in our native country, ruled by a totalitarian government, filled Serena and me with joy. Nevertheless, the reports of the returning American members of the committee were not at all reassuring. They seemed to underscore that our concern for the spiritual integrity of our native church was very much justified. At the same time, we could not completely agree with either of the factions.

Here in the United States the prophetic criticism of the church is not only allowed but expected, especially when certain actions or nonactions of the federal or state government are considered morally questionable. It distressed us that the church in Hungary was deprived of that right. At the same time, since Serena and I were personally acquainted with the church leaders in Hungary, we hopefully assumed that, *in private*, they must have shared their prophetic criticism with members of the ruling group. Of course, even if there was such a private exercise of criticism, it did not satisfy the leaders of the opposition, who demanded that free expression of opinion should be granted to the church.

In principle we could not help but sympathize with such a demand. Yet two things were always at the forefront of our considerations. We had to remember that, like it or not, geography made the USSR, not the United States, Hungary's neighbor, and that the Yalta agreement had pushed Hungary into the Soviet sphere. Therefore, to judge from the safety of America the official church leaders in our Communist-controlled native country would have seemed a cheap and easy kind of sermonizing. Yet for the same reasons we could not encourage the leaders of the opposition either. It was obvious that, much as America was committed to furthering the cause of fundamental freedoms and rights in all parts of the world, any military confrontation with the Soviet Union had to be avoided at all costs.

A New "Hungarian Tragedy"

Why do I describe it? After all, the new "Hungarian tragedy" unfolded before the eyes of the whole world. Not that the world necessarily remembers it. The world is a big place, and too many tragedies happen in it every year; one disaster buries the previous one. And "the world," this great "vague specific," simply stands by the tomb, shakes its head, wrings its hands, and does nothing. The wounds of injustice remain untended; they fester and germinate new tragedies. And thus the vicious cycle is perpetuated by the breeding ground of fallen humanity.

The revolution in Hungary began with a simple demand for bread and freedom. Students, workers, and intellectuals started to clamor for "luxuries" like national independence, free elections, a free press, free communication with other countries, and the assurance of a decent human living. Finally and most loudly, they demanded the withdrawal of all Soviet troops from Hungary, which was long overdue according to the Paris peace treaty. They simply wanted complete neutrality, to be left alone to manage their own affairs.

There were a few heady days. Spring seemed to blossom in October—there was a semblance, a mirage of victory. The Soviet-serving government was helpless, unable to control such a sweeping eruption. But then the Russian tanks proved to be very persuasive. (Tanks usually are.) They rumbled into Budapest and turned it into a battlefield. They crashed into crowds and crushed human bodies, scores of them. Soon the Queen of the Danube, raped anew, lay in ruins again. Thousands fled, and the almost unending line of refugees began to pour into the West.

In the once more devastated country, most of the former leaders of the churches (bishops, chief ruling elders, etc.) were able to retain their offices. The new situation, militarily enforced, obliged them to salvage whatever they could of the ongoing ministry and mission of the church. And in the final analysis, history seemed to have vindicated their "realpolitik."

Now, however, it was their task to prove—while meekly cooperating with the new Communist government—that the purpose of their "realpolitik" was indeed the survival of the church, a church fulfilling its witness and service as both a beachhead and a bridge, not just as a maimed "spiritual satellite."

Repetition of a Relief Action

At the end of 1956 and for all of 1957, Serena and I had only one concern: In what ways could we lend a helping hand, both to our afflicted brethren in Hungary and to the thousands of refugees arriving in America?

Like Karl Barth, I decided to remain silent about the heart-breaking Hungarian situation. I felt it would be unfair and unwise—not to mention presumptuous—to make pronouncements, to mete out judgments and words of wisdom, to offer advice concerning issues and events in which I could not participate on the spot—and a very hot spot at that! At the same time, Serena and I did whatever we could to intervene on behalf of individuals, primarily ministers who had been arrested following the crushed revolution. Eugene C. Blake's office in America and the secretarial offices of both the World Alliance of Reformed Churches and the World Council of Churches in Geneva were very cooperative in these cases.

Quite a few refugee theological students and ministers were eager to continue their studies and pastoral work in America, and we were quite successful in opening up new opportunities for them. But the greatest help we could offer was a new, well-organized relief action on behalf of our brethren in Hungary who were deprived of many things because of the devastation. I asked the bishops of the Reformed Church in Hungary to send me lists of the ministers and church workers who were in the greatest need. At the same time, Serena sent out a plea for assistance to hundreds of American Christians whom we had met at various conferences and on other occasions. Her letter evoked an amazing response: soon hundreds of gift packages were on their way to Hungary.

Certainly great relief was supplied by the material help that reached our suffering fellows. But greater and more beneficial than that were the spiritual effects upon both sides.

Many people in Hungary, embittered by what they regarded as their political abandonment by the West, suddenly began to feel the touch of hands reaching out from America with the soothing message, "You are not alone; history may have betrayed you, but we, your brothers and sisters in America, are with you and for you."

And we received our personal share of blessings from both sides. The essence of the messages coming from Hungary was "We thank our Lord that you are where you are in these times of our need." The letters from *this* blessed land expressed similar gratitude: "How grateful we are for the new friends we found in your native land. Through them we discovered a new understanding of what being a Christian really means. We became so much richer and deeper in our own faith."

Those months in our lives were both physically and emotionally exhausting. Often we worked as dusk became night and night became dawn. The light of our desk lamps paled in the light of the rising sun, which would find us still bent over our tables, sorting, writing, asking, answering, figuring. The *koinonia* of giving and receiving, the fellowship of suffering and compassion, took shape and once again turned into palpable realities before our aching, sleepless eyes. And we felt anew the warmth and the once-and-for-allness of the first Easter sunrise.

18

ON THE ECUMENICAL FRONTIER
(1957–1959)
. . . IN THE AMERICAS

The Call to Unity

During the years following the Amsterdam assembly and especially during the years following the Evanston assembly, the major Protestant churches in America increasingly experienced what Pierre Maury called *"la tristesse oecumenique"* (*"ecumenical sadness"*): not only a painful realization of their dividedness but also their frustrating impotence to overcome it. They began to feel that declarations about Christianity on the awesome level of worldwide assemblies were one thing, but that the implementation of these lofty principles on the local level was something entirely different.

Amid all these uneasy realizations, the North American Conference on Faith and Order was held in Oberlin, Ohio, in 1957. It provided a much-needed stimulus, issuing a call for Christian unity that was clarion clear. It explicitly stressed that Christian unity first and foremost means getting back to the Center that is Christ himself.

Our unity in him is not to be equated with uniformity; it

does not exclude creative conflict. At the same time, it includes various types of creative cooperation among denominations, which in certain cases even lead to organic union. But even organic unions are worthless if they are merely the products of bureaucratic maneuverings. Unless we fully recognize our spiritual oneness in Christ, external union is but a new organization, another empty shell.

At this conference we welcomed for the first time (at least in the United States) the presence of two Roman Catholic theologians. One of them, Gustave Wiegle, was even willing to participate actively in the drafting work of a subcommittee. As chairman of that subcommittee I was delighted by his cooperation. And so we glimpsed a door ajar, ushering us toward real dialogues between Roman Catholics and Protestants.

Contending for the Faith

In the fifties talks moving toward union were in progress between the Congregational Christian Churches and the Evangelical and Reformed Church. The process emphasized the importance of contending for the faith that was once and for all delivered to the saints. This meant that "the faith of our fathers" should never be regarded as a trust fund, an accumulation of faith deposited to our name and merely inherited by us. We must reaffirm it and bear testimony to it as our commonly held personal commitment.

In 1955 a joint theological committee to study basic Christian doctrines was established. I read a paper to the committee called "Historical Doctrinal Bases of the Evangelical and Reformed Church." In it I reviewed both the "Evangelical" and the "Reformed" background of the denomination I belonged to, and looking forward, I called on the members of the uniting churches to participate in a new venture of protest. For the true "venture of faith" means assuming a protesting attitude by placing the accent primarily on its positive character (*protestari* meaning "solemnly affirm") and only secondarily on its negative connotation (*protestari* meaning "solemnly negate or reject"). I called the outcome of such an attitude a "tested testimony." The new statement of faith unanimously accepted in 1959 by the General Synod of the new United Church of

Christ (see the Appendix) turned out to be such a tested testimony. It was a genuine pleasure for me to participate in its drafting.

A Servant Theologian

In the summer of 1959, following the meeting of the General Synod of the United Church of Christ, I hastened from Evanston to Kingston, Jamaica; next to Montevideo, Uruguay; then to Buenos Aires, Argentina; and finally to Sao Paolo, Brazil. In Kingston I lectured to the theological students of the Caribbean Islands and preached in various churches. In Montevideo and Buenos Aires I spoke to many hundreds of Hungarians, most of them refugees of World War II and the Revolution of 1956. In Buenos Aires I also delivered lectures at various Baptist, Lutheran, and Methodist-Presbyterian seminaries.

But the main purpose of my South American trip was to attend as a delegate the council of the World Alliance of Reformed Churches, which met in Sao Paolo. I had made extensive preparations for this council both as a theologian and as an editor. In the May 1958 issue of *Theology and Life* I had published an editorial on the main theme of the upcoming meeting, "The Servant Lord and His Servant People," and I had devoted the entire February 1959 issue to a discussion of the central theme and the subtopics of the conference. In Sao Paolo every participant received a copy of this issue, and its articles were widely used in the various sections.

In my first editorial I specifically stressed that Christian service has nothing in common with "servility" or "servitude." Often it must assume the form of a healthy nonconformity. And whether a Christian serves in a Communist country or among people under colonial subjugation or in a highly industrialized bourgeois society, he will soon learn that to be a "servant of the Lord" means also "sharing in his suffering." Yet in any authentic Christian service, prophetic criticism as articulated in the ministry of rebuke can never claim for itself either the first or the last word. Those belong to another aspect of our service: the ministry of reconciliation.

A second contribution to the Sao Paolo meeting was my essay entitled "The Service of Theology," which appeared in the February 1959 issue of *Theology and Life*. The publication of this discourse must have prompted the executive committee of the World Alliance to ask me to serve as the secretary of the first section of the Sao Paolo Conference, which tackled the same subject. The statement of the council on this topic made good use of my essay.

By the end of the Sao Paolo meeting, I gave thanks to God that I could indeed serve as a servant theologian of the Servant Lord.

19

ON THE ECUMENICAL FRONTIER
(1959–1964):
LIGHT AND UNITY

Light Against Darkness

Light as a Theme. Staying permanently in America entailed certain sacrifices for us. For example, for many reasons beyond my control, I had to give up my original long-range plan to write a two- to four-volume *Dogmatics* or *Systematic Theology.* For this reason I shifted my attention to working on smaller books, in which I hoped still to sum up the essence of my theology.

But what should I choose as the central image around which I could crystalize my thoughts? First I thought of the image of life, because in Hungary I had been regarded as the theologian of life. But I came to the conclusion that "life" as a symbol could be rather diffuse. How about "faith"? Yes, but wouldn't my enduring, deep-seated interest in both the psychology and the theology of faith lure me into producing yet another monograph like those I had already written, instead of a comprehensive work in theology?

In the late nineteen-fifties it finally dawned on me: the symbol of *light* could serve as the most comprehensive image for my purpose. True, the Bible derives the origin of all life from God, but nowhere does it say "God *is* life." The Bible also declares that faith is the gift of God's grace, but it never says "God *is* faith." The image of light, however, completely captures the essence of God: "God *is light* and in him is no darkness at all" (1 John 1:5).

In addition, my personal experience had taught me how disastrous the lack of light can be in our everyday life. I could never forget the desperation that continuous darkness had evoked in us throughout the seige of Budapest. Even unbelievers had begun to pray for the arrival of the day when they could leave the dark, damp, unsanitary shelter, climb the stairs again, and once more enjoy the brightness of the sun. That memory has stayed with me as a constant reminder of our inclination to take everything for granted, especially something as natural as light, both in the form of the physical radiance of the sun and in the form of the spiritual blessings offered to us in "the Light of the World."

And so, long before I learned that the main theme of the Third Assembly of the World Council of Churches (held in New Delhi in 1961) was to be "Jesus Christ: The Light of the World," I had decided to make "light overcoming darkness" the motif of my next work, which I had entitled *Light Against Darkness*. This book, published in the spring of 1961, covered the entire field of theology, and took advantage of the fact that Christianity is an audiovisual religion having a message that must be proclaimed and heard as well as radiated and seen.

Variations on the Theme. In the center of the Christian message is the life of man and the universe—but always in the light of God who himself is Light. Thus the book's main sections focused on the biblical symbol of light, applying its qualities to basic scientific, theological, and socio-ethical issues.

In the works of creation and redemption, both in the Old and the New Testaments, light is a central motif: "Let there be light"; "I have given you as a covenant to the people, a light to the nations"; "I am the Light of the World." In the life of the

Christian, living by faith means "walking in the light." The ministry of the church is a "light-bearing mission." And light comes full circle in our own lives only if we do not keep it for ourselves but *render it back to God* (something we are reminded of by John S. B. Monsell's hymn, "Light of the World We Hail Thee").

The sciences of cosmogony and anthropology, history and sociology, as well as futurology, all point beyond themselves and unavoidably lead us back to the original source of all existence: the Divine Light.

Christ's Church

Evangelical, Catholic, and Reformed. At the end of 1960, Eugene C. Blake preached a sermon at Grace Cathedral in San Francisco in which he outlined a proposal for the reunion of Christ's church. He stressed that "a reunited church must be both reformed and catholic." Soon the General Assembly of the United Presbyterian Church added to these two adjectives a third one: "evangelical." At the same time it initiated exploration of the possibilities for "a united church truly catholic, truly reformed, and truly evangelical."

In the 1962 and 1963 issues of *Theology and Life* I published a series of editorials on the same subject but changed the order of the adjectives, putting "evangelical" before "reformed." Logic, after all, dictates that the church can be "truly reformed" only if it rediscovers itself in the Evangel (Gospel). By the time the eight articles were published in book form (by Eerdmans in 1964), I had reshuffled the order of the adjectives once more, as the title indicates: *Christ's Church: Evangelical, Catholic, and Reformed.*

Using "catholic" as the second adjective indicates that the catholicity (universality) of the church is not to be identified with that made captive in the Roman Catholic Church. What the Reformation did in the sixteenth century was to recapture catholicity in its original sense. As Christians we are all people of the catholic faith. In fact, we all ought to be *Protestant Catholics*, as our witnessing for the Gospel and against false human ideologies should become the permanent style of our everyday lives.

Four F's and Four C's. Christ is the Lord of the truly evangelical, truly catholic, and truly reformed church. His *fullness, freedom, finality,* and *faithfulness* evoke *contrition* in our hearts, the *continuity* of the church, our *concern* for others, and our ever-fresh *commitment* to God. Without these there could be no ongoing re-formation or re-newal.

In the context of the church's continuity I also discussed the three "historic ministries" in the life of the church: the ministry of deacons, presbyters (elders), and bishops. Next I offered a critical appraisal of the various movements toward church union throughout the world. Finally, I proposed ten theses for the reunification of the historic church bodies. These theses were used both in the United States and abroad, especially for the Consultation on Church Union.

Come, Creator Spirit!

In the eighteenth century David Hollaz felt it a spiritual necessity to turn his treatment of each Christian doctrine into a "prayerful sigh," to let his "language *about* God . . . pass expressly into language *to* God." At the end of my discussion of Christ's church, I felt prompted to do the same. Part of my closing prayer read,

> O come, Creator Spirit,
> and give Thy Church the courage
> always to be truly evangelical,
> truly catholic, and
> truly re-formed.
>
> Thou, who hast formed Thy Church,
> come, and re-form it again and anew.
>
> For the sake of Christ
> who is with us and prays with us
> that we may all be one.

It seemed providential that the Frankfurt meeting of the World Alliance of Reformed Churches held in 1964 chose for its central theme the same prayer: "Come, Creator Spirit." And one of its subtopics was the petition "Come, Creator Spirit—for the Calling Together of the Churches."

In discussing this petition in a 1964 issue of *Theology and Life*, I stressed that God's Spirit has formed not many churches but *one* church. We broke it up by various schisms; we even dare to call the pieces "churches." And do we not still covertly cherish the status quo of our present dividedness, even while we publicly implore the Holy Spirit to call us, as "churches," together?

Jesus had to climb the mountain of Golgotha in terrible loneliness as his disciples "forsook him and fled." From our "churches" a much easier task is expected: that they climb the mountain bearing their crosses not alone but together, with the assurance that their extremity, even during their negotiations toward reunion, will prove once again to be but God's opportunity. For his Spirit intercedes for us, and for our prospective union, "with sighs too deep for words" (Rom. 8:26).

Needed: Trialogue

Our negotiations toward union should really be not just dialogue but "trialogue," a point I made in a 1964 issue of *Theology and Life*. Even if the word *trialogue* is not approved by the etymologists, it hits the mark theologically because it points to the presence of not two but *three* participants. In a genuinely theological trialogue, two of the participants move on the same horizontal level, but the third (the divine!) addresses them and talks with them vertically, from on high. Therefore, the basic question is, Are we—Roman Catholics, Protestants, and the rest—ready and willing to let God transform our dialogues into trialogues? Do we let God's Spirit be our chairman, moderator, coach, and referee? Do we accept him as *the* judge over our treasured traditions, and submit ourselves, without reservation, to his verdict?

20

ON THE ECUMENICAL FRONTIER
(1964–1965)
. . . IN EUROPE

At Last, Again in Hungary

After eighteen years of absence (sixteen in Serena's case), Serena and I finally returned to our native country on September 4, 1964. During those years, especially following the events of 1956, it was hard to keep in touch with church leaders, relatives, and friends in Hungary. As the tensions of the Cold War between the West and East grew, and all the outgoing and incoming mail was censored by the Communist state, our correspondence shrank to a minimum. Those who risked writing were in dire need of something, primarily medical supplies. We managed to fill their needs, especially those of ministers and church workers ousted by the government and living below the poverty line. The only greetings I received from Hungary in the late nineteen-fifties and early sixties were from my former students on the occasions of their class reunions. They daringly continued to express their gratitude to the "Western sympathizer," the "dissident" Professor Vassady. Thus Serena and I lived for many years in virtual isolation from our friends.

Then, after Stalin's death, there came a period of cautious liberalization. The presiding bishop of the Reformed Church in Hungary was invited to America by the United Presbyterian Church. He was bold enough to visit us too, spending a couple of days in Lancaster. He assured us that although it was not expedient to criticize the Hungarian government, the church tried to exercise its prophetic role in the form of quiet diplomacy. The state intended to maintain a good relationship with the church. Both parties recognized their ideological differences but also the advantages of cooperation, especially in promoting the cause of social justice and world peace.

The bishop extended an invitation to us on behalf of the Reformed Church in Hungary. He asked us to visit the country, requesting that I preach and lecture at various places and thus strengthen the spiritual ties that bound our two countries together. His only stipulation was that we avoid making critical comments about the government. We readily consented. After all, we would go to edify the church, not to censure the state. We saw ours as a bridge-building mission.

When our train reached the Austrian-Hungarian border, we were sobered by the sight of the forbidding barbed-wire fence separating East from West, the watchtowers with armed guards, the searchlights scanning the countryside. All this was a grim warning to those tempted to try to escape from the East to West. Naturally it dampened our spirits. But our morale improved when we arrived in Budapest and were warmly welcomed by the representative of the Foreign Affairs Department of the church, and later on by all the bishops and chief curates.

Never a Dull Moment

Our six-week stay was filled with exciting days. Not since my speaking tour in America had I been kept so busy. But the two speaking tours were vastly different. In America I had been traveling and speaking all alone. Now, however, in "the old country," Serena was with me, and we visited familiar places. Here was our history—here we had met, married, begun raising our children, worked together, encountered Nazis and Communists, learned to be refugees in a battlefield, lived through the siege of Budapest, and sunk near the "kaput level" of physical survival. No wonder that by the end of our tour we both were emotionally drained and physically exhausted. But it was worth it!

In a nutshell: I preached in the larger cities and churches, and lectured at seminaries to students and faculties. Both of us attended meetings of presbyteries and pastors' conferences, conducted Bible-study groups, and visited charitable organizations and institutions. We saw relatives and old friends, comforted people who had lost their jobs and were now treated as "class aliens," and held discussions with young people to learn as much as we could about their aspirations, hopes, and apprehensions. We gave spiritual support to parents whose children had fled to the West and left them alone, and listened to complaints of retirees and bereaved people. We had exciting conversations not only with honest-to-God Christians but also with honest-to-Marx Communists and atheists. We were indeed, all the time and everywhere, deeply involved.

What we liked the most were the meetings we had with my former students and fellow workers throughout the country. In 1964 there were still about six hundred ministers in Hungary who had been students of mine, and many more with whom I had once worked. Some of my former students had to travel an entire day in order to see us. And we spent hours—in one instance a whole night—immersed in conversation.

One Friday evening we were scheduled to meet a large group of ministers at a conference ground. Our train was delayed, so instead arriving at suppertime as scheduled, we arrived at ten that night. Knowing that most of them had to leave early the next morning, faced with a long Saturday train-ride in order to be back with their congregations by Sunday, we took it for granted that they had all gone to bed. But we were not in a land of clock-watchers. They had waited for us—not even in the building but out in the dark October chill. As our car reached the garden gate, they ran toward us, clapping and cheering. A few minutes later we started our meeting with them, and the hours raced by. Around 3:00 A.M. we reminded them that they had better get some sleep before their long journey home. Their answer was gratifying: "There will be another night for us to rest, but no other occasion to be together with our beloved professor."

All of them were eager to hear about our work in the United States. In the course of our conversation, old memories were refreshed, long-forgotten anecdotes told, reports on their pastoral work given, gratitude for gift packages expressed, many questions raised and answered, and tears and laughter shared. Love glowed throughout the night. And when the rising sun peeked through our window, it found us still together.

By the end of our tour, Serena and I had noted a variety of details about our native land. Budapest was still partly in ruins; certain sections of the city were even more devastated than they had been in 1946. The regrettable events of 1956 had clearly left their mark. The political mood of the city could best be sensed by listening to taxi drivers, waiters, and chambermaids. They were all yearning for more freedom, their longing sometimes masked by humor. The streets were dimly lighted, but public security was strictly enforced. There were no muggings, not even in the darkest streets. There were no Western daily papers available, not even at the larger hotels' newsstands. At that time, once you were in Hungary, you were indeed cut off from the West.

The scarcity of Western visitors, especially American visitors, was quite noticeable. In fact, Serena and I were singled out at the hotel where we stayed: an American flag was placed on our table in the hotel dining room. And so, whether we liked it or not, our presence there immediately caught the attention of everybody else. We had been warned in advance that our hotel room might be bugged, so we were cautious. We shared our observations outside our room—in the hotel lobby or the dining room.

Everywhere we went, the leaders of the church received us graciously. They eagerly acknowledged the importance of our bridge-building mission, and expressed their thanks for whatever we had done for them in the past as well as what we were accomplishing in the present. At the same time, we couldn't help but notice that they wanted to make our presence in Hungary as inconspicuous as possible. In a strangely maneuvered red-carpet treatment, they avoided any advance publicity about our whereabouts and schedule. In various cities we heard the same complaint again and again: "We didn't know that you had been scheduled to preach in our church." And the same accusation: "The church administrators purposely tried to hide you from the public, so hundreds of us were deprived of hearing you." Yet, despite this ecclesiastical hide-and-seek, word of our arrival usually got around. Even without any official advance announcement, the people knew—as if through telepathy—when and where to find us, and they packed the churches and lecture halls.

The day we left Hungary, the bishop of Budapest arranged a final meeting so that the ministers of his district could bid us farewell. They came in droves and filled the auditorium to capacity. It was a poignant occasion. Subdued, quiet. Words can say much, but silence even more. And how eloquently tear-filled eyes can speak! A quick, sudden embrace often cuts to the quick. And a firm, simple handshake can shake you to the core. There were these servants of the Word of God. All of them had been knocked around; some of them had even been kicked around repeatedly by a totalitarian Communist regime. All had been tried by fire and tempered by it. Many of them had seen the inside of prison walls. Now, seemingly free yet walled in by uncertainty, they had to live with the question mark of tomorrow hanging over their heads. They had to tread gingerly, constantly cautious. They not only had to walk a tightrope over the precipice; they were condemned to live on it. One slip of the foot or the tongue, and . . .

There are two often-quoted verses in the New Testament: "Be wise as serpents and innocent as doves" (Matt. 10:16); and "Render therefore to Caesar the things that are Caesar's, and to God the things that are God's" (Matt. 22:21). Both can be cleverly expounded in countless sermons and Bible studies. But to live by these verses daily is a different story. Where is the computer that can distinguish between the things that belong to Caesar and the things that belong to God? Where is the tape measure that can mark the point where wisdom turns into facile rationalization? Where is the scale with a balance that would not be tipped by fear or just plain battle-fatigue?

These men were called to preach the unfettered Word in a fettered church. And somehow, some way, by the grace of God, they managed to do it. Somehow, some way, they remained committed to their call.

At the recent Frankfurt meeting of the World Alliance of the Reformed-Presbyterian Churches, the main theme of our discussion had been "Come, Creator Spirit." Now, in Hungary, one of the ministers questioned the biblical accuracy and reasonableness of this title. "Surely you know," he said, "that the first Christians—those in the catacombs, in lions' dens, in prison houses—never invited or invoked the Holy Spirit in this way. To them it seemed superfluous to ask someone to come who was already there. His presence for them was as constant and as natural as their own breath. So it is with us. The Spirit is a palpable reality, here and now, and ever after. Just as he promised."

Herein lay the secret of the spiritual survival of these ministers. They took the promise and the presence of the Spirit at face value, and then went on working out their salvation and that of their church "in fear and trembling," against enormous odds. Serena and I left Hungary convinced that these weather-beaten and weatherproof servants of our Servant Lord would carry on the mission of the church as both beachhead and bridge, and that the Reformed Church in Hungary would remain a sturdy outpost on the ecumenical frontier.

Italy, Spain, and Portugal

After visiting Hungary we visited various cities in Italy and Sicily. In Hungary we had just encountered the curtailment of certain religious liberties by a secular totalitarian system. And now we were looking forward to visiting Spain and Portugal, where the ecclesiastical totalitarianism of the Roman Catholic Church managed to suppress certain freedoms of the minority Protestant churches. But our primary purpose was to visit

Rome in order to attend several sessions of the Second Vatican Council. The question of religious liberty was on their agenda, a topic very much central to our interests.

I could write page upon page about Vatican II, but a few impressions must suffice: Latin, the official language of the church, in various accents; the formal, restricted order of the proceedings; the top dignitaries of the hierarchy in their ornate robes, members of the highest council of the *governing* church, numerically just a speck, yet endowed with enormous power over the *governed* church; the representatives of the laity restricted to the balcony, relegated to the role of mere onlookers. Indeed, Catholic laity had even less say than the officially invited "observers" from the Orthodox and Protestant churches, who were repeatedly contacted (at least between sessions) by the "experiti" and theologians of the Roman Church.

Through the courtesy of the Roman Catholic bishop of Harrisburg, we were invited to the reception given by the bishops of the United States. Thus we were able to meet personally some of the most prominent Catholic theologians of Europe and America. The bishop of Harrisburg also furnished us with letters of introduction to the archbishop of Seville in Spain and to the patriarch of Lisbon in Portugal. Our visits with these two ecclesiastical dignitaries were memorable.

One Sunday morning I preached to a small Protestant congregation in one of the slums of Seville. I should explain that if you wanted to find a certain Protestant church in Spain, you did not look for a large edifice with a tower or a steeple, or expect to locate it on the main street or in any of the conspicuous squares of the city. You had to go to the poorest section of town and enter the main gate of a tenement building, where you would find yourself in a rectangular courtyard with many entrances to small family dwellings. Over one of these doors you might finally discern the modest inscription *Capilla Evangélica*.

On the afternoon of this particular Sunday, Serena and I were graciously received by Cardinal Bueno y Monreal, the archbishop of Seville, in his magnificent palace. The archbishop started the conversation in Spanish, which we did not speak. I tried German, but he just shook his head. Serena's knowledge of French finally solved the problem. With her help, what we had thought would be a short, formal visit turned into a frank and lively conversation that lasted one-and-a-half hours.

Soon we became immersed in the subject of religious liberty. The archbishop said he was in favor of it, but he also pointed to internal difficulties that would be precipitated by any sudden change in the status quo in Spain. "The Franco government walks on two crutches," he confessed. "One is the military; the other is the Roman Catholic Church. The weakening or strengthening of either one may upset the balance and topple the government. Therefore, a rapid democratization or liberalization could hardly be expected." At the same time, he expressed his personal aversion to any sort of proselytizing.

At the end of our long give-and-take, he asked us if we were interested in seeing his throne room. Of course we were. He disappeared, then returned with a huge key and led us through a long corridor. The petit-point tapestries on both walls of the corridor were only a hint of the beauty we beheld when we entered the spacious throne-room. Everything was gold or gilded, silk or velvet. Hanging on the brocade-covered walls were masterpieces by the world's greatest artists. Our eyes feasted upon works by Michelangelo, Leonardo, Raphael, Tintoretto, and Goya, to mention but a few. Paintings worth several million dollars were hidden from the world, seen only by selected VIPs of the church, and only on special occasions. And in the center of the room stood the golden throne.

Serena immediately took a picture of the archbishop and me next to the throne. When she asked the archbishop to sit on his throne for another picture, he graciously complied. "Don't look so solemn," Serena said to him. "Smile! Think of Jesus Christ and what he did for us!" With this prompting the archbishop smiled broadly, perhaps for the first and the last time in that throne room. He seemed to genuinely enjoy our natural attitude; it was probably a breath of fresh air amid the stuffiness of daily protocol, of being approached by everyone with solemn reverence.

When we finally departed, the archbishop accompanied us down the long flight of stairs and waved good-bye at the large entrance door of the palace. The gatekeeper's jaw dropped. This scene was no doubt a first for him. Who *were* these strangers who were being treated with such unusual courtesy by His Eminence?

Who? In terms of status, we were small potatoes. Members of the "lowly" Protestant church. Sojourners who just a few hours earlier had worshiped in that part of the city where the gatekeeper of this palace would never set his foot. But we were two human beings who dared to approach this high-ranking hierarchical figure as simply another human being, just as much a handful of dust as we are or will be when "dust returns to dust." This is what unlocked his heart and mind as well as his throne room.

We thanked God that no official interpreter had been on hand (probably because our visit took place on a Sunday afternoon). We were convinced that our private audience with the archbishop had encouraged him to tell us things that he would never have divulged in someone else's presence. And in this way we found him to be but another Christian brother on the ecumenical frontier.

After this heartwarming experience, Serena and I went on to Portugal. In Lisbon I addressed the student body of the Presbyterian Seminary, which functioned under the auspices of the southern branch of the American Presbyterian Church. Here we heard still more complaints about the humiliating way in which Protestants were treated by the state and by the Roman Catholic Church, the predominant church of the country. For instance, ministers of the Protestant churches showed us their ID cards, which indicated that officially they were "unemployed." Even though they worked hard as pastors of various small congregations, the state refused to recognize that service as a bona fide occupation.

We were told that the patriarch of Lisbon was scarcely interested in any sort of dialogue or cooperation with the Protestants. However, the introductory letter of the bishop of Harrisburg did open the door for us, and the patriarch received us with formal graciousness. It was obvious that he wanted to keep our conversation on the level of amicable small-talk. But that was not our purpose. Finally we reached a point where I could seize the chance to speak to him about the spiritual blessings of the ongoing conversations between various Christian churches.

"Yes, yes," he replied. "In Portugal we have already entered into dialogue with the Anglican Church."

"I hope you will do the same thing with the other Protestant churches, too," I hastened to comment.

"When the time is ripe for that, we will do so," was his diplomatic answer. He was ready to drop the subject, but we wouldn't let him. I pressed further.

"But mere dialogues are not sufficient. What we all really need is 'trialogue.'"

"I fully agree," he said, looking at Serena. "I am happy that Mrs. Vassady is also included in our conversation."

"Yes," I responded, "but that is still only a trialogue on the human level. When I speak of trialogue, I mean to say that both you and we should give the primary role to the Holy Spirit. If he is bypassed, our so-called dialogues are of no use at all."

He reddened as he hastened to reply, "Of course, of course, the Holy Spirit should also be included."

When we left the patriarch, I said to Serena, "Basically he was a friendly man."

"Oh, yes," she laughed, "a friendly fox with baby-blue eyes."

In the wake of our European experiences we felt even more keenly than ever before that "the hour is coming and now is" (John 4:23) when all true Christians—Roman Catholics, Orthodox believers, and Protestants—will have to enter not only into dialogues but into divine-human trialogues, with the Spirit as moderator of the whole encounter. Thus our united petition should indeed be "Veni Creator Spiritus!" ("Come, Creator Spirit!") Without him our much-touted dialogues will, in Gustave Weigel's phrase, deteriorate into "two sets of monologues for mutual information." Just so much hot air, nothing more.

The Church with Open Doors

Upon our return from Europe, I summed up our observations about religious liberty in three articles that appeared in *Theology and Life* in 1965: "Atheism, 'Catholic Society' and Religious Liberty"; "The Church and the Totalitarian Society"; and "Live Antitheses." But my major concern was the need for *openness* in the church. In the closing pages of my book *Christ's Church*, also published in 1965, I prayed for "a Church with open doors and large windows":

> Gather us, Lord, or scatter us;
> do as Thou deemest right,
> building us all into one Church:
> *a Church with open doors and large windows*,
> a Church that takes the world seriously,
> ready to work and to suffer,
> and even to bleed for it.

Enriched by our experiences, particularly those in Rome, I rejoiced with the best theologians of the world that Vatican II had ended with an open-ended faith and theology. Just as in chemistry the arrangement of atoms in a certain structural formula is represented by an open-ended chain, so the church in its basic structure should never be a closed circle. The climate of an elitist introversion stunts both genuine faith and genuine theology.

The church, if true to its mandate, is bound to be open-eyed, open-minded, open-hearted, and open-handed. This means that in our pluralistic society it should never pursue a policy with rigidly fixed limits, and that under all circumstances, even at its own peril, it should remain an open sanctuary, the house of the Lord of all, always accessible to all (a point I made in an article in *Theology and Life* in 1966).

In his great play *Murder in the Cathedral*, T.S. Eliot expresses this idea more movingly than any theologian could. The would-be assassins of Thomas the Archbishop are approaching. The priests, trying to protect their beloved leader, bar the doors of the Cathedral of Canterbury. Thomas is quite familiar with the strength of those doors. No one could enter them from without unless they were opened from within. And he knows the price he will pay for opening them. Yet he orders his priests to do just that:

> Unbar the doors! throw open the doors!
> I will not have the house of prayer, the Church of Christ,
> the sanctuary, turned into a fortress. . . .
> The Church shall be open, even to our enemies. Open
>   the door!

Fourfold Openness

From my early youth I had striven for openness, but it became more and more of a focal point for me after the Amsterdam assembly. Its manifold potential intrigued me. Nothing is so rewarding as watching a theory unfurl into reality, and to be instrumental in promoting this process.

On September 14, 1966, when Pope Paul VI received me and the president of the student body of Lancaster Seminary in a private audience, I said,

> Our educational trip [to Rome] is motivated by a four-fold openness. . . . First of all, by our mutual openness toward God in our common Lord and Savior, Jesus Christ; secondly, by our openness toward the self-awareness, the mission, and the renewal of the church; thirdly, by our openness toward other churches, particularly to the Roman Catholic Church, for the sake of our common witness and service; and finally, by our mutual openness toward the world, being aware that the Christian parish is bound to perish unless it regards the whole world as its parish.

In response the pope grasped my right hand with both of his hands and said several times, "We all must pray and work for church unity." After I had returned to Lancaster, a letter arrived from the secretary of state of the Holy See, informing me that "His Holiness was warmly appreciative of your thoughtful presentation."

My next project was to spell out in detail the essence of that presentation in a series of articles that appeared in *Theology and Life* in 1966. The all-inclusive title of this series was "God, Church, and World: Clues for Conversations and Co-operation between Orthodox, Roman Catholics, and Protestants." It consisted of four articles on four basic issues: (1) "Revelation, Scripture, and Tradition"; (2) "The Nature, Mission, and Renewal of the Churches"; (3) "The Church, the Churches, and Reunion"; and (4) "The Church in the Modern World." This was the last comprehensive literary venture of my active professorship in the field of ecumenics.

21

RETIREMENT

Two Memorable Days

At the end of the 1972–73 academic year, having served as a theological professor for forty-eight years, on two continents and in nine seminaries, I reached the age of mandatory retirement. For a few days, May 24 and 25, every event turned out to be a "last occasion."

I ended my last class period with the students by quoting the words of Dietrich Bonhoeffer before he was hanged by the Nazis: "This is now the end, but for me a new beginning." And I added that on the ecumenical frontier all "ends" turn into "new beginnings." This is always a comforting thought at a time of many inevitable "lasts."

On the evening preceding commencement day I delivered the baccalaureate sermon. My theme was "Faith Growing into Faithfulness" ("Be faithful unto death, and I will give you the crown of life"; Rev. 2:10). Afterwards the students gave me an ornate hardwood candlestick with this inscription engraved upon it: "From the students of LTS to Dr. Béla Vassady, a light in the darkness"—a complimentary reference to my book *Light Against Darkness*.

The next day, at the commencement exercises, I was officially declared professor emeritus of the seminary and presented with a "memoir" of my professorship. I was also given a sterling-silver medallion engraved with the watchword of the seminary: "Preach the Word!" This was the first time that the seminary had given such a medallion to any of its professors.

The student newspaper, *The Seminarian*, published a special issue for the occasion and—what I liked the most—recalled that besides all of my academic degrees, what I had cherished the most was being called a "V.D.M." ("verbi divini minister," "servant of the Word of God").

At the alumni banquet the president of the seminary handed me an album containing hundreds of letters from numerous groups and individuals—from the leaders of national church bodies that I had served, both in Hungary and in the United States; from the faculties of the seminaries where I had taught; from the World Council of Churches and the World Alliance of Reformed Churches; and from former associates and former students serving as ministers throughout the world. Of course, I enjoyed reading the words of affection and gratitude from former students, colleagues, and fellow workers. I was especially touched by some of the tributes from those with whom I had traveled and worked on the ecumenical road for many years. For instance, W. A. Visser 't Hooft, honorary president of the World Council of Churches, wrote,

> The World Council of Churches has a very great debt of gratitude to the twenty-eight men who were chosen in 1937 to bring the Council into being and who served from 1938 to 1948 as the Provisional Committee of the World Council of Churches in Process of Formation. Professor Vassady was one of the twenty-eight. . . . We owe so much to these twenty-eight because they had the vision and acted on it. Thus the churches affirmed their fundamental unity in Christ at the very time when the nations were drifting apart.

A few weeks after these events Serena and I sold our house and left Lancaster for Ann Arbor, Michigan, so that we could live near to our two daughters and their families. The fact that I had really retired dawned upon me only in Ann Arbor. What could not quite penetrate during the last days of celebration and confusion suddenly struck me: Serena and I had indeed irrevocably reached the penultimate stage of our earthly activities. We had now entered a classroom not as teachers but as pupils. And we had to enroll in a course to learn the not-too-easy lesson of making haste slowly.

Making Haste Slowly

On the eighth of August we arrived in Ann Arbor. Our lovely apartment faced the slowly flowing Huron, and we decided to keep pace with the course of the river.

During the first years of retirement, I served as supply pastor for churches in Port Huron, Clinton, and Kalamazoo, and preached from time to time in many other places. The "hit-and-run preacher" was still very much alive in me. But what I liked best was participating in the continuing education of the laity. I did so at the First Presbyterian Church of Ann Arbor, which asked me to serve as its "theologian in residence" and opened up a series of marvelous opportunities for both Serena and me.

"Sundays at 11:00" was the name given to the seminar courses that followed the first morning service. Each course lasted at least four to six weeks. Since the majority of the congregation consisted of highly qualified professional people, their pointed questions were always thought-provoking and invigorating. The series of lectures included "The Christian in the Making," "Dietrich Bonhoeffer: A Man for Others," "Theologians of the Twentieth Century," "Courage to Be Christian," "Milestones in our Christian Pilgrimage," "Karl Barth: The Man and His Theology," and "Back to Basics in Theology."

Fond as we were of Ann Arbor and of our elder daughter, Naomi, who lived there, in 1980 we made the decision to move to Grand Rapids so that we could live closer to our younger daughter, Timea. She not only held a full-time job but also was raising two teenagers single-handedly, and we hoped to be of help to her.

Here too we continue our occasional supportive ministries of preaching, lecturing, and counseling. The emphasis in all we do, however, is on "occasional," without any pressure of "must."

As we continue to learn the art of making haste slowly, we turn into prospectors unearthing the hidden treasures of leisurely busyness. How beneficial is walking rather than jogging, not only for our bodies but for our minds! How we relish doing our own pacing and spacing, taking our own sweet time for deliberations, time to observe and time to weigh. We prize our freedom to be selective in all our activities; to distinguish between the ephemeral and the permanent; to reject the tawdry and the trendy, however enticingly packaged they may be; to leave the relentless pursuit of prominence to those who don't have the vaguest idea how dwarfing the rush for self-importance really is.

We had our share of the hustle and bustle at the foot of the mountain, and of the frustration of craning our necks to see only a part, a patch, of it. But now that we have the luxury of keeping our distance, we can let our eyes roam the mountain's height and width, its peaks and valleys. We can see it as it is—at least from our viewpoint—while never forgetting that what we perceive is not the whole, for every mountain has another side. But keeping our distance from the turmoils of active life does not make us distant from them, and we hope to God it never will. A larger perspective does not make us lazy. Instead, it sharpens our acuity, pricks our curiosity, and whets our appetite to explore the other side of the mountain.

Leaving the "madding crowd" is a far cry from shedding involvement; it only changes its quality and dimensions. Reducing group activities means increasing our time to develop our individual relationships much more fully. In other words, we are becoming increasingly one with mankind, especially with those who "limp" with us along the path of God's Word.

For a Christian, mandatory retirement can never mean

stagnation. His advance may be slower, but he is advancing nevertheless. Slowing in pace enhances pressing forward spiritually. His eyesight may become dimmer, and his physical motor may be more and more frequently in need of repair. But with the eyes of his faith he is able to perceive, better than ever before, that "marvelous light" into which he was called.

22

GOING HOME
(IN THE SEVENTIES)

Four Trips to Hungary

All our lives Serena and I were propelled both mentally and physically into a sort of perpetual motion, partly by the force of history and partly by our own yen for exploration. Though we traveled a great deal, we were never happy-go-lucky tourists, and we hardly ever went just for the sake of vacation. We always had a special reason, a goal in sight, an assignment to attend to, an official obligation to fulfill. Even after retirement, our globe-trotting continued.

Visiting Hungary in 1975: Going to a Funeral

On the World Day of Prayer in 1975, Serena was just getting ready to leave for a community service for which she was scheduled to speak when the phone rang. A cablegram from Hungary informed us of her mother's death. Serena was shaken by the news, yet she felt it was her responsibility to go and deliver her message to that large community gathering.

A few weeks later, after so many years, we were once more on our way to Hungary. It was a soul-stirring experience to meet many of our old friends at the funeral. We stayed for six weeks in order to sell the condominium that Serena inherited.

Selling it was one thing, but getting the money was another. State regulations prohibited transmitting the proceeds of the estate from Hungary to the United States. They had to be deposited in a "frozen forint account" and could be withdrawn only in limited installments and used by the heirs only within Hungary. This restriction virtually obligated us to make three more trips to our native country. We accepted it as a God-given opportunity to continue our bridge-building mission between the West and the East.

Visiting Hungary in 1976

Leading a Church Group.   Our second trip was well-organized in every respect. Sponsored by the United Presbyterian Church's "Journeys for Understanding," we led a study group of thirty-five American Presbyterians to our native country. This group included ministers, educators, church workers, elders, and deacons. Their introduction to the church situation in Hungary began in Geneva, at the headquarters of the World Council of Churches, and continued as they were briefed by the leaders of the church in Budapest, Sárospatak, and De-brecen. The presiding bishop of the Reformed Church addressed the group on the delicate topic of Marxist-Christian cooperation. The past and present connections that Serena and I had enabled us to open doors for them, to introduce them to unique events and experiences and special places off the beaten path. We enjoyed many memorable experiences, but two were particularly moving.

Probably the most memorable was a Sunday we spent in a rural community—Nyírbátor—in a 600-year-old church that had become Reformed in the sixteenth century. During the Counter-Reformation it had been ruthlessly forced back into the Roman Catholic Church. But it had succeeded, at a price of heroic sacrifice, in shaking off the Roman yoke and once more embracing the faith of the Reformation.

As the church service began, I faced the soberly dressed members of the congregation, most of them sturdy farmers of my motherland, all of them speaking only my mother tongue, the Magyar language. Then I looked at my American friends, whose motherland was the United States and whose mother tongue was the English language. And I said to myself, "These people here are all gathered together as members of the one holy catholic church, about which Cyprian, Augustine, and John Calvin had rightly stated, 'You cannot have God for your Father unless you have the Church for your Mother.'"

There we were, all bound together as children of the same spiritual mother. And so, on the spur of the moment, I abandoned the original topic of my address and spoke to this congregation about God's great and gracious gift to us all as manifested in mother's milk, in our respective motherlands, and in our mother tongues. Yet beyond all these, I noted, is the church universal as our all-embracing spiritual mother. Though I didn't mention the word *ecumenical*, I felt that I managed to drive home what that word really means: we have been redeemed by the same one blood of Jesus Christ; we are all blood brothers and blood sisters in him; and all of us have the same spiritual mother, the one holy catholic church.

The other particularly memorable event occurred in Debrecen. In one of the city's parks is a commemorative column that stands between the large Reformed Church and the Reformed College. Engraved on it is the picture of a seventeenth-century galley, and under it the names of those Hungarian Protestant ministers who were driven by the ruthless force of the Counter-Reformation to march through Austria to Trieste, then down to Naples, Italy, where they were sold as galley slaves. Many of them perished. Those who survived were finally liberated by a Dutch admiral, Michael de Ruyter.

Since 1976 marked the three-hundredth anniversary of this event, our American Presbyterian group decided to place a wreath at the foot of this column. As usual, advance publicity about this event had to be avoided. The local authorities wanted to deter any massive gathering of the local faithful.

Our group moved quietly from the college to the column.

We sang the hymn of the galley slaves: "Lift thy head, O Zion, weeping, / Still the Lord thy Father is." A. K. Stevens, a professor emeritus of the University of Michigan, delivered a short, moving address. Then the group placed its wreath at the foot of the column. On the ribbons of the wreath, written in both English and Hungarian, was the declaration "The Word of God is not fettered."

In the meantime some passersby had gathered and called to others, and by the end of our small ceremony our little group was surrounded by many of the local people. Some of them just stared. Some wept silently, then turned and hurried away.

During every phase of our trip through Hungary, we could not help making the same basic observation: facial expressions and silences said so much more than the carefully selected words of "official" greetings and information.

Family Reunion. Shortly after the Presbyterian group left Hungary, the three Vassady offspring and our oldest grandson, Andrew, arrived from America. Nearly thirty years had passed since three skinny, undernourished, bewildered Hungarian children had left their ravaged country for the United States. And now they returned as well-developed, attractive *American* adults. Yes, as Americans in every way—except for their unquenchable love for their native land. Herein lies the greatness of America: its naturalized citizens are never expected to forswear love for the country of their birth. In fact, the opposite is true. Those immigrants who quickly and callously, almost flauntingly, forget their native land easily lose the trust and respect of native Americans.

We had taught our children to cherish and preserve their mother tongue and Hungarian culture. Since all of them had married Americans who spoke only English, this had not been easy. Nevertheless, Naomi, who had been thirteen when she left Hungary, retained an astoundingly flawless knowledge of the Magyar language. Béla, Jr., and Timea, four and six years younger, had some difficulties initially, but a few days spent in Budapest quickly took care of that. Andrew, our grandson, the first in our family with the birthright to become President of the United States, had previously spent seven profitable months in a school in Sárospatak, and took to Hungarian like a duck to water. So all of us were well-equipped not only to see but also to hear, to understand and communicate, and to fully benefit from this unique experience.

And benefit we did. What a family reunion that was at the Budapest airport! So similar to yet so vastly different from those historic moments twenty-nine years earlier at La Guardia. Indeed, our family has had its share of tears and laughter, of big lows and big highs. Through these experiences our children have learned that emotions are nothing to be ashamed of; it is neither childish nor weak to express them. In fact, only strong persons dare to cry. Thus, during the three short weeks of their stay in Hungary, they dared to hug the old oak tree they had once loved to climb next to our villa in Debrecen. They dissolved in tears at the reunion with my former students (by this time all elderly ministers), who reminisced of times past with lumps in their throats. And how enthralled they were when I, accompanied by a gypsy band, serenaded their mother with the same love song I had sung to her on the first night of our honeymoon!

Sometimes we all just stood quietly together, drinking in the sight of Budapest, its lights reflected on the waves of the Danube. Or we leaned out of the windows of the tower room of the castle at Sárospatak to look down at the surrounding land—land not quite ours anymore, yet always ours. We were home yet prepared to leave for home, feeling not one bit divided in our hearts, neither two-faced nor schizophrenic.

By mid-July we were all back in America, resuming our lives here. We returned with a deeper love for our native land as well as for our adopted country. That trip bred a decision on the part of Béla, Jr., that in time he richly fulfilled. Thenceforward, he decided, he would devote a great deal of his time as a historian to researching, writing, and lecturing in the field of Hungarian-American relations.

Visiting Hungary in 1977 and 1978

Researching and Lecturing.   Our third and fourth visits to Hungary, in 1977 and 1978, were filled partly with research and partly with lecturing.

Curiously enough, the research had to do with my own past. I gave myself the mandate to recover—or rather to rediscover—numerous editorials, articles, and essays that I had published in the thirties and early forties but had long since forgotten about. Now I had them microfilmed or photocopied to assure the accuracy of data for this autobiography.

In 1977 I was asked to deliver lectures at the seminaries in Budapest and Debrecen about my theological journey. And in 1978 the seminary in Budapest wanted me to speak on two additional topics: "Providence and Predestination" and "God's Instruments and Agents."

The first of these was a recurrent topic in my theological pilgrimage, a subject peculiarly alive in the spirit of Reformed people in Hungary. In the vicissitudes of their political history as well as their church history, amid trials and tribulations throughout the centuries, they had clung to their assurance of God's gracious election, and the purposefulness of his providence proved to be their greatest comfort.

However, I felt that the second subject was even more timely for present-day Hungary, because now the Christians there have to find their bearings in the framework of an atheistic Marxist society. In my lecture I stressed the point that in the world there are, by and large, two sorts of people living side by side: those who are mere *instruments* or tools of God, and those who are his voluntary *agents*, his bona fide servants.

People belonging to the first category vary greatly. Some have no interest in God at all; some worship a false deity; some sneer at God, even vehemently fight the True and Only One. Yet whatever they do, the King of kings has the power to use them according to his inscrutable purpose. Militant and philosophical atheists, honest agnostics, hypocritical Christians, self-righteous moralists—God can forge them all into his instruments. They do not have the faintest idea that he is using them, but he is. This world has many people—like Cyrus and Darius, Pharaoh and Pilate—who are unwittingly doing the will of God.

The other group, the agents of God, is a less complicated lot. They know "whom they have believed," and live and act (in Visser 't Hooft's phrase) "under the pressure of their common calling." Even if they do not hold any office in the church, their simple witness and genuinely dedicated service can be very contagious. And the Lord God, who has the power to turn stones into living sons of Abraham, can, through the witness of these emissaries, turn unwitting instruments into willing agents, into knights fully armored, wholly dedicated to serve the King of kings.

A Golden Diploma. During our fourth visit, my native church and my alma mater, the Reformed Theological Seminary at Debrecen, honored me with a golden diploma. Present for the occasion were the members of the Collegium Doctorum and well-known theologians from abroad, among them a metropolitan from Russia and a professor of theology from Princeton, New Jersey. This was a touching tribute, commemorating the fiftieth anniversary of my earning a "Doctor of Sacred Theology" degree, *summa cum laude.* The press pointed out that this event was a "first" in the four-hundred-year history of Hungarian Protestantism. In his presentation of the diploma, the dean of the faculty appraised and praised my ecumenical endeavors to promote the causes of church unity and world peace.

As the focus for my acceptance speech I chose Proverbs 25:11: "A word fitly spoken is like apples of gold in a setting of silver." I knew that I was addressing a church shackled by its geographical location and political situation, a church in which the Word of God in the words of men could not always be freely expressed, and therefore not always "fitly spoken." And so I stressed that the mission of the church is the same everywhere: to proclaim God's Word and to live up to it. Nowhere is this an easy task. Hindrances and obstacles vary from place to place, from country to country, from continent to continent, from century to century, but they exist everywhere. Yet the freely and fitly spoken Word is our ultimate hope. Without it there can be no church unity, no social justice, and no world peace.

That very same day we learned that the conclave of cardinals in Rome had just chosen the Polish archbishop Woytila to be the next pope of the Roman Catholic Church. Somehow I sensed immediately that the theological, social, and political background of John Paul II and his forthcoming reign would have a tremendous impact on the entire world, but especially on the countries of Eastern Europe.

In Search of Identity

No church can be truly *the* church, living up to its divine calling, without being constantly in search of its own identity. Sometimes this search goes on unnoticed. But there are periods when it becomes conspicuous—in fact, assumes saving proportions. That is what happened in our native church during and after World War II.

Our four trips to Hungary in the seventies gave us the chance to "stop, look, and listen," to appraise and to draw certain conclusions about the church of our native land. We tried to be scrupulously objective, which is never an easy task, especially when one is emotionally involved. But being aware of this made us particularly careful to check and recheck our opinions. Sometimes we even played devil's advocate against our own evaluations. One can never be fully accurate, but we hope we managed to capture the truth as realistically as is humanly possible. This section and the following one consist of two things, interwoven and indivisible as they are: historical facts and human insights.

In 1945, when Budapest was still partly under siege, Pastor Albert Bereczky emerged from his shelter and declared, "I have accepted God's grace to live and to serve, and this is my *continuous liberation.*" In 1948, as elected bishop of Budapest, he spelled out to the entire church what such a continuous liberation really means: in the face of a new totalitarian power, the church must learn "how to walk the narrow road."

That same year Karl Barth was invited to Hungary for the second time. He lectured on the *real* church, and after his return to Switzerland exhorted those he had addressed:

> By the mercy of God you have been offered a unique opportunity. When do the good days of the church begin, if not in moments when, both theoretically and practically, the Gospel is its only source and comfort? . . . Such opportunities can slip by irrevocably. Let me appeal

to you, not merely for your own sake, but with all the other churches in mind: Do not let the opportunity that is now being offered to you slip by!

The vital and haunting question is this: Has the Reformed Church in Hungary let that "unique opportunity" slip by during the last thirty-five to forty years?

In October 1948 the state signed an agreement with the leaders of the church. This assured the church a chance to search for its identity, to repent of its sins of the past—and, thus purified, to renew its faith. At that time Hungary was already annexed to the Eastern bloc of nations, headed by a newly established, Soviet-educated Communist government, a government that, despite its iron-fisted totalitarian power, was still seeking to confirm its foothold in a basically anti-Communist nation.

First of all, it had to deal with a church still afire with evangelistic zeal. The spiritual blessings of its great awakening (1945–1947) penetrated every part of the church body. Its leaders, having themselves been seared by the fire of renewal, were willing to duly accept the rule and rights of Caesar, although not at the price of shortchanging God (Matt. 22:17–21). In the spring of 1948 they boldly declared, "The goal of our church is to be a free church, obedient only to Christ, its divine Lord."

Of course, the fatal flaw in making such agreements is that they are subject to differing interpretations. What is full freedom in the exercise of religion? We all know what that means in America, but in Hungary the government meant merely that the doors of the sanctuaries would be open for Sunday worship. Though this freedom was granted, our native church had to relinquish all its parochial schools except the Reformed Gymnasium in Debrecen. Further, all free religious organizations and federations had to be disbanded, and be confined to and restructured within the body of the church. All this in exchange for the freedom to worship.

But can you call "free" that which is subtly controlled? True, to hear the Word of God read from the pulpits is in itself a precious privilege. But now its interpretation had to become selective and prudently cautious. And while the sermons loudly lashed out at the sins of the past, they risked not even a whisper of criticism concerning the present. Usually these sermons were critically toothless; they were expected to undergird and promote the current state projects.

Such projects were not necessarily bad or evil. To say that whatever a Communist-Socialist state does is wrong or harmful would indeed be a prejudiced assertion. In its own way and by its own method—which we may not agree with—the Hungarian government has done much good in certain areas, with impressive results. In fact, with the blessings of the state, the church has been able to increase its philanthropic work, to make it more effective and pervasive than ever before.

In all fairness, another fact must also be pointed out: strange as it may sound, while the church has been more restricted in its internal affairs, it has made significant strides in its theological growth and ecumenical outreach. In ecumenical dimensions it has been able to establish close relations with the World Council of Churches and other interchurch organizations. It now participates in the various interchurch dialogues, promoting the causes of European security and world peace.

Nevertheless, though apparently heading in the right directions in these respects, the churches of the Eastern bloc lack something that we in the West so often take for granted: the free, unhampered expression of conscience and conviction.

Release and/or Coercion

An Assessment. By and large, there are two main types of relationships in our social and corporate life. The first breathes the fresh air of freedom. The second must constantly inhale the fetid air of coercion. The church, if it is real, is the prime example of the first; the totalitarian state is the prime example of the second.

The great awakening in the Protestant churches of Hungary at the end of the war gave rise to free and spontaneous

community (*koinonia*). Soon, however, a new political collectivism started to wield its weapons of coercion, and through
intimidation paved the road of regimentation. And the more
the churches submitted to this regimentation, the more they
were bound to become servile to a regimenting state and, in
and through that state, to a regimenting world power.

In the case of the churches in Eastern Europe, that regimenting world power is, of course, the Soviet Union. No
wonder that, ever since the incorporation of these nations in
the Eastern bloc, the leaders of these churches have become increasingly vocal on the subjects of basic human rights, social
justice, world peace, disarmament, and the dangers of nuclear
holocaust. Their declarations have one-sidedly favored and
sometimes loudly praised the Soviet Union as the only law-
abiding, justice-seeking, peace-making world power. Oddly
enough, in all this the state per se remains in the background.
Without lifting voice or finger, it exercises its "obey or else"
kind of power strictly through the church authorities.

As the church leaders have changed, the newly elected
bishops have had to be pre-approved by the Communist totalitarian state. Formally and constitutionally the free election of
church leaders is still observed, but virtually everybody knows
in advance for whom each congregation is expected to vote.
Thus the freedom of the congregations to elect bishops for the
various church districts exists only on paper.

All this sounds and looks bad. It invites the simple—
indeed, simplistic—conclusion that the bishops must be lack-
eys of the state. Thus, in order to save their own skins or to
augment their own power, they would deliberately lead the
churches into submission. But neither an unequivocal yea nor
an unequivocal nay would be the true answer to such
imputations.

In the last three to four decades, from the end of the
turbulent war years to the equilibrium and relative prosperity
of today, there have been about three turnovers in the
bishoprics.

The hardest decisions fell upon those who, in 1948, had
to make the agreement with the state. They were promptly
accused of selling out the church to the Communist state. Yet

the alternative they had faced was to drive the church into the catacombs. An unyielding resistance to the state's demands would have meant losing even their right to free worship. A resounding "no" would have seemed heroic for the moment, but the long-range effects upon the church would have been devastating.

A church consists of people, all sorts of people, who cannot all be expected to endure a lasting martyrdom. The bishops felt that even a diminished and controlled church above ground could do more than a fractured one underground.

Were they right? And to what extent? Were all those compromises absolutely necessary? These are academic questions—now. Answers differ. Who was right or wrong is anybody's guess. But subsequent events and the permanent geopolitical situation of Hungary have borne out the decision of the bishops of the forties.

Those who succeeded them have not had to face such momentous decisions. They simply maintain the status quo. They are swift with disciplinary action whenever a minister shows more independence than would be "healthy" or whenever anyone "steps out of line." They all have vocal friends and silent enemies. Some of them are more feared than loved. Some invite resentment by throwing their weight around. Neither they nor the "faithful" can forget that they wear the bishop's mantle not by the free votes of the people but by the "grace" of the state. No wonder they have a tendency to give a bit more to Caesar than to God. Their argument is that their obedient service to the state pays dividends that benefit the church. They can point to improvements that could never have come about without the financial aid and, more generally speaking, the blessings of the state. And as the years have passed the state has undoubtedly given the church more and more "rope" to move around. But although the rope is longer, it is still a rope tied to a fence-post.

Nothing is easier than to judge. At the same time, nothing is more difficult than to judge. Much as we strive for it, objectivity is a rare commodity. Applying our viewpoints to situations entirely alien to ours can never be fair. Viewpoints are bound to differ, depending on which part of the planet we inhabit. The atmosphere surrounding us shapes them.

With the passage of time, people who live in countries of controlled thinking become less and less aware that their ideas, opinions, and convictions are the products of the pressure, propaganda, and perspectives they have to live with. Stress and conscious or subconscious fear seep into the very fiber of their existence. This is just as true of those who live and work at the top of the ecclesiastical ladder as of those who live at its foot.

Therefore, it would be woefully one-sided for us to accuse the present leaders of the Reformed Church with deliberately driving their church into servitude for their own ulterior motives. On the other hand, such a judgment is still one side of the whole truth, and thus it cannot be discarded as altogether unjust. Though we grant the bishops every benefit of the doubt and even our understanding and sympathy for their difficulties as they try to play a complicated game, the evidence cannot be ignored. Too many signs and witnesses point out that, under the guise of ecclesiastical discipline and Christian obedience, they steer the church into a degree of submission to secular authority.

If this evaluation of the Hungarian church and its chief "shepherds" seems to be ambivalent, it is so because the whole situation is contradictory and ambiguous. In our complicated world, right and wrong cannot be cut-and-dried. We can no longer permit ourselves the luxury of seeing everything in black and white. Gray areas shadow much of our worldscape, and in our global village we can scarcely avoid venturing into these shadows. Whenever we do, we cannot help judging whatever we see according to our own conscience and convictions. We are prayerfully aware that to keep a completely balanced judgment is impossible. The more painstakingly we strive for balance, the more the undoubtedly existing yet undetectable imponderables make us tread warily.

Christ's warning "do not judge" is often misunderstood because it is only half of the message. We have the right—in fact, it is our Christian responsibility—to dare to pronounce judgment. But only—and this is indeed a big "only!"—after we have dared truly and honestly to pass judgment upon ourselves. (As Matthew 7:5 says, "First take the log out of your own eye, and then you will see clearly to take the speck out of your brother's eye.") Only after we have undergone such difficult self-surgery will we be able to observe others with a measure of clarity, humility, and understanding.

A Few Concluding Notes. After forty years of East-West tensions, the ghost of Yalta still keeps haunting. It was at Yalta in 1945 that Churchill and Roosevelt agreed to the military, political, and economic paramountcy of the Soviet Union in Eastern and Central Europe. They did so for the sake of temporary advantages, trusting that Stalin would keep his promises regarding basic human rights and democratic procedures. Thus they unwittingly gave the Soviet Union a chance to transform those nearby countries, one by one, into "political satellites." Since this transformation they have been called "captive nations" whose restoration to freedom is still "unfinished business." But the unfinished business of whom? It is a moot question with vague and evasive answers. One thing is certain, however: the spiritual undergirding of this task is the responsibility of the churches.

The church, if it is real, lives and moves and has its being in an unfathomable experience best described as "liberating captivity." ("Make me a captive, Lord, and then I shall be free.") This experience serves as a matrix for its prophetic mission. An authentic church is bound to pronounce God's judgment upon any and all sorts of captivities. Therefore, one of its mandates (as discussed earlier) is to be a beachhead church, a prophetic critic, but never to regard this purpose as an end in itself. Its passing of judgment, however true and right, must always be subservient to its redemptive and communal work. The beachhead church finds its *raison d'être* by being also a bridge church. In other words, its acts of holy nonconformity must always go hand in hand with its deeds of reconciliation.

How beneficial it would be to make this the central theme for certain ecumenical gatherings! Would it not be more edifying if instead of just pityingly calling these East European churches "captive churches," we would extend to them again and again an invitation: "Come, share with us all your successes and failures as you try to be both a beachhead and a bridge, both a critic and a reconciler, in your own social and political surroundings. And we will also speak to you about our own successes and failures (because we too have both) in our own setting." Honest sharing would lead to mutual and invaluable spiritual support.

In some ways an autobiography is not the right place for expounding upon such matters. Nevertheless, two more ideas, not new but nearly forgotten, still beg to be mentioned.

The first of these two ideas involves the principle of sisterhood and its practice on the grass-roots level. Genuine sisterly relationships should be established between certain congregations belonging to East European and Western churches. Their mandate would be to correspond with each other, to visit one another, to get to know each other's problems, yearnings, and sorrows. Neither world assemblies of churches nor confessional councils nor even such annual gatherings as the Stockholm Conference for Confidence-Building and Disarmament and the Karlov Vary Talks could serve as substitutes for such encounters on the local level.

One should never underestimate the thrust and power of local congregations, especially when they are mobilized by sisterly meetings between congregations from the East and the West. They may have a greater impact on their own local and state governments than certain ecumenical and international gatherings do, and through those governments exert greater influence upon even the world powers.

The second idea relates to the younger generations in both socialist and capitalist countries. Their longing for justice and peace is overwhelming—not only because they have much more to lose in the event of war than those whose years on this earth are numbered, but also because they "travel light," unencumbered by the bag of hatred, prejudices, and bitter memories that still burdens the older generations. So let me suggest that churches, seminaries, church-related colleges, and other educational institutions organize and establish exchange fellowships in both East European and Western countries. Particularly those young men and women who major in social studies, philosophy, and/or the political sciences and have a special interest in Christian ethics should be given the opportunity to continue their postgraduate studies for a few years in countries of different (and even opposite) persuasions. During their stay they could get acquainted with the steps that have been taken by their hosting churches and/or states in the interest of social justice and global peace. Such firsthand knowledge would then make them better equipped to work in a more unbiased way for the same goals in their own countries. And in later years these young men and women could organize their own "world association" that would bind them together throughout their entire lives, to the benefit of the whole world.

Homeward, in Each and Every Way

Beginning in 1975, Serena and I crossed the Atlantic Ocean eight times. Flying toward Hungary, we happily said, "We are heading homeward." But on our return trips to America we said the same thing. It struck us that both countries were our own; we felt at home in each of them. Yet, ultimately, we were but "strangers and sojourners" in both. Therefore, whether eastward or westward, our flights were always a mixture of joy and sorrow.

Again and again the inevitable question arose: "After all, what is 'home' for us?" And the inevitable answer always came: "Both and neither." For in the deepest sense each direction meant and will always mean the same thing. Because in each and every way we were, we are, and yes, we always will be homing pigeons on their homeward journey.

And wherever we go, Psalm 139 keeps reverberating in us:

> If I ascend to heaven, thou art there!
> If I make my bed in Sheol, thou art there!
> If I take the wings of the morning
> and dwell in the uttermost parts of the sea,
> even there thy hand shall lead me,
> and thy right hand shall hold me.

23

AGAIN IN TRAVAIL
(IN THE EIGHTIES)

The Uncorked Bottle

The text of the first sermon I wrote as a student of divinity was Romans 8:22–23: "We know that the whole creation has been *groaning in travail* together until now; and not only the creation, but we ourselves, who have the first fruits of the Spirit, *groan inwardly* as we wait for adoption as sons, the redemption of our bodies" (italics mine). More than fifty years later, at my retirement, my parting words to the members of the seminary faculty were taken from Galatians 4:19: "My little children, with whom *I am again in travail* until Christ be formed in you" (italics mine). And during the decades in between, I preached many sermons on the eschatological discourse of Jesus. In Matthew 24:7–8 he proclaimed that before the end will come, "Nation will make war upon nation, kingdom upon kingdom; there will be famines and earthquakes in many places. With all these things *the birth-pangs* of the new age begin" (NEB, italics mine).

The dawning of the nuclear age makes these biblical allusions poignantly relevant.

Homo sapiens has reached a dangerous point in his development. Like the fisherman of the Arabic fairy-tale, he was able to uncork the bottle and release the genie from it, but now cannot recapture the genie and reseal the bottle. God the Creator hid nuclear energy in the womb of Mother Nature. Our technical expertise grew sufficient to release it, but now our knowledge is woefully inadequate to harness it.

Indeed, knowledge is not wisdom. Having half-digested the fruit consumed in the Garden of Eden, we keep on strutting in the role of the Creator. Alas, the babies we so proudly conceive are born with various birth defects. Our latest offspring, nuclear weapons, bear the mark of the demonic and, just as in the horror movies, are rapidly developing into full-grown monsters. The arsenal continues to grow, and our technological advancement, coupled with our human fallibility, drives us each day nearer to the precipice. It is indeed a miracle of a long-suffering God that this planet is still in one piece.

Frantically searching for a means of survival, we look for man-made panaceas. Frightened, we engage in peacemaking procedures that lead only to temporary appeasement, not to a just and lasting peace. Or, what is even worse, we throw ourselves with a horrifying kind of hope into a mushrooming armaments race.

Wedged into a predicament with apparently no exit, the questions are now daily thrust upon us. What should we Christians do? Should we shout patriotic slogans like "Better dead than red"? Or, haunted by "nukemares," should we mutter between chattering teeth, "Better red than dead"? Neither of these alternatives is compatible with our Christian faith. But what then?

That Reassuring "Again"

When Paul scolded the Galatians with "I am afraid I have labored over you in vain," in the same breath he also called them his "little children" with whom he was "again in travail." Though they disappointed him, he refused to give up on them.

The word *travail* means toil; difficult, burdensome work; anguish resulting from hardship. But it also means the labor and pangs of childbirth. In other words, it is a fruit-bearing pain, and its result is new birth, life, celebration.

Paul's voice and mission is—or ought to be—also the voice and mission of the church. Just as he saw in the recalcitrant Galatians his "little children" over whom he labored and agonized unceasingly, so should we, as the church, treat all human beings as "God's children," with no distinctions and no exceptions.

As Christians we have the option of regarding the ongoing conflict between the world powers as one form of the travail in which "the creature is waiting to be freed." But we also recognize that these bloody birth-pangs are at the same time a manifestation of mankind's redemptive history. Tormenting, yes, yet redemptive wherever the church reaches out to all humans until Christ be formed in them.

To be in travail again and again with all the inhabitants of this globe is the overriding mission of the church.

The Heart of the Gospel

The tangible purpose of redemptive travail is reconciliation. This is what the world needs the most, and what our generation desperately craves. For all ages but especially for ours, the message and ministry of reconciliation is "the heart of the Gospel" (as the 1967 confession of the United Presbyterian Church aptly states).

In its everyday usage, *reconciliation* is a rather colorless word. It pops up in high-minded speeches because it sounds noble, but it is seldom taken seriously. It usually boils down to simplistic suggestions: "Nations should stop quarreling with each other"; "Factions should smooth out their differences"; "Estranged people should become friends." But who should take the first step toward the other? Why should I be the one to do that? And what should I do if my approach is not reciprocated? Such questions remain unanswered.

However, the same powerless word emerges as an all-embracing force as soon as it reflects the Spirit of the Gospel. The Bible teaches that reconciliation is God's own act (2 Cor. 5:19). By dying for me on the cross, he restored the divine-human relationship that I had broken. And when I grasp the magnitude of his deed, I am so filled with gratitude that I am bursting with a desire to do something in return. And what else could be my answer, my meager reciprocation, than to do for his children what he did for me?

If I am a Christian, I never forget that reconciliation starts with God, but is reflected in my actions. It has two movements: a vertical one, from God to man, and a horizontal one, from man to man. Should I disregard the first, the second would become powerless. No matter how noble my attempt, how sincere my outreach, if it is based on my own initiative, prompted by my own humanitarian fervor, kindled by my own idealistic expectations, it will peter out in disillusionment. Disappointed by rejection, I too may withdraw into a cocoon of hurt feelings or, worse still, revert to hostility.

If, however, I am practicing reconciliation fully aware of its source, by God's grace I will persevere. If I keep my eyes focused constantly on the cross, I will not lose sight of the fact that I am only a catalytic agent, called to transmit God's overwhelming unconditional love even to my enemies.

Does this Christian, biblical approach to reconciliation hold the answer? Would it assure us happy results? That would be too much to hope for. Let us come down from the mountain into the dusty valley of reality and face the difficulties staring at us.

Barriers to Reconciliation

The ministry of reconciliation is not merely a high-sounding calling of some church functionaries somewhere out there. All members of the church should share in this task, not only corporately but individually. You are the church; I am the church. And that is where the first difficulty sets in.

Even if we are born-again Christians, we cannot shake the frustrating contradictions of our own nature. My part in reconciliation starts with a complete surrender of myself to God, a repeatedly needed submission to him. Sometimes I can do it quite easily; at other times I cannot, hard as I try.

Then too, reconciliation means an unconditional self-identification with all of humanity. This is a great deal to expect, because that includes every man and woman of every possible description: the rich and the poor, the exploiter and the exploited, the oppressor and the oppressed, the victim of racial discrimination and the victim of reverse discrimination, the upholder of unjust social structures and the downtrodden subjected to them. Reconciliation means identifying even with the world powers as they threaten each other and us, as they manufacture newer and deadlier weapons designed to blow us into smithereens.

How can I fit into this picture? How can I be an agent of reconciliation when I have an arsenal of secret weapons of my own prejudices, memories of personal injuries, nightmares of injustices against my own nation or social group? How can I reach out to those who inflicted such pain? And how can I learn not only to forgive but also to forget? Where will I get the strength to overcome the thorny barriers hedging my own soul?

The only way to do it is to return again and again to Golgotha and to the empty tomb. To try to recapture afresh the vital reality of the "good news," which in our hectic "Christian" life so easily sinks into the quagmire of theory.

We encounter the second barrier in our own church, in the fact that a great percentage of our churchgoing people do not have the foggiest idea about the Christian meaning of reconciliation. Sunday School teachings and sermons expounding it either did not hit home or sooner or later became old hats shoved to the back shelves by vastly more important church activities.

Thus, though the word *reconciliation* is widely used in our communities, the interpretation of it has badly degenerated. Some regard it as an empty, theoretical principle; others perceive it as a precision instrument that, if skillfully handled, may lead to earthly security; still others think it a magic word, a mantric "om" that by sheer repetition may generate peace and assure survival.

What a deterrent this "Babelism" in spiritual semantics proves to be in our ministry! How discouraging is the frequent discovery that we do not speak the same language, that we sit in the same pew and listen to the same Word of God, but understand and interpret it so differently!

And if this "little" problem with our brethren is not enough, let us go one giant step further. Let us step into the arena of present-day international relations and meet those leaders who are atheists or anti-Christians. Try to explain the Christian meaning of reconciliation to members of the Soviet politburo, to the Chinese government, to African or South American dictators, to Castro, to Arafat, or to Khomeini. Try to explain it to so many terrorist groups. "Legion" is the name of those who would interpret our Christian approach of reconciliation as the sign of some foolish, milk-toast meekness, as evidence of weakness, a signal of giving in, giving up, or backing out. They would surely attempt to exploit our attitude. After all, it is easy to outwit the meek.

Beyond Defeat—Victory

If we are fully aware of all these barriers to our reconciling ministry, what should we do then? Should we throw in the towel? Should we stoically resign ourselves to the "fact" that, after all, reconciliation is a distinctly divine act that happened once on the cross but could hardly be re-enacted in human dealings?

But let us stop and take heart. After all, the *real* accomplishment on Golgotha became known only later, even to the disciples. At first the crucifixion spelled nothing but defeat. An "idealistic fool" who with his miraculous power might have become the success story of his age, the pampered hero of his people, became instead a lonely, forsaken man hanging on a cross. But lo, beyond the cross, there glowed the open tomb. Beyond defeat, total victory.

And this is exactly what Christ promised us too: first defeat, then victory. When and how, it is not ours to see. What we have to accept is that our labor may seem to bear no fruit. But we must steadfastly believe that, guided by the Spirit, whatever we say and do will somehow, some way seep into nooks and crannies and take root. Even the most tightly closed minds are not hermetically sealed. Here and there will be pockets of understanding, long stopped-up ears bent to listen, shut eyes opening for a look, even if only out of curiosity at first.

Alas, in this age when we are hungering for prompt fulfillment, we find it hard to patiently "wait upon the Lord" and his slowly—perhaps very slowly—unfolding plan. In our present state of affairs, what we want to see more than anything else is some practical, visible guarantee of long life and security. On this earth, of course!

This is exactly one of the points at which the church, by and large, is failing to live up to its true calling.

Peace: Perishable and Imperishable

With the escalation of the nuclear scare, the church has become more and more vociferous in championing peace. Putting on the armor of its spiritual authority, it fights rapidly growing military spending and the development and proliferation of nuclear weapons. In the narthex of churches one often finds a display of leaflets clamoring for a nuclear freeze. This has indeed become one of the hottest issues of our day. Unilateral, bilateral, multilateral—whatever its adjective, a freeze seems to be the surest way to peace. And peace is defined as insurance for long life, safe life, secure life. This is what everybody wants.

Basically, there is nothing wrong with that. The instinct of survival is part of the law of nature, the desire of all humans regardless of ideological differences. To work for the preservation of life is our God-given responsibility. Woe to us if we forget it.

But this is only one side of the coin. What the church frequently neglects nowadays is to point out the other side as well. Engrossed in fighting human causes on the horizontal level, it fails to focus light on the divine.

Jesus once said to his disciples, "Peace I leave with you; *my* peace I give to you; *not as the world gives* do I give to you. Let not your hearts be troubled, neither let them be afraid" (John 14:27; italics mine). We see hardly any awareness among Christians of such a peace, yet *there is* such a peace. By the grace of God our family had a taste of it in the cellar shelters of Budapest during World War II. Though the bombs were shaking the ground *around* us, *in* us there was peace, total and absolute. The kind that passes all understanding. If the church spent more energy pointing to this imperishable divine peace, the scramble for perishable earthly peace would become less frantic.

We must also ask how many of us good, churchgoing Christians believe truly and unconditionally in life eternal? If we did, could this earthly life be so terribly, overridingly important? Would we be so totally obsessed with its prolongation, its maintenance at all costs? One hears more and more sermons about how to live here and now, but fewer and fewer about how to die here and now.

For the apostles, dying and resurrection were the topics of every message. Eternal life was securely built into the temporal one; death was nothing but a gateway between the two. Its familiar, natural nearness eradicated fear, even in the face of persecution and martyrdom. This fearless faith was the cornerstone of the early church, a cornerstone often neglected and eroded in these days.

Would such a faith mean that the church should stop working for peace on this earth and for the preservation and prolongation of this life? Heaven forbid. But it should maintain a sense of proportion, keep things in proper perspective. It should muster the courage to raise—and answer—the taboo question "What if not?"

Even If Not

In a story in the Book of Daniel (3:1–30), King Nebuchadnezzar orders his subjects to prostrate themselves before the golden image he has erected. Three men, worshipers of the true God, refuse. Outraged, the king threatens to throw them into a fiery furnace unless they obey. "And who is the god that will deliver you out of my hands?" he asks them mockingly. They answer, "Our God whom we serve is able to deliver us from the burning fiery furnace; and he will deliver us out of your hand, O king. *But if not*, be it known to you, O king, that we will not serve your gods or worship the golden image which you have set up" (italics mine).

Indeed, we have a God who can save us from the fiery furnace of a global holocaust. And we believe that he will. But at the same time, we also believe that his power and wisdom far surpass our understanding, and for reasons unfathomable to us, he may decide to let our bodies perish in a nuclear war. If we fully trust him, we have to come to terms with that frightening "What if not?"—however difficult that may be.

At the beginning of this chapter I quoted certain phrases from our Lord's predictions about the events preceding the end of the world. "Nation will rise against nation"; there will be "wars and rumors of wars."

It is a hard-to-digest paradox of our faith that, while on the one hand we are called to do our utmost to bring about reconciliation and work for peace, on the other hand we must come to terms with the fact that the sinfulness of human nature cannot evolve into sinlessness. As long as mankind exists, sin will exist, and as long as sin exists, there will be wars. Even at the very end.

Will such an end come soon, in the form of a fiery nuclear furnace? Is it near, or still far away? No one knows, and no one should speculate. All we can be sure of is that there will be an end, though it will by no means be "the end of the world" for those who know about a "world without end."

A dear young friend of ours was dying of cancer. Her pain was excruciating. During our last visit we could hardly see her because of the multitude of tubes inserted into her wasted body. Yet shortly before she died, she found the strength to jot down the following words for us: "I am not afraid of the future, for God is already there."

Rejoicing in Hope

Travail and reconciliation, war and peace, living, dying, then living again! Overwhelming issues! How difficult it is to face them candidly, without the veneer of cheery platitudes. No matter where we turn, our own inadequacy stares back at us. We must recognize that—and then find our comfort in the final ringing sentences of the message of the Evanston assembly:

We are not sufficient for these things. But Christ is sufficient. We do not know what is coming to us. But we know who is coming. It is he who meets us every day and who will meet us at the end—Jesus Christ our Lord. Therefore we say to you: Rejoice in hope.

24

THE PAST IS PROLOGUE

Remembering and Laboring

In the early hours of Memorial Day 1958, our expectant older daughter, Naomi, knocked on our bedroom door and said, "Mommy and Daddy, the pains have just begun. We better go to the hospital." By noon our first grandchild was born, and the new mother quipped, "For me, Memorial Day turned out to be Labor Day."

The symbolic meaning of that remark stayed with me. Could the Memorial Day of our life, the time of remembering, ever be separated from the pain of travail? We must take a close look at our past and examine it, not in order to dwell on either its praiseworthy achievements or its agonizing failures, but to discern that ultimately it has been a birth experience, a series of pains worth enduring, a price to be paid for new life.

The writer of the Letter to the Hebrews does not say that Jesus Christ is the same yesterday, today, and *tomorrow*. Instead, with a leap of faith, he bypasses "tomorrow" and declares that Jesus is the same yesterday, today, and *forever*. We are assured that in him our fragile, shaky tomorrow is already firmly anchored in an unshakable and unfathomable forever. In this sense, our past is indeed always a prologue to eternity.

Recounting and Reckoning

In the first chapter of this book I indicated that the word *confession* has two meanings. First, it is a declaration of our faith in God. Its second but by no means secondary meaning is an acknowledgment of our sins against God and against our fellowmen.

I hope I have already manifested the first type of confession, unequivocally admitting that I have nothing that I did not receive. Above all else, God's greatest gift to me is indeed faith itself, saving faith. And I like to believe that, even if I have faltered and failed many times, I have never lost sight of it or stopped being grateful for it.

But now, in this final chapter, I feel compelled to face squarely the second, rather unpleasant demand of confession. This requires that I confront myself, really look at myself. No one has better expressed how discomforting such a look can be than Saint Augustine in his *Confessions*: "You took me from behind my own back where I had put myself all the time that I preferred not to see myself. And you set me there, before my own face, that I might see how vile I was. . . . I saw myself and was horrified."

The more one fancies himself a Christian, the more disturbing such an eyeball-to-eyeball encounter can be. Yet, no matter how one twists, turns, and tries to wiggle away, the plain fact remains: confessing one's faith cannot be done without confessing one's sins. Therefore, after all these chapters of recounting, the time has now come for a chapter of reckoning, and for travail in the deepest sense of the word.

Being in travail with others is an often upsetting existential involvement. But to be in travail with oneself is always an agonizing personal predicament. It cuts to the quick.

Godly Griefs

Mark Twain spoke of us all when he wrote, "Man is the only animal that blushes. Or needs to." Genuine repentance is our vertical blush in the sight of God. And its matrix is "godly grief" leading to salvation.

Confessing our sins is never easy. And for those of us who are both ministers and theologians, it is doubly difficult. After all, "men of the cloth" are by and large thought to be possessed of many virtues and expected to be free of short-comings. Our public puts us on a pedestal whether we want to be there or not, and it becomes our moral and spiritual duty— that is, our pastoral obligation—to remain there. Our fall would disillusion many who see in us a safe anchorage for their often leaky boats.

Since I became a "Reverend" at an unusually early age, I had to meet this obligation at a stage when some of my former classmates were still merrily sowing their wild oats, barely giving a thought to their future. I was thrown into a situation with a tailor-made identity that I had to live up to.

That Domineering "It." To be sure, the decision to become a theologian was my own. I relished roaming the avenues of research that my profession opened up before me. Everything seemed to be in apple-pie order. And yet I had the nagging feeling that the very theologian in me, so eager to pursue his studies, had relegated to the background a more important search: to find his own spiritual identity.

At one point in this book I wrote about the freedom fight of the theologian and his conquest of the psychologist and the philosopher. I regarded this struggle as my Copernican Revolution. But it certainly didn't effect a complete about-face. For the theologian who took over the turf still kept me shackled to an "I-It" relationship that hindered my soaring into the realm of the "I-Thou" relationship. In other words, theology as an "It," an object for my scrutiny, ruled over me more than the "Sovereign Thou," the God of Abraham, of Jacob, of Jesus Christ, and (supposedly) of Béla Vassady. Only later did I learn about the pitfalls of theology as a scientific and profes-sional undertaking. First I had to fall into practically all of them.

In principle I knew quite well that "a conceptualized God is no God"—indeed, I often taught and preached this truth.

Yet in practice that theoretical God often took the place of the living Lord. I had to recognize this again and again. Each recognition would bring forth a new travail with the more-or-less abstract theologian in me, and I would pray that my "godly" vocation would not prevent the formation of Christ within me.

I also had to learn that, even if I regarded myself as a "pilgrim theologian" who consciously abhorred any closed system of thought, I was still prone to evaluate many things from a warped and sometimes rigid perspective. The vibrant Christian life is so rich and diverse that it is impossible to define it in terms of propositional truths, let alone to encage it in any formula. Such efforts are always detrimental to the divine-human encounter as well as to our human relationships on the horizontal level.

Just how inclined I was to fall for this temptation dawned upon me when I read a poem that Serena wrote shortly after we were married. The gist of it was, Do not attempt to squeeze me into your system. I suddenly realized how her many-splendored personality eluded and defied any definition or equation. Neither my psychology nor my theology could catch up with it. (Indeed, they never did, thank God.)

Two Selves in Me.   No doubt the unusually early advances and "successes" in my career tempted me to build up certain convictions of superiority and brought forth my special brand of cocksureness. This then spilled over into self-confident pronouncements. Yet, at the same time, if caught in the vise of some ulterior consideration, I often lent an ear to the voice of the insecure man in me, and thus lost my bravado and failed to speak out frankly and boldly at the most opportune times about highly important issues. The memories of some of those lost opportunities still haunt me. My description of man-the-sinner as afflicted with both an insecure and a cocksure self was undoubtedly the result of honest self-analysis. Unfortunately, the mere diagnosis of a virus does not eradicate it. Sometimes the circumstances of our very lives proliferate it.

Ministers, for instance, and to an even greater extent professors of the "sacred science of theology" are rarely exposed to contradictions or provocations (certainly less often than, say, politicians). The pulpit and the professorial chair surround them with an aura of infallibility. In many cases their utterances remain unchallenged. Pride, self-deception, and complacency can then easily find cover—even nourishment— behind the invisible shield of such authority.

During the forty-eight years of my professorship, I found myself again and again in situations in which mine was the only voice, my pronouncement was the final word. Have I succeeded in not exploiting, unconsciously, these pre-rogatives of mine? Hardly. I had to learn and endlessly relearn that the three great virtues in life are humility, humility, and once again, humility (to borrow Cyprian's insight). This learning process became the "continuing education" in my life. For whenever I thought that I had finally succeeded in being humble, I had to find out how difficult it was not to be proud of my humility.

It is God's costly grace that keeps teaching me this lesson.

The Pitfalls of Egocentrism. Even the very writing of this theological autobiography makes me vulnerable to the dangers of self-deception. It is hard to dwell upon one's own life without being snared by narcissism. After all, in an autobiography the "capital I" is the chief performer. (Just look at how many times I have had to use it so far!) It unavoidably holds center stage. Furthermore, here and there my script exudes the "sweet smell of success."

In chapter two I exclaimed, "Get behind me, self-centeredness and pride! Let this message radiate through every page: 'Our competence is from God.'" Have I been able to avoid the pitfalls of egocentrism? To answer this definitely, with either a complacent "yea" or a breast-beating "nay," would be hypocritical.

There is a little poem whose author's name escapes me, but as I worked on this book a fragment of it kept echoing in my mind "Just stand aside, and let yourself go by, / Think of yourself as *he* instead of *I*." I have tried to follow this advice in my writing. But it saddens me that in my living I have left it so often unheeded. "Standing aside" and "letting myself go by" just did not jibe with my nature.

Mishandling Time.   Throughout my life I have been an active person—in many instances, overly so. And the nature and purpose of my activities seemed not only to justify my relentless work schedule but to make it praiseworthy. In the end I had practically no time for anything or anybody else. The older I grow, the more my handling—or rather, mishandling—of time grieves me. I grabbed it so tightly for professional purposes that I almost choked the life out of it.

This interfered first of all with the time I spent with my students. In my professional life I constantly had to decide whether I should devote more of my time to research and writing or to the pastoral care of my students. I was inclined to *do* the first while *saying* that a theological professor should regard his students as if they were members of his congregation—that is, his primary consideration should be sharing their basic problems and tending to their needs. The researcher in me most frequently gained the upper hand over the pastor in me. The realization of this failing, especially after my retirement, has grieved me more and more. And yet many letters from former students testify to the opposite. They recall remarks I made that I forgot long ago. But they did not forget them because somehow those remarks hit home. Such instances should be registered under the caption "The Workings of the Holy Spirit." Indeed, the credit is God's, not mine.

My professional ambitions also interfered with the time I spent with my family. For me it is even more grievous to remember how much more time I should have spent with them. I let the pursuit of my career and my official responsibilities cloud my perspective and scramble my priorities in this vital area.

It seemed so natural to me that my so-called "Christian obligations" should overshadow the personal obligations to my wife and our children. It seemed perfectly reasonable that Serena should take over the majority of the responsibilities usually allotted to "the man of the house," that she should spare me so many vexing problems and time-consuming decisions. Even the children accepted it as natural that Daddy had no time for this or that, even though "that" turned out to be a picnic or a trip canceled at the last minute because Daddy had something more important to do.

Looking back, I find it amazing that in spite of all this my family remained loving and close-knit. Part of the explanation must have been the welding power of common suffering. After all, few families went through the kind of trials and tribulations that ours did—not only because of the war but because its dread-filled years were so quickly followed by those long, dreary months of aching separation.

All this should have taught me a lesson. After our euphoric reunion in the United States, I should have started to resist certain peremptory demands of my vocation. I should have turned down at least some speaking invitations. I should have said "no" to certain Sunday engagements so that I could have spent weekends with my family. I should have left my study door open more often and let the outside sounds of domestic life invade and penetrate my seclusion. I should have—but I did not.

Such misplaced priorities could have played havoc with our family unity. They could have—but they did not. My only explanation is that, separations and disruptions notwithstanding, there was always an underlying power that bound us together: the living Word of the living God.

Waverings in Family Devotions. My professional commitments also altered the course of our family devotions. Before I left Hungary in 1946, Serena and I agreed that both of us would read the same chapter in the Bible each day. We kept our promise. Because Serena included the children in her devotions, they knew that not only God was with them during this difficult time, but their Daddy was with them in spirit too, even though he was thousands of miles away. For them to know this became a great spiritual boon. And for Serena and me it was a very special blessing that helped both of us to bear the burden of aloneness. No matter where I was—on an airplane or a train, in the noisiness of a terminal or the privacy of my hotel room—it was always a reinvigorating experience to open my Bible and read it together with my constant fellow-travelers, my wife and our children.

After the family came to the United States, we maintained our daily family devotions for several years. Reading the same Bible verses in two languages, English and Hungarian, was most enriching. It instilled in the children the awareness that their Lord is a multilingual God who speaks to everyone in his or her own tongue. The language may differ, but God's message is the same.

As the children grew older, however, we reached a fork in the road. The proliferating demands of their social life and school activities started to interfere. Our after-supper devotions became more hurried, more formal, even half-hearted. Serena and I had to decide if we should rigidly enforce the ritual, or if the time had arrived to ease up, to let the children "do their own thing" and leave the rest to the Lord. We decided on the latter and never regretted it. Parents can lay the human foundations, but they should let the Lord build the house. When our flesh and blood near the threshold of adulthood, they must be allowed to work out their own salvation alone, to leave behind the "faith of their fathers" and find their very own. And if all goes well, they will find that the two happen to be the same.

Serena and I continued our devotional Bible readings on a fairly regular basis. But now new temptations started to creep in. We had both developed into "word-aholics." Since both of us were overloaded with speaking and preaching engagements, we began to use our Bible readings to hunt for verses to fit our assigned topics. We tended to forget that we ourselves were in constant need of hearing God's living Word speak to us personally. We had to learn again and again that only after the Word penetrated our own souls, pierced our own hearts, could we try to interpret it to others. We should never try to tailor the Word to the message, but always let the Word *be* the message. Otherwise, dry bones start to rattle in even the best-composed sermons and speeches.

Misguided Prayers. By the same token the rattling of dry bones can also be heard in the most resounding and exquisitely chiseled public prayers. Often I was tempted to aim my public prayers horizontally, as missiles directed at an audience or congregation, rather than vertically, as sighs of repentance and gratitude sent up to God. Time and again I had to recognize that even "good" prayers can be deadening unless they grow out of personal walks and talks with God. Occasionally my private "conversations" with God may consist of only a sigh or a half-conscious but joyous awareness of his presence—or a fleeting pain caused by the lack of such awareness. Channels may be clogged now and then, but never permanently. Sooner or later the "living waters" break through and clean away the mud.

Stored-up Theology. I am still limping along the road to the discovery that unless theology has a ring of immediacy it cannot be called theology. It can live up to its name only if its message is gathered daily, as the manna was, sometimes in green pastures, at other times on rocky land. Should its truths and insights be hoarded and stored away, only worms would feed on them. They would prove unfit for human consumption.

Unfortunately, even a pilgrim theologian has a tendency to become static, bogged down in the knowledge he diligently garnered and stored in his granary, deluding himself that he has it all, that he has arrived. But thank God for Peniel, for new nights and new dawns, and new wrestlings by the gorge. And thank God for new dislocations of the pilgrim's thigh, for that healing hurt that sends him forth, no matter how lamely, toward the Goal.

Attitude of Gratitude

Godly griefs are good for the soul. But they are genuine only if steeped in gratitude.

Thanks be to God that he so graciously spared me from the potentially harmful consequences of my failings. Neither my sins of omission nor commission have cast a shadow on either my personal or professional life. God has let me have more than I have deserved of the respect and devotion of those with whom I have worked. And what a blessing that no generation gap exists in our family, and the abiding love of our three fine adult children, by now parents themselves, warms my sunset years.

God made me a living proof that "[his] power is made perfect in weakness" (2 Cor. 12:9). He keeps on teaching me never to take anything for granted. The dimmer my vision, the more clearly I can see the outlines of his unfathomable mercy, and the more I learn to receive all things and each day from him with an ever-deepening attitude of gratitude. And so I remain especially grateful to him for three main occurrences in my life.

First, I am thankful that I happened to be the progeny of a mixed marriage between a Protestant and a Catholic. Because of this I experienced spiritual travail already in my teens, and so I resolved as a youth to work for church unity after I grew up.

Second, I am thankful that God enlisted a Christian man from America to bring me to this country to study at the age of nineteen. This enabled me to make all sorts of comparisons, and thus to overcome not only racial and national prejudices but continental and hemispheric prejudices as well. This new vista broadened my horizons and taught me to appraise everything from a worldwide perspective. And this shift in viewpoint ocurred when ecumenism was still regarded by many as a passing vogue or an ephemeral utopian theory.

Third, the cornucopia of my gratitude spills over as I raise my voice of praise to the Almighty for the greatest blessing of all: my wife, Serena. For more than half a century she has been and still is the most enriching and sustaining force (after God) in my earthly existence. In fact, I could hardly have written this book without her cooperation. Her talent, insight, and dedicated labor are an integral part of it. This book by its very nature needed a lighter touch than that I have used all my life in my professional writings, and Serena's creative restyling has informed every page. The shared experiences of our more-than-fifty-year-long togetherness made it seem natural that "my" autobiography should be the fusion of the two of us. And, indeed, so it is.

"God of Grace and God of Glory"

I have always liked the hymn "God of Grace and God of Glory" by Harry Emerson Fosdick. It serves as a source of inspiration to any pilgrim, theologian or otherwise. It pulsates with the honesty of repentance as it changes into thankful obedience, with the experience of forgivenness as it helps motivate our own forgiving, with the confession of our faith and our sins as the thrust of the Gospel transforms them into mission and ministry. We feel ourselves perennially drawn from the "God of Grace" to the "God of Glory." We make a lifelong journey from God to God. Paradoxically, we walk with him and are accompanied by him until finally we arrive in his glorious presence.

Mind-boggling? Yes. But oh, how very reassuring!

Serena and I sometimes talk wistfully about how good it would be if we could die together and reach the "God of Glory" hand in hand. Of course, beyond such childish daydreams, we know full well that even if on this earth we must let go of each other's hand, it will not make any real difference.

One day, or on two different days—how far apart, only God knows—our earthly motors will give out. And then, regardless of temporary separation, *we shall limp together into eternity.*

Now we see God "in a mirror dimly," but then and there we shall see him "face to face": the "God of Grace" and the "God of Glory." We shall reach him and limp no more.

Alleluia! Amen.

APPENDIX

Statement of Faith of the United Church of Christ, 1957–1959

We believe in God, the Eternal Spirit, Father of our Lord Jesus Christ and our Father, and to his deeds we testify:

He calls the world into being,
   creates man in his own image,
   and sets before him the ways of life and death.

He seeks in holy love to save all people from aimlessness and sin.

He judges men and nations by his righteous will declared through prophets and apostles.

In Jesus Christ, the man of Nazareth, our crucified and risen Lord,
   he has come to us,
   and shared our common lot,
   conquering sin and death
   and reconciling the world to himself.

He bestows upon us his Holy Spirit,
   creating and renewing the church of Jesus Christ,

binding in covenant faithful people of all ages,
tongues, and races.

He calls us into his church
to accept the cost and joy of discipleship,
to be his servants in the service of men,
to proclaim the gospel to all the world and resist the
powers of evil,
to share in Christ's baptism and eat at his table,
to join him in his passion and victory.

He promises to all who trust him
forgiveness of sins and fullness of grace,
courage in the struggle for justice and peace,
his presence in trial and rejoicing,
and eternal life in his kingdom which has no end.
Blessing and honor, glory and power be unto him. Amen.